MEDIA POLICY AND GLOBALISATION

MEDIA POLICY AND GLOBALISATION

Shashi Kant Swami

CYBER TECH PUBLICATIONS
4264/3, Ansari Road, Daryaganj, New Delhi-110002 (India)
Ph.: 011-23244078. Fax: 011-23280028
E-Mail: cyberpublicationsdelhi@yahoo.com

MEDIA POLICY AND GLOBALISATION

Shashi Kant Swami

First Edition 2009

Published by :

G.S. Rawat for **Cyber Tech Publications**
4264/3, Ansari Road, Daryaganj, New Delhi-110002 (India)
Ph.: 011-23244078. Fax: 011-23280028
E-Mail: cyberpublicationsdelhi@yahoo.com

Printed at : Asian Offset Printers

Preface

Media and communications has played a vital role in globalization by being an enabler of globalization and a transformation agent of social, cultural, and political structures. The paper discusses two possible futures for the media and communications component of globalization: the commercialization of media sectors and outputs creating media and communications products or fulfilling more human needs and rights through media and communications. The latter is least likely to occur unless a more balanced distribution of power amongst the multilateral system, government, private sector, and civil society is established working to promote the human rights agenda. The paper suggests international institutions should use the global media framework to put the needs of people first, and so reforming the structure of global governance is necessary to change the way media and communications is governed towards a more social direction.

Undersigned is confident enough that this work of him is unique and it has its own style and way of presentation. The book has been kept in easiest possible language and has been included with latest information and data of the related field. Your valuable suggestions and complaints if any are always welcome.

—Author

CONTENTS

1

Media: Recent Studies

Media studies has a short history but a long past. Though the name is not more than three decades old, the central intellectual problems of media studies have been pursued in a variety of intellectual traditions over the course of the twentieth century (and before). Looking backwards, we are in a good position to discover ancestors in the American progressives (Chicago), the effects tradition (Columbia), critical theory (Frankfurt), and British cultural studies (Birmingham). This class attempts to give a guided tour through this thicket and to help you become familiar, comfortable, and even fluent with theoretical vocabulary and questions that have been historically important in the formation of media studies.

Of all the times in history to be studying the mass media, this is probably the best. Not only the dizzying technological and economic upheavals within the media industries themselves make it so, but also the outpouring of theory, argument, and research on the mass media from diverse academic fields. Theories about mass communication have never been more plural--or more contentious. The area of knowledge we provisionally call "Mass Communication Theories" is an unsettled terrain, something of a frontier, and frontiers are known for adventures and dangers, lawlessness and open vistas. This course does not pretend to offer more than a survey of important landmarks.

It will deal with central traditions of study, topics of debate, and conceptual problems in media studies, with a bias toward the United States. You will not learn everything you need about mass communication theories, let alone social theory. Recent work is slighted in this course (but not in other courses). Your development into a social theorist of media, culture, and society will likely take your entire program at least.

I assume that mass communication theory is best understood as a branch of social theory. Not only does mass communication theory historically mimic the main currents of social theory, but the concept of communication is central to efforts to understand modern societies: indeed, the attempt to theorize "society" and "communication" arise in the same moment, as reflected in Cooley's Social Organization, for instance. The class aims to help you begin to theorize about mass communication and society and to introduce you to a variety of positions. Part of the Iowa tradition is that every scholar, whatever his or her particular method, area, or topic, should be a theorist, and a theorist is (to give a minimalist definition), one who argues, gives reasons and makes connections to larger problems.

Theory is not only something that people do in their armchairs; it is an art that every scholar, if not citizen and human, should cultivate. "All anthropoi naturally desire to know," said Aristotle. This class is an invitation to theory.

Our approach will be historical. A chief way to study theory is via the history of theory. All theory is a rapprochement with the past of theory. Further, historical narration, as many recent theorists have claimed, is both a political and intellectual task. It is not a matter of stringing events or milestones together, but of claiming a lineage, and thus staking a claim to the present. Readings for this class have been chosen for cartographic rather than cutting-edge qualities--their ability to help anchor a cognitive map of ideas.

This class also aims to help serve as a preparation for the qualifying examination in media studies. It is something of a theory survival course. It aims to introduce you to the vocabulary and intellectual style and basic issues of social theory in general, to the world of theoretical talk in which you will be immersed here. We will also pursue, in passing, what could be called the philosophy of scholarship--why we should theorize, publish, teach, and what it is all for. The personal resources that give rise to theory are precious and need fostering.

OBJECTIVES

1. Introduce students to the history and development of mass communication theory.
2. Detail what is meant by theory, why it is important, and how it is used.
3. Detail several of the most influential traditional and contemporary mass communication theories.
4. Improve students' skill at applying mass communication theory to their own use of the media.

Communication is the process of creating shared meaning. Communication between a mass medium and its audience is mass communication, a primary contributor to the construction and maintenance of culture. The precise relation of culture to mass communication and its function in our lives has long been debated. Because of the power mass communication has in shaping culture, it presents us with both opportunities and responsibilities. Media industries must operate ethically or risk negatively influencing the culture in which they exist. Consumers likewise have the responsibility to critically examine media messages. Both technology and money shape the mass communication process. Innovations in technology bring about new forms of media, or make older forms more accessible. As profit-making entities, the media must respond to the wishes of both advertisers and audience. Ultimately, though, the consumers choose which forms of media they support and how they react to the messages that face them. Technological and economic factors such as convergence and globalization will influence the evolution of mass communication.

1. The model of communication that is expressed as "Who Says What in Which Channel To Whom With What Effect" was developed by

   (A) James Carey.

(B) Marshall McLuhan.

(C) Wilbur Schramm.

(D) Harold Lasswell.

2. A friend nods in agreement at something you've said. This is an example of:

(A) feedback in interpersonal communication.

(B) feedback in mass communication.

(C) noise in interpersonal communication.

(D) encoding in interpersonal communication.

3. It is imprecise to speak of "source" and "receiver" in communication because

(A) there may be more than one of each.

(B) there is much variation in what constitutes a source and receiver.

(C) if the receiver isn't listening, the source can't be a source.

(D) communication is an ongoing, reciprocal process.

4. Because it is imprecise to speak of "source" and "receiver" in communication, Osgood and Schramm replaced these concepts with ____________ in their model of communication.

(A) interpreters

(B) encoders

(C) decoders

(D) participants

5. Network executives read the overnight ratings for a new television series. This is an example of

(A) feedback in interpersonal communication.

(B) feedback in mass communication.

(C) noise in interpersonal communication.

(D) encoding in interpersonal communication.

6. An example of ______________ occurs when your newspaper gets wet and it is difficult to read page 1 because page 2 bleeds through.

   (A) feedback in interpersonal communication

   (B) feedback in mass communication

   (C) noise in interpersonal communication

   (D) noise in mass communication

7. Movie box office figures are an example of

   (A) instant and direct feedback in interpersonal communication.

   (B) instant and direct feedback in mass communication.

   (C) delayed and inferential feedback in interpersonal communication.

   (D) delayed and inferential feedback in mass communication.

8. People who belong to a bounded culture

   (A) do not generally get along with people outside that culture.

   (B) choose not to participate in the dominant culture.

   (C) usually identify themselves as members of that culture.

   (D) are generally looked down on in the United States.

9. Social scientists are engaging in ________ research when they study advertising's contribution to the creation of a consumer culture.

   (A) micro-level

   (B) transmissional

   (C) critical

   (D) ritual

10. An individual who believes that a breakdown of traditional values will be the inevitable result of the spread of the Internet is said to believe in

(A) technological determinism

(B) manifest destiny

(C) technological despotism

(D) latent destiny

11. The purchase of 20th Century Fox by Australian company News Corp is an example of

(A) concentration of media ownership.

(B) globalization of media.

(C) audience fragmentation.

(D) erosion of distinctions among media.

In preliterate cultures knowledge was passed on orally. With the advent of writing, literacy became more highly valued than memory. After Gutenberg; and invention of the printing press, literacy spread to all levels of society and by the mid-19th century, a middle class with discretionary time and income had emerged, providing a mass audience of readers. Mass media helped to unify the diverse cultures of the United States. Television in particular was instrumental in transforming our country into a consumer economy. Understanding the ways in which media impact individuals and society is an important aspect of media literacy. Other elements include an understanding of the process of mass communication and an awareness of media content as a "text" that provides insight into contemporary culture.In order to develop our media literacy, we must be able to understand the process by which media sends messages and learn to analyze those messages. This requires an ability and willingness to analyze media messages, a knowledge of genre conventions, and an ability to distinguish emotional from reasoned reactions. By increasing our critical awareness, we can make better choices from among media content.

1. You are most likely to find a griot in

(A) literate cultures.

(B) preliterate cultures.

(C) dominant cultures.

(D) bounded cultures.

2. In oral or preliterate cultures

(A) there is a clear division of labor among members.

(B) memory is devalued.

(C) myth and history are intertwined.

(D) language is very general.

3. In literate cultures

(A) there is a clear division of labor among members.

(B) elders are revered for their experience.

(C) myth and history are intertwined.

(D) role and status are rigidly defined.

4. Gutenberg was a ___________ by trade.

(A) clergyman

(B) goldsmith and metallurgist

(C) merchant

(D) painter

5. Books were the first mass-produced product, speeding the development of:

(A) powerful monarchies throughout Europe.

(B) a more powerful literate clergy.

(C) magazines.

(D) capitalism.

6. Increased leisure time and expendable income are two products of:

(A) the Industrial Revolution.

(B) the Protestant Reformation.

(C) advances in steam-powered printing presses.

(D) the decline of literate cultures.

7. Literacy is the ability to
   (A) effectively and efficiently comprehend and utilize a given form of communication.
   (B) read and write at a college level.
   (C) deliver an effective oral presentation.
   (D) participate in trade and commerce.
8. The ability of television to influence important foreign policy decisions by appealing to people's emotions has been called _______ by Madeleine Albright.
   (A) binding culture
   (B) the third person effect
   (C) multiple points of access
   (D) the CNN effect
9. Genres refer to
   (A) communication strategies employed by preliterate cultures.
   (B) different types of feedback in mass and interpersonal communication.
   (C) categories of expression within the different media, for example, the evening news and documentaries.
   (D) bounded cultures' ability to limit expression.
10. Production values refers to
    (A) the characteristic, distinctive, standardized style elements of a given form of media expression, for example the up-beat music that introduces the local evening news.
    (B) categories of expression within the different media, for example, the evening news and documentaries.
    (C) the specific internal language of a given medium, for example the choice of lighting in a soap opera.
    (D) the common assumption that media messages affect others, but not ourselves.

The Internet was inspired by Joseph C.R. Licklider's vision of a nationwide network of computers, and further developed by the U.S. military. Personal computers made the Internet available to non-institutional users. The most common uses of the Internet are accessing World Wide Web files, using e-mail, and participating in mailing lists and USENET groups. It is difficult to estimate the number of Internet users. Usage continues to increase with teenage girls now the fastest growing group of users. The development of on-line commerce has been controversial, since many of the original Internet users object to their medium being overtaken by commercialization. MP3, audio file compression software, is a form of convergence that is changing the distribution of music dramatically.

The Internet allows every user to become a publisher. This property has raised First Amendment issues related to misinformation, online pornography, and copyright protection. Privacy is another concern, regarding both online communication and easy access to personal information. The Internet is increasingly being used as a political forum in which citizens can communicate directly with elected officials, but runs the risk of closing out those who lack sufficient media literacy.

Most of the early literature printed in North America was political or religious in content. Technological advances in printing and increases in literacy led to the flowering of the novel in the 1800s. Due to the cultural importance of books, censorship has been a controversial issue. There are now several categories of books, including trade, professional, el-hi, higher ed, and mass market paperbacks.Although publishing houses were traditionally small businesses, most books today are published by huge conglomerates. At the same time, independent bookstores are increasingly giving way to chains. Electronic publishing is broadening the options for aspiring writers. Although illiteracy is rare in America, aliteracy, unwillingness to read, has caused some to wonder if books are a dying medium. The success of the Harry Potter books, however, has turned this trend around and helped bring about a rebirth of reading.

Newspapers as we know them date back to the seventeenth century. Even before the Revolutionary War, American newspapers largely maintained independence from government control. The first mass circulation newspaper was the New York Sun, emerging in 1833 and selling for one cent a copy. Groups such as Native Americans and African Americans also used the medium at this time to express views outside the mainstream. Competition in the 1880s led to the rise of yellow journalism.

Newspaper chains began forming in the 1920s, and have grown more numerous over time. The advent of television brought further changes to the medium. Today, metropolitan dailies are losing readership as suburban and small town papers grow in popularity. Nevertheless, chains control 82% of all circulation. Civic journalism and changing technology are two important issues for all newspapers. Editors are also facing the dilemma of giving younger readers the soft news they want or losing them as customers.

The magazine was introduced to America in the mid-18th century. Factors such as increased literacy and industrialization fueled growth in the industry after the Civil War. The medium was an important force for social change in the early 20th century, due to the muckrakers. After the coming of television, magazines continued to prosper through increased specialization.

Of more than 22,000 magazines in operation today, the top 800 consumer magazines account for three-quarters of the industry's revenue. Since space is sold on the basis of circulation, research groups such as the Audit Bureau of Circulation and Simmons verify a magazine's circulation numbers. New types of magazines, such as Webzines and synergistic magazines, are currently emerging. In order to compete with the specialization of cable television, many magazines are now seeking global audiences. Advertisers are becoming increasingly influential over the stories that appear with their ads.

Movies began with the sequential action photographs of Eadweard Muybridge in 1877. Narrative films were introduced around the turn of the century. Film soon became a large, studio-controlled business on the West Coast. The industry weathered the Great Depression, only to be forced into change with the coming of television.

Today, major studios produce most movie revenue, though independent films are often more innovative. Rather than take chances, the blockbuster mentality of the big studios leads them to rely on such strategies as concept films, sequels and remakes, and movies based on television shows.

Convergence of film with other forms of media has allowed new methods of distribution and exhibition. Digital video is beginning to open up new methods of production. The practice of product placement often effects artistic decisions, which a media literate person can learn to detect.

The technology for radio was developed in the late 19th century, at about the same time that sound recording was being perfected. The medium was used in the early decades of the 20th century for point-to-point communication, and in 1920 KDKA made the first commercial radio broadcast.

Advertising became the economic base of radio in the 1920s. Because it offered free entertainment, radio became increasingly popular during the Great Depression. This time was known as the golden age of radio, until television began to overtake it in popularity after World War II.

Radio is successful today largely because it is local and specialized, which appeals to advertisers as well as listeners. The recording industry, on the other hand, is primarily controlled by four major companies.

The two industries have changed and prospered due to technological advances such as digital recording and convergence of radio and the Internet. Controversial music file-sharing software such as Napster may transform the recording industry, in spite of legal attempts to shut it down.

Although methods of television transmission were developed as early as 1884, television first began to gain popularity after World War II. The 1948 television freeze allowed time for the FCC to develop a plan for growth, and by 1960, 90% of American homes had a television.

The business of television is still dominated by the networks, but new technologies are beginning to erode their power. Cable, VCR, DVD, the remote control, direct broadcast satellite, digital video recorders, digital television, and the Internet have diminished networks' authority and changed the relationship between medium and audience.

News staging is an ethical issue being debated by media literate viewers. Staging can range from giving the false appearance that a reporter is on the scene to re-creating or simulating an event, all for the purpose of holding the audience's attention.

Public relations is difficult to define, because it can involve publicity, research, public affairs, media relations, promotion, merchandising, and more. In its maturation as an industry, public relations has passed through four stages, culminating in advanced two-way communication. Some 200,000 people work in public relations in the United States, in 4,000 firms and in in-house PR operations. They typically carry out 14 activities, including publicity, communication, public affairs, and government relations. PR is not the same as advertising, in part because of its policy-making component.

Globalization, specialization, and converging technologies are trends in public relations. An important issue in the industry is ethical standards, one example being the proliferation of video news releases and their challenge to media literate consumers.

Advertising dates back thousands of years. Changes caused by industrialization and the Civil War fueled its growth, with magazines being an important vehicle for advertising. Radio, then television, changed the nature of advertising, as commercials in turn changed the nature of each medium. Although many see advertising as a critical aspect of our capitalistic society, others find it intrusive, deceptive, and demeaning to our culture.

The 6,000 advertising agencies in the United States are paid either through retainers or commissions. Types of ads include retail, direct market, institutional, and public service.

The link between seeing an ad and buying the advertising product is tenuous at best.

New methods of cyberadvertising have developed over the past several years, such as transaction journalism and intermercials. Other important developments are increasingly fragmented audiences and globalization.

There are many theories of mass communication. The paradigms of these theories shift as new technologies and new media are introduced. Mass communication theory has passed through four eras.

The era of mass society saw media as all-powerful and audiences as defenseless against their effects. In the era of the scientific perspective, research showed that media affected some people much more strongly than others, often according to social characteristics.

The era of limited effects theory included several theories, including attitude change theory and the uses and gratifications approach. Recognizing the power of media effects, theorists discussed agenda setting, dependency theory, and social cognitive theory. Contemporary mass communication theory can be called the era of cultural theory.

Media effects are seen as shaped by audience members involvement in the process and reality is seen as socially constructed. Gerbnerís cultivation analysis and critical cultural theory are two important examples of contemporary theories.

Media industry researchers debate whether media effects are diminished when audiences know that content is only make-believe and whether media reinforce preexisting values or are replacing them. Social scientists test the explanations of various theories advanced to answer these questions by doing research.

Quantitative research methods include experiments, surveys, and content analysis. Experiments sacrifice generalizability for control and the demonstration of causation. Surveys sacrifice casual explanations for generalizabilty and breadth. Qualitative methods include historical, critical, and ethnographic research. Researchers use methods such as the analysis of primary and secondary sources and the undertaking of participant-observer studies.

One of the most studied effects issue is the impact of mediated violence. Researchers have studied the link between violent media content and subsequent aggressive behavior, with social learning theory discrediting the notion of catharsis. There is, however, disagreement regarding the exact interplay of content and behavior.

The impact of media portrayals of different groups of people and the impact of the media on political campaigns are two other effects issues that have been studied. Freedom of the press is established by the First Amendment of the Constitution. This protection extends to all forms of media but can be suspended in cases of clear and present danger and to balance competing interests, as in the conflict between a free press and a fair trial.

Libel, slander, and obscenity are not protected. Other specific issues of media responsibility include definitions of indecency, the impact of deregulation, and copyright. Social responsibility theory is the idea that to remain free of government control, the media must serve the public by acting responsibly. This does not free audiences from their responsibility to be media literate.

Applied ethics is the practice of applying general ethical guidelines and values to a specific situation. Self-regulation by the media often results in ethical dilemmas involving such issues as truth and honesty, privacy, confidentiality, and conflict of interest. Media professionals have established formal standards of ethical behavior, though some people object that they are ambiguous and unenforceable.

Almost since radio's inception, signals have been broadcast internationally in order to circumvent government control. Today, so much entertainment is popular internationally that many countries have laws limiting the amount of airtime devoted to foreign content.

The effects of a country's political system on its mass communications can be broken into five concepts: Western, Development, Revolutionary, Authoritarianism, and Communism. Regardless of the concept, most radio and television programming follows the model of the United States, though other countries might use the media to enforce different social messages.

The advent of satellites and the Internet has thwarted the attempts of governments to control the media. UNESCO has called for the establishment of international rules that allow governments to monitor media content, but Western nations reject this limitation on the freedom of the press. The global village is bringing world communities closer together, but often at the expense of native cultures.

2

Theories and Introduction

CULTIVATION THEORY OF MASS MEDIA

"Cultivation analysis concentrates on the enduring and common consequences of growing up and living with television. Theories of the cultivation process attempt to understand and explain the dynamics of television as the distinctive and dominant cultural force of our age. Cultivation analysis uses a survey instrument, administered to representative samples of respondents.

The responses are analyzed by a number of demographic variables including gender, age, race, education, income, and political self-designation (liberal, moderate, conservative). Where applicable, other controls, such as urban-rural residence, newspaper reading, and party affiliation are also used.

Cultivation analysis is a part of the Cultural Indicators (CI) research project. CI is a data base and a series of reports relating recurrent features of the world of television to viewer conceptions of reality. Its cumulative content data archive contains observations on over 4,500 programmes and 40,000 characters coded according to many thematic, demographic and action categories."

"...specifies that repeated, intense exposure to deviant definitions of 'reality' in the mass media leads to perception of the 'reality' as normal. The result is a social legitimisation of the 'reality' depicted in the mass media, which can influence behavior. (Gerbner, 1973 & 1977; Gerbner et al., 1980.)"

Gerbner first introduced cultivation theory in 1969 with his work Toward "Cultural Indicators": The Analysis of Mass Mediated Public Message Systems. Gerbner begins developing cultivation as a structural piece for the long-term examination of public messages in media influence and understanding. He notes in the introduction that "the approach is based on conception of these message systems as the common culture through which communities cultivate shared and public notions about facts, values, and contingencies of human existence". Gerbner clarifies that his objectives are not with "information, education, persuasion, and the like, or with any kind of direct communication 'effects.'" More accurately, his concern remains with "the collective context within which, and in response to which, different individual and group selections and interpretations of messages take place". Nonetheless, Gerbner's works present a social psychology theory on communication effects, and consequently, on persuasion as related to mass media.

Gerbner speaks of the "cultivation of collective conscious" in relation to the rapid growth of media outlets (in particular, television) and the capacity of mass media to transcend traditional "barriers of time, space, and social grouping". Cultivation then describes the process in which entire publics are affected by content on television. Potter (1993) notes Gerbner's intentions for using "cultivation" as an academic term to define his interest in "the more diffuse effects on perceptions that are shaped over a long period of exposure to media messages". "Cultivation," rather than "long-term effects" indicates the emphasis on the constant nurturing, exposure, and consistent incorporation the viewing public experiences through mass media channels.

COMMUNICATION CONTEXTS

Humans communicate with each other across time, space, and contexts. Those contexts are often thought of as the particular combinations of people comprising a communication situation. For example, theories of interpersonal communication address the communication between dyads (two people). Group communication deals with groups, organizational communication addresses organizations, mass communication encompasses messages broadcast, usually electronically, to mass audiences, intercultural communication looks at communication among people of different cultures, and gender communication focuses on communication issues of women and between the sexes. Newer contexts include health communication and computer-mediated communication.

Contexts of communication are best thought of as a way to focus on certain communication processes and effects. Communication context boundaries are fluid. Thus, we can see interpersonal and group communication in organizations. Gender communication occurs whenever people of different sexes communicate. We can have mass communications to individuals, group, and organizations.

Using communication contexts as a means to help us study communication helps us out of problems some people associate with the intrapersonal context (some say the "so-called" intrapersonal context). Some people facetiously say intrapersonal communication exists when someone talks to themselves. It's more accurate to define intrapersonal communication as thinking. While thinking normally falls within the purview of psychology we can recognize that we often think, plan, contemplate, and strategize about communication past, present, and future. It is legitimate to study the cognitive aspects of communication processes. So, even if some people call those cognitive aspects of communication thinking, it can be helpful to allow the context of intrapersonal communication to exist, thereby legitimating an avenue of communication research.

COORDINATED MANAGEMENT

The Coordinated Management of Meaning theorizes communication as a process that allows us to create and manage social reality. As such, this theory describes how we as communicators make sense of our world, or create meaning. Meaning can be understood to exist in a hierarchy, depending on the sources of that meaning. Those sources include:

1. raw sensory data -- the inputs to your eyes and ears, the visual and auditory stimuli you will interpret to see images and hear sounds;
2. content -- interpreted stimuli, where the words spoken are understood by what they refer to;
3. speech acts -- content takes on more meaning when it is further interpreted as belonging to a speaker who has specific communication styles, relationships with the listener, and intentions;
4. episodes -- in common terms, you may think of this as the context of the conversation or discourse where when you understand the context you understand what the speaker thinks he or she is doing;
5. master contracts -- these define the relationships the communicating participants, or what each can expect of the other in a specific episode;
6. life scripts -- the set of episodes a person expects they will participate in; and
7. cultural patterns -- culturally created set of rules that govern what we understand to be normal communication in a given episode.

Persons use two types of rules to coordinate the management of meaning among those seven levels of meaning. First, we use constitutive rules to help understand how meaning at one level determine meaning at another level. Second, we use regulative rules to help us regulate what we say so that we stay within what we consider to be normal communication in a given episode.

The first concept most students learn about the meaning of meanings is the Semantic Triangle. This label refers to the three part connection among a referent, a reference, and a symbol. The referent is the thing, such as my cat Baxter. The reference is the thought I have of Baxter, a 12 year old grey tabby who loves to lounge on my computer keyboard. The symbol is the word "Baxter." Notice that if I am talking about Baxter I have selected the referent and have control over the reference and symbol. However, if I talk to you about Baxter lounging on my keyboard you will not understand my meaning until you understand the thing (the referent) I am speaking of and the thoughts (references) I have of that thing.

The Semantic Triangle allows for some ambiguity. After all, it is not possible for you to know exactly what my thoughts are. Still, there needs to be ways for people to help make sure they are understand by others, especially when referents, references, or symbols are new to one or more of the communicators. There are four ways in which we help each other understand what we mean:

1. Definitions -- these tell others what is in our heads, or what we mean when we use a certain word;
2. Metaphors -- metaphors allow us to talk about something unfamiliar in terms of something else that is familiar. Metaphors also allow us to merge two concepts whose result is a third concept. For example, I could speak of Baxter as a furry bundle of energy.
3. Feedforward -- this is the process of providing feedback to ourselves before we even speak, so that we help ourselves choose the best way to communicate in a given situation to a given audience; and
4. Basic English -- the set of 850 words out of which any person can effectively communicate ideas, simple or complex.

Semiotics is concerned with signs and their relationship with objects and meaning. One way to view signs is to consider them composed of a signifier and a signified. Simply put, the signifier is the sound associated with or image of something (e.g., a tree), the signified is the idea or concept of the thing (e.g., the idea of a tree), and the sign is the object that combines the signifier and the signified into a meaningful unit. Stated differently, the sign is the relationship between the concept and the representation of that concept.

For example, when I was a child I had a stuffed animal. OK, it was a stuffed green rat, but it was a smiling rat. That rat was the signifier. Think what a stuffed animal could signify to a child. In my case, it signified safety, warmth, and comfort. So, when I walked into my room and looked at my stuffed green rat it was a sign to me that everything was OK. Notice that the signifier and the signified cannot be separated and still provide a meaningful basis for the sign.

Today, that stuffed green rat is just a memory to me. I cannot even recall what I named it. In fact, as time passed that rat became a sign of something else. The rat is still a signifier but it signifies my early childhood when the world seemed calm, safe, and inviting. Now the rat could be considered a sign of my youthful innocence, long past and hard to remember, just like the name of that rat.

SYMBOLIC INTERACTIONISM

Symbolic Interactionism is based on three assumptions:

1. communication occurs through the creation of shared significant symbols,
2. the self is constructed through communication, and
3. social activity becomes possible through the role-taking process.

You can get a basic grasp of this theory by learning its keywords and how they fit together.

I -- the active portion of the self capable of performing behaviors.

Me -- the socially reflective portion of the self, providing social control for the actions of the I.

Self -- the combination of the I and the Me. Self is a process, not a structure. The I acts and the me defines the self as reflective of others.

Self-indication -- experience and feedback as the I acts and the Me observes the I from the role of the Other. The Me then gives direction regarding future action to the I.

Generalized Other -- the typical members of a society or culture.

Specific Other -- the idea of a specific person outside the Self.

Role Taking -- putting oneself in the place of another, or waling in someone else's shoes. We learn to Role Take by Play and Games.

Play -- activity where a child is both the self and an other, without recognizing the self. The child plays both roles without recognizing the self in either role.

Game -- interaction where the child has the attitude of all the others involved in the game. The child is the self but can recognize the other's perspectives. Thus, behavior is not a response but an interpretive process. The individual can comprehend the self only through interaction with other people.

Gesture (nonsymbolic) Interaction--an impulsive and spontaneous action in the sense of a reflex response (e.g., pulling your hand away quickly when after it touches something hot).

Symbolic Interaction -- an interpretation of a symbol.

Symbol -- the representation of one thing for another thing.

Significant Symbol -- a symbol that has shared meaning (e.g., the words in a language).

Mind -- a social, behavioral process in which the human being is capable of acting toward and even creating his or her environment, or objects in the environment.

ATTRIBUTION THEORY

Attribution Theory assumes that people try to determine why people do what they do. This search for a reason behind behavior allows people to attribute causes to behavior. A behavioral cause could be situational, where a person had to do something because of the situation they were in. A behavioral cause could also result from something unique to person. Examples of those unique attributes include, but are not limited to:

1. the person's desire to perform the behavior (e.g., they did it because they wanted to do it),

2. the person's whim (e.g., they did it because they felt like doing it),
3. the person's ability (e.g., the person is capable of doing the behavior),
4. the person's sense of obligation (e.g., the person did it because they felt they had to or should do the behavior), and
5. the person's sense of belonging (e.g., the person did it to fit in with a group of people important to the person).

A person seeking to understand why another person did something may attribute one or more causes to that behavior. However, a three-stage process leads up to the final attribution:

1. the person must perceive or observe the behavior,
2. then the person must believe that the behavior was intentionally performed, and
3. then the person must determine if they believe the other person was forced to perform the behavior (in which case the cause is attributed to the situation) or not (in which case the cause is attributed to the other person).

CONSTRUCTIVISM

Constructivism makes three assumptions regarding communication:

1. all communication is intentional
2. communication is goal-driven
3. negotiation comes into play with shared interpretation (meaning)

Constructivism focuses on individuals rather than interactions. It tries to account for why people make the certain communicative choices. Constructs are the basis of constructivism. They are dimensions of judgment and can be thought of as filters, files, templates, or interpretive schemes. They are domain specific, almost exclusively focusing on interpersonal message variations. Constructs are assumed to change over time, following Werner's Orthogenetic Principle (impressions start globally, undifferentiated, and unorganized then get more complex, abstract, differentiated, and organized as people develop).

Constructivist research uses the Role Category Question to find constructs embedded in free response writing, often about a person the writer likes and a person the writer dislikes. The more constructs a person uses the more cognitively differentiated they are. Cognitive differentiation is a subset of cognitive complexity, which measures the organization, quantity, and level of abstractness of the constructs a person holds about another person. Cognitive differentiation measures only the quantity of constructs but still predicts the degree to which a communicator is person centered and other oriented. Constructivism claims that the more cognitively differentiated a person is the more likely they are to be a competent communicator (one who intentionally uses knowledge of shared interpretations to express meaning is such a way as to control another person's interpretations of some event, object, person, etc.).

Constructivist research shows moderately strong correlations between the organizational level of a person and cognitive differentiation, persuasive ability, and perspective taking. Smaller correlations have been found between organizational level and self monitoring.

ELABORATION LIKELIHOOD MODEL

The Elaboration Likelihood Model claims that there are two paths to persuasion: the central path and the peripheral path. The central path is most appropriately used when the receiver is motivated to think about the message and has the ability to think about the message. If the person cares about the issue and has access to the message with a minimum of distraction, then that person will elaborate on the message. Lasting persuasion is likely if the receiver thinks, or rehearses, favorable thoughts about the message. A boomerang effect (moving away from the advocated position) is likely to occur if the subject rehearses unfavorable thoughts about the message. If the message is ambiguous but pro-attitudinal (in line with the receiver's attitudes) then persuasion is likely. If the message is ambiguous but counter-attitudinal then a boomerang effect is likely.

If the message is ambiguous but attitudinally neutral (with respect to the receiver) or if the receiver is unable or not motivated to listen to the message then the receiver will look for a peripheral cue. Peripheral cues include such communication strategies as trying to associate the advocated position with things the receiver already thinks postively towards (e.g., food, money, sex), using an expert appeal, and attempting a contrast effect where the advocated position is presented after several other positions, which the receiver despises, have been presented. If the peripheral cue association is accepted then there may be a temporary attitude change and possibly future elaboration. If the peripheral cue association is not accepted, or if it is not present, then the person retains the attitude initially held.If the receiver is motivated and able to elaborate on the message and if there are compelling arguments to use, then the central route to persuasion should be used. If the receiver is unlikely to elaborate the message, or if the available arguments are weak, then the peripheral route to persuasion should be used.

THEORY OF SOCIAL JUDGMENT

The key point of the Social Judgment Theory is that attitude change (persuasion) is mediated by judgmental processes and effects. Put differently, persuasion occurs at the end of the process where a person understands a message then compares the position it advocates to the person's position on that issue. A person's position on an issue is dependent on:

1. the person's most preferred position (their anchor point),
2. the person's judgment of the various alternatives (spread across their latitudes of acceptance, rejection, and noncommitment), and
3. the person's level of ego-involvement with the issue.

Consider the course choices available to you next term. For the sake of argument, let's say you have four required courses to finish but have one three credit hour elective remaining. What courses open to you would you definitely not enroll in, no matter what? Those courses fall in your Latitude of Rejection. Do you think anyone could persuade you to take a class that falls in that latitude? Not likely. And, the more ego-involved you are in the decision to enroll in your course (the more you care about that decision) the larger your Latitude of Rejection will be. Persuasive messages that advocate positions in your Latitude of Rejection will be contrasted by you. That is, they will appear to be further away from your anchor point than they actually are. That's not good news for the would-be persuader.

Now consider the courses that you really don't have an opinion about, that you don't have positive or negative feelings toward. Those courses fall in your Latitude of Noncommitment. It's possible that someone could persuade you to enroll in one of those courses, but you'd have to learn more about the course first, at least enough until you an opinion, or judgment, about it. Now, consider all those courses you would consider enrolling in. Those courses fall in your Latitude of Acceptance. A person with good arguments might be able to persuade you to take one of those courses, especially if, in your judgment, the course is similar to your anchor point course. Persuasive messages that advocate positions in your Latitude of Acceptance will be assimilated by you. That is, they will appear to be closer to your anchor point than they actually are. That's good news for the would-be persuader.

If you are persuaded, then the further a message's position is away from your anchor point, the larger your attitude change will be. But remember that it is very unlikely that you will be persuaded out of your Latitude of Rejection. So, once a message enters that region and moves away from your anchor point, the amount of your attitude change decreases.

THEORY OF SOCIAL PENETRATION

Social Penetration Theory asserts that as relationships develop persons communication from superficial to deeply personal topics, slowing penetrating the communicators' public persona to reach their core personality or sense of self. First viewed as a direct, continuous penetration from public person to private person, social penetration is know considered to be a cyclical and dialectical. Relationships have normal ebbs and flows. They do not automatically get better and better where the participants learn more and more about each other. Instead, the participants have to work through the tensions of the relationship (the dialectic) while they learn and group themselves and a parties in a relationships. At times the relationships is very open and sharing. Other time, one or both parties to the relationship need their space, or have other concerns, and the relationship is less open. The theory posits that these cycles occur throughout the life of the relationship as the persons try to balance their needs for privacy and open relationship.

Persons allow other people to penetrate their public self when they disclose personal information. The decision to disclose is based on the perceived rewards the person will gain if he or she discloses information. If a person perceives that the cost of disclosing information is greater than the rewards for disclosing information then no information will be disclosed. The larger the reward-cost ratio the more disclosure takes place. If you think to the relationships you have been in you will probably find that in almost all of them more disclosure took place at the outset of the relationship than at any other place. That happens because people initially disclose superficial information that costs very little if another person finds it out. It matters little if you know that I enjoy all types of music but especially enjoy listening to blues, saxophone jazz, and straightforward rock-n-roll.

It gets a bit more personal when I start explaining why I like those types of music, so I, like most people, will wait until you reciprocate and tell me your favorite types of music before I allow you more visibility into who I am. The deeper I allow you to penetrate my self, the more affective information I will disclose to you. The closer you get to my core self the higher my perceived costs will be for disclosing that information. Thus, it is not likely that I will disclose very personal information to very many people.

UNCERTAINTY REDUCTION THEORY

The Uncertainty Reduction Theory asserts that people have a need to reduce uncertainty about others by gaining information about them. Information gained can then be used to predict the others' behavior. Reducing uncertainty is particularly important in relationship development, so it is typical to find more uncertainty reduction behavior among people when they expect or want to develop a relationship than among people who expect or know they will not develop a relationship. Consider how you try to reduce uncertainty about someone you have just met and want to spend more time with. Now consider how you try to reduce uncertainty about people you meet on an elevator. There are three basic ways people seek information about another person:

1. Passive strategies -- we observe the person, either in situations where the other person is likely to be self-monitoring* (a reactivity search) as in a classroom, or where the other person is likely to act more naturally (a disinhibition search) as in the stands at a football game.
2. Active strategies -- we ask others about the person we're interested in or try to set up a situation where we can observe that person (e.g., taking the same class, sitting a table away at dinner). Once the situation is set up we sometime observe (a passive strategy) or talk with the person (an interactive strategy).
3. Interactive strategies -- we communicate directly with the person.

* Self-monitoring is a behavior where we watch and strategically manipulate how we present ourselves to others.

GROUPTHINK

Groupthink occurs when a homogenous highly cohesive group is so concerned with maintaining unanimity that they fail to evaluate all their alternatives and options. Groupthink members see themselves as part of an in-group working against an outgroup opposed to their goals. You can tell if a group suffers from groupthink if it:

1. overestimates its invulnerability or high moral stance,
2. collectively rationalizes the decisions it makes,
3. demonizes or stereotypes outgroups and their leaders,
4. has a culture of uniformity where individuals censor themselves and others so that the facade of group unanimty is maintained, and
5. contains members who take it upon themselves to protect the group leader by keeping information, theirs or other group members', from the leader.

Groups engaged in groupthink tend to make faulty decisions when compared to the decisions that could have been reached using a fair, open, and rational decision-making process. Groupthinking groups tend to:

1. fail to adequately determine their objectives and alternatives,
2. fail to adequately assess the risks associated with the group's decision,
3. fail to cycle through discarded alternatives to reexamine their worth after a majority of the group discarded the alternative,
4. not seek expert advice,
5. select and use only information that supports their position and conclusions, and
6. does not make contingency plans in case their decision and resulting actions fail.

Group leaders can prevent groupthink by:

1. encouraging members to raise objections and concerns;
2. refraining from stating their preferences at the onset of the group's activities;

3. allowing the group to be independently evaluated by a separate group with a different leader;
4. splitting the group into sub-groups, each with different chairpersons, to separately generate alternatives, then bringing the sub-groups together to hammer out differences;
5. allowing group members to get feedback on the group's decisions from their own constituents;
6. seeking input from experts outside the group;
7. assigning one or more members to play the role of the devil's advocate;
8. requiring the group to develop multiple scenarios of events upon which they are acting, and contingencies for each scenario; and
9. calling a meeting after a decision consensus is reached in which all group members are expected to critically review the decision before final approval is given.

ORGANIZING

Karl Weick writes of the process oriented organizing, rather than the structural oriented organization. Communication is key to the organizing process because it is a large factor in the sense-making process people use when they organize.

The sense-making process is an attempt to reduce equivocality, or multiple meanings, in the information used by the people in the organization. When information is handled by the organizers they go through the stages of:

1. enactment -- where they define the situation and begin the process of dealing with the information,
2. selection -- where they narrow the equivocality by deciding what to deal with and what to leave along, ignore, or disregard, and
3. retention -- where they decide what information, and its meaning, they will retain for future use.

In both the selection and retention stages there are additional processes. These processes depend on double interacts. An act occurs when you say something ("Can I have a popsicle?").

An interact occurs when you say something and I respond ("No, it will spoil you dinner."). A double interact occurs when you say something, I respond, then you respond to that, adjusting your first statement ("Well, how about half a popsicle?"). Double interacts works in:

1. assembly rules -- the operating procedures (e.g., all requests for information from the media must be handled by the Corporate Communications Dept., requests for pay raises must be made through your immediate supervisor, etc.) used by the company to choose what to do maximize the likelihood of achieving the goal at hand, and in the
2. behavior cycles -- sets of double interacts the organization uses to facilitate the selection and retention process. Examples of behavior cycles include staff meetings, coffee-break rumoring, e-mail conversations, internal reports, etc.

Weick sees the the organization as a system taking in equivocal information from its environment, trying to make sense of that information, and using what was learned in the future. As such, organizations evolve as they make sense out of themselves and their environment.

MUTED GROUP THEORY

Muted Group Theory is a critical theory because it is concerned with power and how it is used against people. While critical theories can separate the powerful and the powerless any number of ways, this theory chooses to bifurcate the power spectrum into men and women.

Muted Group Theory begins with the premise that language is culture bound, and because men have more power than women, men have more influence over the language, resulting in language with a male-bias. Men create the words and meaning for the culture, allowing expression of their ideas.

Women, on the other hand, are left out of this meaning creation and left without a means to express that which is unique to them. That leaves women as a muted group.

The Muted Group Theory rests on three assumptions:

1. Men and women perceive the world differently because they have different perception shaping experiences. Those different experiences are a result of men and women performing different tasks in society.
2. Men enact their power politically, perpetuating their power and suppressing women's ideas and meanings from gaining public acceptance.
3. Women must convert their unique ideas, experiences, and meanings into male language in order to be heard.

The premise and assumptions leads to a number of hypotheses about women's communication:

1. Women have a more difficult time expressing themselves than do men.
2. Women understand what men mean more easily than men understand what women mean.
3. Women communicate with each other using media not accepted by the dominant male communicators.
4. Women are less satisfied with communication than are men.
5. Women are not likely to create new words, but sometimes do so to create meanings special and unique to women.

Muted Group Theory does not claim that these differences are based in biology. Instead, the theory claims that men risk losing their dominant position if they listen to women, incorporate their experiences in the language, and allow women to be equal partners in language use and creation. Language is about power, and men have it.

FACE

Erving Goffman wrote about face in conjunction with how people interact in daily life. He claims that everyone is concerned, to some extent, with how others perceive them. We act socially, striving to maintain the identity we create for others to see. This identity, or public self-image, is what we project when we interact socially. To lose face is to publicly suffer a diminished self-image.

Maintaining face is accomplished by taking a line while interacting socially. A line is what the person says and does during that interaction showing how the person understands the situation at hand and the person's evaluation of the interactants. Social interaction is a process combining line and face, or face work. Brown and Levinson use the concept of face to explain politeness. To them, politeness is universal, resulting from people's face needs:

1. Positive face is the desire to be liked, appreciated, approved, etc.
2. Negative face is the desire not to be imposed upon, intruded, or otherwise put upon.

Positive politeness addresses positive face concerns, often by showing prosocial concern for the other's face. Negative politeness addresses negative face concerns, often by acknowledging the other's face is threatened. Anytime a person threatens another person's face, the first person commits a face-threatening act (FTA). Face-threatening acts come in four varieties, listed below in order from most to least face threatening:

1. Do an FTA baldly, with no politeness (e.g., "Close your mouth when you eat you swine.").
2. Do an FTA with positive politeness (e.g., "You have such beautiful teeth. I just wish I didn't see them when you eat.").
3. Do an FTA with negative politeness (e.g., "I know you're very hungry and that steak is a bit tough, but I would appreciate it if you would chew with your mouth closed.").

4. Do an FTA indirectly, or off-record (e.g., "I wonder how far a person's lips can stretch yet remain closed when eating?"). An indirect FTA is ambiguous so the receiver may "catch the drift" but the speaker can also deny a meaning if they wish.

Of course, a person can choose not to threaten another's face at all, but when a face must be threaten, a speaker can decide how threatening he or she will be.

CULTIVATION THEORY

According to Cultivation Theory, television viewers are cultivated to view reality similarly to what they watch on television. No one TV show gets credit for this effect. Instead, the medium of television gets the credit.

Television shows are mainstream entertainment, easy to access, and generally easy to understand. As such, they provide a means by which people are socialized into the society, albeit with an unrealistic notion of realty at times, particularly with respect to social dangers.

Television seeks to show and reinforce commonalities among us, so those who regularly watch television tend to see the world in the way television portrays it. Compared to actual demographics, women, minorities, upper-class, and lower-class people are under-represented on television shows. At the same time, the percent of people who work in law enforcement and violent crime are over-represented.

People who are heavy watchers of television assimilate this information and believe that the world is a dangerous, scary place where others can't be trusted. This is known as the "mean world syndrome." Further, heavy watchers of to blur distinctions between social groups such as the poor and the rich, urban and rural populations, and different racial groups.

Those TV watchers also identify themselves as political moderates but answer surveys similarly to how political conservatives answer the surveys. Not everyone is successfully cultivated by television. Those who watch little television are not affected. Likewise, people who talk about what they see, especially adolescents who talk with their parents, are less likely to alter their view of reality to match what they see on television.

THE SPIRAL OF SILENCE

The Spiral of Silence is a model of why people are unwilling to publicly express their opinions when they believe they are in the minority. The model is based on three premises:

1. people have a "quasi-statistical organ," a sixth-sense if you will, which allows them to know the prevailing public opinion, even without access to polls,
2. people have a fear of isolation and know what behaviors will increase their likelihood of being socially isolated, and
3. people are reticent to express their minority views, primarily out of fear of being isolated.

The closer a person believes the opinion held is similar to the prevailing public opinion, the more they are willing to openly disclose that opinion in public. Then, if public sentiment changes, the person will recognize that the opinion is less in favor and will be less willing to express that opinion publicly. As the perceived distance between public opinion and a person's personal opinion grows, the more unlikely the person is to express their opinion.

Consider the case of Dennis Rodman, one of the stars of the Chicago Bulls basketball team. Mr. Rodman has consistently been an incredible competitor and rebounder for the Detroit Pistons, San Antonio Spurs, and Chicago Bulls. Over the years he attracted a large fan base, but watched it fall in recent years as he got "weirder" or more "individualistic" (depending on how you interpret his behavior).

Fans in San Antonio welcomed Mr. Rodman when he first arrived, but vocal supporters were hard to find just before he was traded to Chicago. At the start of the 1996-1997 season Mr. Rodman's stock was high in Chicago, falling off somewhat after the "kick the cameraman" incident. I wish him well, but if the public becomes displeased with him the Spiral of Silence will strike his supporters once again.

STANDARD FORMAT FOR A SOCIAL SCIENTIFIC JOURNAL ARTICLE

Social scientific research reports and journal articles are designed to describe what researchers did, why they did it, how they did it, what they found, and what that means.

While all journals have their specific requirements, all research reports and journal articles follow the same standard format. The format is standardized to make it easy for readers to study research presented in a variety of journals.

The speed with which you read journal articles and the understanding you gain from those articles will increase once you become familiar with the standard format.

1. *Title:* The title should be brief but clearly describe the focus of the research described in the article.
2. *Author(s):* The names of all authors is given. The institutional affiliation is also given, sometimes with the authors' names, sometimes at the bottom of the first page, sometimes at the end of the article, and sometimes at the end of the journal.
3. *Abstract:* The abstract is a brief summary of the article designed to give the reader an overview of what the researchers did, how they did it, what they found, and what it means.
4. *Introduction:* This section describes all prior research and theories that all relevant to the study described in the article. That prior literature is integrated to form the basis of an argument(s) supporting why the present study was conducted. The introduction also introduces and argumentatively supports whatever research hypotheses and/or research questions are addresses in the study.

5. *Method:* This section describes what the researchers did. The section is written in sufficient detail and precision to allow a reader to replicate the study. There are exceptions to this principle of replication (e.g., lengthy surveys are not normally included, complex and detailed instructions to experimental subjects are often summarized, etc.). The method section contains as many of these five subsections as are appropriate for the study:

   Subjects: The demographics of the persons used in the study.

   Apparatus: Detailed description of special equipment used, if any, in the study.

   Procedures: Detailed description of what the researchers and subjects did.

   Design: Description of the type of experimental design used in the study.

   Materials or Measures: Description of which testing and measuring instruments were used, and how they were used if differently than their normal use.

6. *Results:* This section describes what the researchers found. You will often find this section to be a mixture of statistical reports, tables, and prose describing those numbers.

7. *Discussion:* This section provides the authors' the opportunity to tell what their research results mean, both to the study and to the world at large.

8. *References:* A list of all works (e.g., books, articles, personal communication, etc.) cited in the study. Most, and usually all, of the cited works will be cited and discussed in the introduction section of the article.

Readers familiar with statistical analyses and the theories, prior research, and methodologies used in field related to the article should have no problem understanding the article. Readers lacking familiarity with field related theories, research, and methodology usually have some difficulties grasping the big picture of the study, but if the article is well written the readers can understand enough to understand the gist of the study.

Readers unfamiliar with statistical analyses fare worse. These readers often entirely skip the Method and Results section, relying solely on the Introduction and Discussion sections. When read alone, the Introduction and Discussion sections can work well to provide the reader with an overview of the study. However, these sections generally stay at a higher level, leaving the details for the Method and Results sections. Often, the prize is in the details.

Certainly, the Results section contains the basis for determining the validity of information in the Discussion section. Readers lacking statistical analyses expertise will be best served by taking a course on experimental design and statistical analysis, preferably in the same discipline as the journal articles they read (e.g., readers of communication articles benefit from an experimental design and statistical analysis course offered by the communication department, readers of psychology articles benefit from an experimental design and statistical analysis course offered by the psychology department, etc.).

ABSTRACT

An abstract is presented to the reader before the beginning of an article. The abstract briefly tells what the researchers did, how they did it, what they found, and what that means. More specifically, an abstract of an social scientific study will describe:

1. the problem being investigated or question being answer,
2. the subjects, along with key information about those subjects,
3. the experimental method(s) used,
4. the results of the study, including statistical significance levels; and
5. what the results mean, both in the study and with regard to prior research, theories, and the world outside the research lab.

A properly written abstract will convey all that information in about 100 to 120 words. There should be no reason to refer to the article to understand jargon, abbreviations, or other oddities in the abstract.

Use abstracts to gain a first glance into journal articles. When you are researching a particular topic you can usually tell if a journal article pertains to that topic just by reading the abstract. If you determine that the article is relevant then be sure to read the entire article. Be aware that when a journal article reports multiple significant findings only the most important four or five will be mentioned in the abstract. When writing about a journal article never rely solely on the abstract (unless you absolutely cannot find the journal article, then be sure to cite the abstract, not the article).

3

MEDIA CONTROL: OPEN COMMUNICATION TECHNOLOGIES

"The conditions associated with a particular class of conditions of existence produce habitus, systems of durable, transportable dispositions, structured structures predisposed to function as structuring structures, that is, as principles which generate and organize practices and representations that can be objectively adapted to their outcomes without presupposing a conscious aiming at ends or an express mastery of the operations necessary in order to attain them. Objectively 'regulated' and 'regular' without being in any way the product of obedience to rules, they can be collectively orchestrated without being the product of the organizing actions of a conductor" (Bourdieu, p. 53)

The above quote by Bourdieu, when viewed from the perspective of the society as the 'habitus', is quiet informing (in theory as well as in practice) of media's interplay with the social structures within which they are embedded. As we have seen throughout our course readings, media technologies-as important instruments at various levels of communication processes in the society, have encountered resistance by various cultural and social norms, and somewhat mixed response from economical and political forces because of their profit making potentials or power generation ability. More then any other type of technology, media and communication technologies have been the subject of public and scholarly debates because of their intrinsic characteristics to be able to convey (asynchronously) content across time and space (at distance), inscribed in form of data, information, images, knowledge, and wisdom, in mediums such as books, data tape drives, CD-ROMS, video and audio tapes, etc. Additionally, synchronous communication has enabled instantaneous communication among people (e.g. telephone, audio and video conferencing, online chat) enabling efficient, but not necessarily effective exchange of information, ideas, thoughts, and concepts.

The pervasive and widespread use of media technologies, often used ubiquitously for symbolic purposes, is also used by the governing elites to maintain the status quo and ensure stability. The necessity to reproduce and maintain a stable state, the habitus (to borrow from Bourdieu whose habitus concept is similar to the stable state produced and maintained by the hegemonic ideology), requires ways for disseminating cultural and political material of the dominant ideology. Similarly to how Bourdieu describes the functioning of the habitus, Gitlin defines the status quo as hegemony, "a ruling class's (or alliance's) domination of subordinate classes and groups through the elaboration and penetration of ideology (ideas and assumptions) into their common sense and everyday practice," and contends that it "is systematic (but not necessary or even usually deliberate) engineering of mass consent to established order" (Gitlin, 1980, pp. 253). Further, elaborating on the aspect of hegemony and clarifying the composition of the elite, mostly government, corporate establishment and those institutions that produce cultural artifacts, Schiller (1996) explains their economic reason for cooperation: "The American economy is now hostage to a relatively small number of giant private companies, with interlocking connections, that set the national agenda. This power is particularly characteristic of the communication and information sector where the national cultural-media agenda is provided by a very small (and declining) number of integrated private combines. This development has deeply eroded free individual expression, a vital element of a democratic society" (Schiller, 1996, p. 44).

This paper will attempt to elaborate on the interplay between media and communication technologies, and social structures and forces (social, cultural, economical, political), whether institutionalized or not, emphasizing that both the content and the channels of communication through which the content is distributed are important factors in the production, maintenance and further reproduction of the artifacts of the dominant ideology. I will argue that the content that is being represented and recorded, when conveyed via open communication (such as the Internet), can show us the liberating potentials of various media technologies. As such, communication technologies are situated as important actors in the process to displacing or shifting the status quo.

MEDIA CONTROL

"The conditions associated with a particular class of conditions of existence produce habitus, systems of durable, transportable dispositions, structured structures predisposed to function as structuring structures, that is, as principles which generate and organize practices and representations that can be objectively adapted to their outcomes without presupposing a conscious aiming at ends or an express mastery of the operations necessary in order to attain them. Objectively 'regulated' and 'regular' without being in any way the product of obedience to rules, they can be collectively orchestrated without being the product of the organizing actions of a conductor" (Bourdieu, p. 53)

The above quote by Bourdieu, when viewed from the perspective of the society as the 'habitus', is quiet informing (in theory as well as in practice) of media's interplay with the social structures within which they are embedded. As we have seen throughout our course readings, media technologies-as important instruments at various levels of communication processes in the society, have encountered resistance by various cultural and social norms, and somewhat mixed response from economical and political forces because of their profit making potentials or power generation ability. More then any other type of technology, media and communication technologies have been the subject of public and scholarly debates because of their intrinsic characteristics to be able to convey (asynchronously) content across time and space (at distance), inscribed in form of data, information, images, knowledge, and wisdom, in mediums such as books, data tape drives, CD-ROMS, video and audio tapes, etc. Additionally, synchronous communication has enabled instantaneous communication among people (e.g. telephone, audio and video conferencing, online chat) enabling efficient, but not necessarily effective exchange of information, ideas, thoughts, and concepts.

The pervasive and widespread use of media technologies, often used ubiquitously for symbolic purposes, is also used by the governing elites to maintain the status quo and ensure stability. The necessity to reproduce and maintain a stable state, the habitus (to borrow from Bourdieu whose habitus concept is similar to the stable state produced and maintained by the hegemonic ideology), requires ways for disseminating cultural and political material of the dominant ideology. Similarly to how Bourdieu describes the functioning of the habitus, Gitlin defines the status quo as hegemony, "a ruling class's (or alliance's) domination of subordinate classes and groups through the elaboration and penetration of ideology (ideas and assumptions) into their common sense and everyday practice," and contends that it "is systematic (but not necessary or even usually deliberate) engineering of mass consent to established order" (Gitlin, 1980, pp. 253). Further, elaborating on the aspect of hegemony and clarifying the composition of the elite, mostly government, corporate establishment and those institutions that produce cultural artifacts, Schiller (1996) explains their economic reason for cooperation: "The American economy is now hostage to a relatively small number of giant private companies, with interlocking connections, that set the national agenda. This power is particularly characteristic of the communication and information sector where the national cultural-media agenda is provided by a very small (and declining) number of integrated private combines. This development has deeply eroded free individual expression, a vital element of a democratic society" (Schiller, 1996, p. 44).

This paper will attempt to elaborate on the interplay between media and communication technologies, and social structures and forces (social, cultural, economical, political), whether institutionalized or not, emphasizing that both the content and the channels of communication through which the content is distributed are important factors in the production, maintenance and further reproduction of the artifacts of the dominant ideology. I will argue that the content that is being represented and recorded, when conveyed via open communication (such as the Internet), can show us the liberating potentials of various media technologies. As such, communication technologies are situated as important actors in the process to displacing or shifting the status quo.

Evident from Gitlin's and Schiller's arguments is their emphasis on the necessity of free and open communication among the masses if there is to be any deliverance from the 'claws' of the media. On the contrary, it is the one-way communication (radio, TV, cable) utilized by the elites to achieve the subordination and dissemination of the hegemonic ideology. Fiske (1996) further elaborates this in his argument that surveillance technology is also used as means to discern the norms and regulations necessary to maintain the hegemony ideology: "Norms are crucial to any surveillance system, for without them it cannot identify the abnormal. Norms are what enable it to decide what information should be turned into knowledge and what individuals need to be monitored" (Fiske 1996, p. 220). Fiske's technologised surveillance of the physical goes hand-in-hand with surveillance of the discourse (what issues are raised on TV, radio, etc.) "because unequal access to those technologies ensures their use in promoting similar power-block interests" (Fiske 1996, p. 218). The important point brought forth here, directly or indirectly, is the identification of the closed, unidirectional (with masses on the receiving end) and restricted access of communication technology.

These aspects are identified as necessary characteristics for the maintenance and reproduction of the hegemonic ideology, enabling the elites to set the form, format and content of the public discourse (broadcasting, TV, radio, press, etc.), and as importantly decide who can participate. Therefore, it can be argued that this manifestation of communication technologies, entangled in the web of one-way communication and used by the elites for power control and dissemination of material in support of the hegemonic ideology, has shaped the traditional scholarly and public discourse, as well as their practical use, to view communication technology as intrinsically embedded with features, characteristics and functionalities, for reinforcing and aiding the hegemonic ideology.

This biased view, that communication technologies are inherently suited to help media control, is troublesome and factually wrong. For example, the scholarly and public discourse on early cable technology shows that cable access was intended for use unlike it is being used today (for dissemination popular consumer culture through its various formats with the aims of making profit). Streeter (1997) argues that cable "had the potential to rehumanize a dehumanized society, to eliminate the existing bureaucratic restrictions of government regulation common to the industrial world, and to empower the currently powerless public" (Streeter 1997, p.228). He further notes that the cable system had the potential to enable two-way communication and interactivity, but apparently failed to do so due to the social (un)response on the part of the audience: "Cable television was something that could have an important impact upon society, and it thus called for a response on the part of society; it was something to which society could respond and act upon, but that was itself outside society" (Streeter 1997, p. 225). And then adds that cable should not be viewed as an "autonomous entity that had simply appeared on the scene as the result of scientific and technical research" (Streeter 1997, p. 225). Here we see a distinction between the current social status of cable as profit making machinery and its potentials to have become socially responsible technology that would have empowered the audience with two-way open communication.

The above suggests that the communicative aspects of the production and reproduction of the dominant ideology, including the production of consent in the audience/consumer or citizen, are identified by media and communication technologies characterized by closed, one-way communication. This provides the elites with the ability to control the public discourse by selectively choosing the issues of discussion, and at the same time is able to control the access to the discourse: "But communication and information technology does not merely circulate discourse and make it available for analysts, it also produces knowledge and applies power" (Fiske 1996, p. 217). This process ensures conformity with the accepted cultural, social, economical, and political norms of the dominant ideology: "focus on communication technology both as ways of engaging in discourse struggles and, through their surveillance capability, as ways of producing a particular form of social knowledge and thus of exerting power" (Fiske 1996, p. 217)

That the various media and communication technology exhibit characteristics of closed systems with one-way communication can be hardly argued. However, the proper question to ask is: why is the communication technology so restrictive and a closed system that can be so easily controlled (deliberately or otherwise) by the elite? First, lets ask the following question regarding how does media fit in the economic system. Do the existing media/communication technologies exhibit characteristics that make them a better fit for the capitalistic free market (economy whose ultimate goal is the bottom-line, i.e. profit), rather than empowering the publics/audiences with information to better participate in representative democracy? Second, are the exhibited characteristics intrinsic to a particular technology embedded in the technology itself, or they are a result of the features and functionalities which designers embellished a particular technology?

To answer the above questions, I first turn to Schiller (1996) who argues in favor of original purpose and design: "When military or commercial advantages are the motivating forces of research and development, it is to be expected that the laboratories will produce findings that are conducive to these objectives. If other motivations could be advanced, the common good, for instance, different technologies might be forthcoming" (Schiller, p.71). Schiller's idea of the original purpose is also supported by the adaptive structurations theory (AST) that differentiates between technology's spirit (the original intent as thought by the designers who might be operating 'outside' of the hegemonic control, relatively speaking) and its subsequent functionality due to the appropriation process as the technology becomes embedded in institutionalized social structures. As such, more then often the existing socially and politically brokered power structures reflect themselves in the structure of the technology: "Information technology is highly political, but politics are not directed by its technological features alone" (Fiske 1996, p. 219).

The AST might appear in contradiction to Schiller's argument that the social use of technology is determined by the original purpose: "What the evidence here demonstrates is the strong, if not determining, influence of the original purpose that fostered the development of each new technology. The social use to which the technology is put, more times that not, follows its originating purpose" (Schiller, p. 71). The seemingly contradictory arguments need to be scrutinized in light of the social constructionist theory and technological determinism applied together. Neither one can explain the interplay of communication technology and society alone. The argument is that if a particular technology was designed to serve the corporate interest, most of its features will be driven to maximize the profits. In contrast, if a group of people designs technology for open communication and democratic access to information, the technology in question will have such features as to enable ease of access to information and make it hard for that technology to be used for restrictive purposes.

But again, it is not the technology per se; it is the social structures that tilt the design, development, and subsequent use of the technology for particular purposes. Unfortunately, most of the communication technology in use today has been built and appropriated for profit making activities and perhaps is unfit to support activities related to participatory democracy.

For example, the development of cable as medium of communication was relatively uneventful until the media corporations saw potentials for profits via advertising. As the fight of discourses got under way between government officials, media corporations and the liberal progressive forces, the elite elements appeared on the scene controlling and moderating the discourse: "The talk about cable ... was characterized by a systemic avoidance of central issues and assumptions, and by a pattern of unequal power in the discussion of its outcomes: the discourse of the new technology was shaped not so much by full fledged debate as by the lack of it" (Streeter 1997, p.222). Thus, the future of the cable technology was affected by the social structures and institutions, striping away from its technological potential the ability to become a technology that could link the masses and bring them together. The communication's technological determinism and social constructionism are interrelated in circular and iterative nature. It is hard to conceptualize isolated technology that is not being affected by the social structures, but constantly affects the same:

> *"As Raymond Williams has shown, this assumption of autonomous technology is characteristic of much though about television and society, and constitutes a false abstraction of technologies out of their social and cultural context" (Streeter 1997, p.225)*

> *"Such speculations naively assumed that telecommunication could magically resolve the power relations among people that caused racist, poverty, and international strife" (Streeter 1997, p.227)*

Even when a particular communication technology changes the social structures, it does not necessarily mean that such changes will be progressive and liberating. Streeter argues that relations in social structures are created by people and can only be changed by the people themselves, suggesting that even if technology has changed some structures, the changes have been appropriated by the elite and incorporated in the production and reproduction of the dominant ideology: "The constrains were not caused by old technological limits, nor can they be eliminated by new technologies: they were caused by relationship between people and can be overcome only by changing relations between people" (Streeter 1997, p.240). Or, as Fiske has put it very succinctly: "Technology may determine what is shown, but society determines what is seen" (Fiske 1996, p. 221). If technology's role in the society is determined both by its own characteristics and by the moderating characteristics of its social surroundings, what might be there that causes a particular technology to become a closed system, one-way communication, disseminating content which is controlled by the stakeholders whose primary concern is to advertise to the consumers or in the case of the government control its citizen through selective and strategic communications?

Arguing that one way communication by media companies (TV, cable, radio, movies) is a very important ingredient in the process of reproduction of the dominant ideology, because it is able to control the discourse by controlling the content and restricting the access to the discourse, Gitlin suggests that the centrally controlled one way communication (one-to-many) must disappear and be replaces by many-to-many communications if we wish to empower the masses (Gitlin, 1972, pp. 363). He further contends that a possible "revolutionary movement must aim to transform mass media by liberating communications technology for popular use (Gitlin, 1972, pp. 363). Apparently, Gitlin believes and posits the open communication (many-to-many) as a possible antidote to the hegemonic ideology.

Therefore, it can be argued that the communication technology, which is constantly modified and affected by the social structures in which it is embedded, while at the same time influencing and modifying those same social structures, has the potential to shift or displace the center of gravity (i.e. the status quo, the habitus) through its characteristics of open communication, which can induce mass communication amongst the masses themselves empowering them with many-to-many communication relatively outside of elites' controls.

Constrained by the historical discourse and practicality of most of the communication technology used for one way communication and for profit making purposes, Schiller is skeptical that such technology can be of any benefit to the society: "The customary argument that commerce and profit seeking go hand-in-hand with social benefit, is still to be demonstrated after hundreds of years of contrary experience" (Schiller, p.71).

At this point I would like to argue that the newest media technology, the communication facet of the Internet, exhibits characteristics of open communication that could position it as potential antidote to hegemonic ideology. As it has been argued above, whoever controls the content can control the scope of the public discourse, and whoever controls the access to the mass communication technology can practically control the voices that can debate the already restricted content/discourse. Unfortunately, TV, radio and cable technologies have been socially (various social and institutional structures) constructed such that both content and access control are in the same hands.

However, the Internet, especially the website portion of it (ability to publish) and the email discussion lists exhibit characteristics contrary to those of earlier technologies (as shaped by the social structures). For example, almost anyone can publish anything on the Internet, relatively speaking, without the fear that the server hosting firms might block the website (apart from criminally related material). In addition, the masses, can freely organize into groups of citizens, consumers, special interests groups, hobbyists, etc., and advocate their causes openly. This is partially enabled by the ability to establish many-to-many communication via email discussion lists. These two examples show that the content is not necessarily controllable by corporate power, and that the access to that content is not restricted by any corporate power. As matters of fact, both are subject to the ability to pay for Internet access, however, many libraries provide free Internet access for interested individuals. From the traditional technologies, public cable access channels resemble the above cases. However, most communities seldom use public cable access channels. When used, they are marginalized by not being included in programming listings (e.g. TV Guide) with the rest of cable and broadcast channels.

What social conditions and circumstanced led to the development of the Internet technologies which seem to exhibits open content and open communication properties, unlike the TV, radio and cable that have remained one-way communication channels? Why haven't then the same social structures and forces restricted various Internet technologies to be used for one-way communication only?

The apparent power to reach the masses, as well as the ability to interact with them, could not have escaped the elite. All of a sudden, as the number of Internet users increased manifolds each year, previously uninterested media corporations (there were repeated public claims that profit cannot be made with this new technology) invaded the Internet landscape, using it not much different than the TV: "Whether deceptively labeled as 'entertainment,' 'news,' 'culture,' 'education,' or 'public affairs,' TV programs aim to narrow and flatten consciousness-to tailor everyman's world view to the consumer mentality, to placate political discontent, to manage what cannot be placated, to render social pathologies personal, to level class-consciousness" (Gitlin, 1972, pp.345). The obviousness of the above is that almost all commercial sites support their Internet presence by online advertising. Yes, one can choose to visit a web site only to be bombarded by advertising, similar to TV advertising. However, studies have shown that web site visitors are increasingly becoming aware and do not necessarily get influenced by advertisements. This is a bit different from the TV. A visitor can still view the page without wasting time, whereas on TV you either watch the commercials or need to switch the channel.

In other words, the Internet, fueled by the open content and open communication, in its infancy and during its development until mid 90s, before it become obvious that it can be used by corporation for making profit, was truly the liberating technology alluded by Gitlin.

To think that the elites were so naive to overlook Internet's potential as mass medium is at best naivety itself. They could not have also overlooked the potential for the masses to utilize the Internet to organize themselves outside elite's control, however, perhaps the elite thought that any such conflict should be domesticated as Gitlin suggests: "What permits it to absorb and domesticate criticism is not something accidental to the liberal capitalist ideology, but rather its core" (Gitlin, 1980 pp. 256). Then, it seems that the inevitable happened, as many times before: "The hegemonic ideology changes in order to remain hegemonic; that is the peculiar nature of the dominant ideology of liberal capitalism" (Gitlin, 1982, pp. 450).

The elite moved to utilize the open communication technology, taking control over various aspect of it. Internet users still have to access the Internet via commercial entities that use online advertising as a profit stream. Various mergers and acquisition have occurred between traditional media and online industry, successfully trapping the masses to a particular content. Yet, it is still easier to escape the online advertisers than those on TV.

Corporations find this very problematic, as it is hard to centrally control a technology that was build to be managed in distributed fashion. Therefore, they have turned more than ever before to manage the access to the Internet technology and control the Internet visiting habits (through content portals) of the masses.

Despite these attempts by corporations, if a group of people wants an Internet presence, with potential readership/viewership of all who have access to the Internet, it can do so with minimal cost. The same cannot be said for the TV, the radio or cable. Whether the possibility for inexpensive presence on the Internet and its potential mass viewership will remain so, only the future will tell.

What could change? The unimaginable could happen. Governments can for example restrict who publishes what in their country by requiring licenses to operate a website. Obviously, for it to be effective the entire world has to enact the same laws since it is easy to move website servers around the world. Next, imagine that by some 'strange' imagination a judge rules that a US firm that provides Internet access can be held responsible for the content published by its customers. If such ruling is to be enforced, it could require that a corporation first approve each websites' content.

This could potentially lead various Internet access and Internet hosting providers to utilize their central role to their advantage. Why was the Internet build with open communication in mind? Adherents of the theory of hegemony could argue that this is contrary to the theory. If the Internet contains such power that can be used as an antidote to hegemony, why did the elite allow it to be developed in the form it is? Did they intent it or is it an unintentional byproduct of government's action to create communication network that can sustains nuclear attack by creating a very distributed communication network?

The Internet and its open communication and open content technologies and principles are still in the infancy. Whether the open concepts will remain part of the Internet in the future remains to be seen.

If previous communication technologies are any indication, we might expect the same with the Internet. However, as I have attempted to show in this paper, the Internet communication technologies have more or less embedded in their technology some characteristics that lend themselves to be used for open communication where the masses can communicate amongst themselves without the corporate media's oversight.

Claiming that there are embedded characteristics in a given technology sounds like technological determinism. That would be an oversight. One needs to look at the social, political, economical, and cultural factors that have helped construct those characteristics in the first place so they could be embedded in the underlying Internet technologies. Further, as time goes on, the social situatedness of the Internet technology could change and the social structures of the future might modify, change or even restricts the initially acquired and embedded open communication and open content characteristics of the Internet. Alternatively, if the open characteristics of the Internet take strong hold in society and overcomes the already entrenched hegemonic forces as they are embedded deeply in various social structures, it might empower the masses to shift and displace the status quo and thus bring forth more representative democracy.

JARGON BUSTING

Typical of an emerging technology, the Semantic Web literature is veiled in a bewildering array of-technical jargon. So much so that a time-pressed researcher might be forgiven for concluding that the Semantic Web is something for geeks and that it has no bearing on real work and real people; that it (unrealistically) requires everyone to create all online content in the RDF (Resource Description Framework)

Semantic Web language. This, of course, could not be further from the truth. Take the Weblogs (Blogs) phenomenon as an example. Few users of Weblogs are aware that they are publishing, syndicating and aggregating data onto the Semantic Web as well as the human-readable Web. Weblog technology revolves around the RSS (Rich Site Summary or RDF Site Summary) family of languages that vary in their human-readability but are united in their machine readability.

This resultant machine processibility is exploited to connect even the most human-centric RSS vocabularies into the Semantic Web directly, or through automated transformation to RDF. Weblogs thus form a valuable (and vast) source of richly interconnected information that requires little or no knowledge of the Semantic Web in order to create and use it.

For the information researcher, the Semantic Web view of this data enables seamless fusion of Weblog data with data from completely different sources such as dictionaries, thesauri, catalogues, databases as well as the 'traditional' Web. Where all this will lead is uncertain but the jargon is no obstacle to its creation and use.

BOTTOM-UP REVOLUTION

What seems certain is that both evolution and revolution will occur, and that the latter is all too easily overlooked. For instance, given the proliferation of data about data (metadata) that underpins the Semantic Web, it is tempting to focus in on the obvious prospect of a better-than-Google search engine. Such a "semantic search" engine is able to determine whether the query "orange" refers to the colour, the fruit, the mobile phone company, or a chemical weapon used by the United States.

As clever and useful as this may be, it is only an evolutionary enhancement of something that is already possible on the Web today. By looking in a little more detail at what is happening on the Semantic Web today, it is possible to gain a deeper insight into where revolution is starting to occur. In this article we will do just that; we will take a look at one of the most exciting new developments on the Semantic Web. Joined-up information about people, emanating not from some centralistic database but from individuals themselves.

In many ways, the explosive growth of social networking software, sites and data is representative of the way the Semantic Web is emerging. Weblogs were the first wave of this evolution/revolution; they allowed individuals to publish data in a sufficiently structured format for machine processing of that data to be relatively trivial.

Communities formed around weblogs in a bottom-up fashion, defined implicitly through syndication and through the lists of other weblogs ("blogrolls") that frequently accompanied weblogs. The next step, perhaps more revolutionary than evolutionary, is to explicitly define these (and other) communities in a way that is more easily machine processible.

The Friend Of A Friend (FOAF) project is one such initiative that is making this possible and, like weblogs, it does this from the bottom up.

One of the aims of the FOAF project is to improve the chances of happy accidents by describing the connections between people (and the things that they care about such as documents and places).

FOAF is a vocabulary for describing people, used analogously to Dublin Core metadata for documents. The idea is to use FOAF to describe the sorts of things you would put on your homepage-your friends, your interests, your pictures-in a structured fashion that machines find easy to process. What you get from this is a network of people instead of a network of web pages: the Web now contains descriptions of real things in the world-people-and because the Semantic Web is designed to be open and extensible, information about what these people do (their calendar), what they own (cars, houses, pets), what they create (documents, pictures, weblogs), can all be described as well.

Several million FOAF documents are out there on the Web already, created both by individuals and by various social software and networking sites.

FOAF documents can be created by hand, but increasingly, FOAF is being created from existing databases or by mining the existing Web.

When people need to know something and the area is outside their expertise, they need a way into the information landscape.

They need to find out what the main topics of interest are; who is well thought of; what where the important issues and papers in the area. People often serve as conduits for this type of information, with personal contacts serving as a way into an area and the key individuals within a field serving as a way of finding the main issues.

FOAF applications cannot replace the subtle social interactions which characterise personal information exchange, but they can help to make connections that might not otherwise have occurred: for example, by enabling certain sorts of information to be accurately processed by computers and therefore much easier to search.

Privacy and trust are clearly issues in FOAF as with all digital information on the Web or elsewhere. Organisations of various sorts already intensely mine the Web for information about individuals, email spammers being the most frequent example. FOAF includes protection against email spammers but in wider terms the very network of connections described in FOAF is likely to be its greatest asset in assessing reliability and quality of digital information on the Web.

CONCLUSION

From the perspective of the information researcher, the Semantic Web promises to provide and exploit joined-up information that goes way beyond the Web's traditional page-to-page links. Analysing the impact this will have on the day-to-day work of information professionals is not trivial. As with most new technologies, the Semantic Web is likely to create entirely new ways of working while simultaneously rendering others obsolete.

Applications like FOAF are at the vanguard of the Semantic Web, enabling a glimpse of what might be achieved. Their implicit and explicit definition of social networks offers the information researcher a wealth of new channels into the information cloud around individuals and communities.

4

Mammography and its Significance

Continuing controversy surrounds screening mammography, particularly for women 40 to 49 years of age. Newspapers are potentially important sources of information on this topic, but it is not known whether they provide well-founded and objective information and recommendations.

DESIGN

Cross-sectional descriptive study.

Setting: 6 top-circulation U.S. newspapers, 1990 to 1997.

MEASUREMENTS

Number of articles about screening mammography, issues covered by the articles, information sources, content and sources of quotes, recommendations cited in articles, and presentation of risks and benefits.

RESULTS

The most common theme of newspaper articles about mammography was screening for women 40 to 49 years of age. Thirty-one percent of the articles presented information without citing a source or justification. Quotes and recommendations in the articles were approximately twice as likely to support as to express reservations about mammography for women aged 40 to 49 years. Recommendations changed little over time and rarely reflected changes in recommendations of national organizations. Of the 102 articles describing the benefits of mammography, 95% expressed them in relative terms and 11% expressed them in absolute terms.

- Newspapers tended to overrepresent support for screening mammography for women aged 40 to 49 years. Reports would have been improved by identification of all sources for information cited, less reliance on relatively few sources, and discussion of benefits in absolute as well as relative terms. Medical journalism may benefit from identification of standards similar to those used for reporting medical research.

Newspapers are important sources of information about scientific and medical topics, not only for the general public but also for the scientific and medical communities and for policymakers. They can provide a forum for opinion and debate, give advice and make recommendations, set the public agenda by identifying newsworthy topics, and affect public policy and medical and scientific research.

Journalists' criteria for judging the quality of reporting may differ from those of a scientist or clinician, and newspapers generally value stories that are seen as exclusive, exciting, or controversial. Journalists often aim for "balance" by presenting both sides of an issue. They may draw on a range of sources for scientific or medical reports but are not necessarily in a position to judge their sources' relative merits, particularly since few journalists have specialist scientific or medical knowledge. In addition, while most scientific journals require disclosure of conflicts of interest, such conflicts are not always identified in newspaper articles. Studies of the accuracy and completeness of newspaper reporting of scientific issues have found that most newspaper articles contain errors of varying seriousness or omit important information and include little scientific explanation or critique of the quality or relevance of scientific evidence.

Breast cancer is the most commonly diagnosed cancer in women and receives considerable press coverage. The use of screening mammography for the early detection of breast cancer has increased in the past 30 years. Trials have shown a 25% to 30% reduction in mortality rate for women screened in their

50s and 60s. This is equivalent to 1 case of breast cancer prevented for every 270 women screened every 2 years from 50 to 69 years of age. No trial has provided conclusive evidence that screening in women younger than 50 years of age would reduce deaths. Recent meta-analyses suggest that screening may reduce mortality in women 40 to 49 years of age, but the reduction is smaller and takes longer to appear than in older women. The potential adverse effects of screening younger women are also greater.

For more than 20 years, the appropriateness of mammography at different ages has been debated and women have received various recommendations. In the late 1980s, most authorities agreed that women 40 to 49 years of age should be screened regularly. However, after an international workshop considered the latest trial evidence in 1993, the National Cancer Institute (NCI) stated that there was insufficient evidence to recommend routine screening in this age group and advised women to discuss their need for mammography with a physician.

Over the next few years, several organizations agreed with the NCI, while others continued to recommend regular mammography. In early 1997, a National Institutes of Health (NIH) consensus conference concluded that there was still insufficient evidence to support routine mammography screening for women 40 to 49 years of age. The subsequent outcry from political, professional, public, and media sources was followed 2 months later by an NCI recommendation supporting routine screening for these women.

From a public health perspective, breast cancer screening in women 40 to 49 years of age may have less impact than other approaches, such as improving screening rates among women 50 to 69 years of age, socioeconomically disadvantaged women, or older women. Some commentators feel that the mammography debate diverts attention from our lack of knowledge of the causes of breast cancer and how to prevent it.

The public has been largely unaware of the uncertain scientific basis of much accepted medical practice. Different types of scientific evidence have differing degrees of reliability, and presentation of this complex issue is challenging for both specialist and nonspecialist writers. Decisions are often made by balancing risks and benefits and can be strongly influenced by how these variables are presented.

Framing benefits in relative terms (for example, percentage reduction in risk) can give an overly optimistic impression, particularly if the underlying incidence of events is low. Including information about absolute benefits (for example, the absolute reduction in risk for or numbers of deaths) allows the effect of no intervention to be taken into account. Evidence shows that policymakers, clinicians, and the public favor interventions whose benefits are framed in relative rather than absolute terms.

Our goal in this study was to examine how mammography screening is presented in newspapers, given that scientific uncertainty still surrounds this important topic. We were interested in information about risk and benefit, how the debate was framed, citation of recommendations, quotes and information provided, and journalists' sources.

METHODS

We conducted a cross-sectional descriptive study to examine newspaper reports on screening mammography published from 1990 to July 1997. Six of the 10 U.S. newspapers with the highest circulations were selected. We chose to examine USA Today, The New York Times, Los Angeles Times, The Washington Post, Chicago Tribune, and Houston Chronicle to include papers from different geographic areas of the United States.

In July 1997, we searched the Nexis online database (Lexis-Nexis, Dayton, Ohio), which includes a full-text newspaper archive, for articles published from January 1990 through July 1997. We used the search term "mammogra!", which identified all articles containing such text words as "mammography," "mammogram," and so on. We obtained the full text of all articles that included some reference to screening mammography. One author reviewed the full text of each article and decided whether to include the article in the study.

To be included, articles had to have any aspect of screening mammography as their main topic or had to include at least 100 words about screening mammography even if it was not the main topic. Letters, book or television reviews, articles fewer than 50 words long, and duplicate articles (identical or nearly identical articles appearing in more than one newspaper) were excluded.

All other articles, including opinion or editorial pieces, were included because they form part of the picture that newspapers present to the public. To assess the effectiveness of our search method, we compared the results of a hand search of every copy of The Washington Post and USA Today for 1996 with the results of the database search.

A coding instrument was developed to abstract the article content. Two of the authors tested the instrument on three samples of newspaper articles.

The instrument was revised after each testing until acceptable agreement between coders was obtained. Most items were dichotomous variables, requiring a yes-or-no response.

The main areas covered by the content analysis were the article characteristics; the themes addressed in the article in relation to mammography; sources of information; persons quoted about mammography, their affiliation, and the content of the quotes; recommendations about mammography cited or made by the writer; and the ways in which the risk for breast cancer and benefits of mammography were described.

Two of the authors coded all articles independently, using a standardized codebook. Overall interrater agreement was 95% (= 0.87). Disagreements were resolved by discussion.

We recorded the actual recommendation cited or made regarding mammography but did not record the organization from which it originated because such organizations were frequently unnamed.

Recommendations about screening mammography made by U.S. government-related or health-related organizations were compared with recommendations made in newspaper articles during the same period.

STATISTICAL ANALYSIS

Data were entered into a database (Access, version 2.0, Microsoft Corp., Redmond, Washington) and were analyzed by using SAS, version 6.12 (SAS Institute, Cary, North Carolina). The main analyses used were means and frequency distributions.

Role of the Funding Sources

The funding sources had no role in the design, analysis, or interpretation of the study or in the decision to submit the study for publication.

Results

The Nexis search identified 2722 articles, 225 of which met the inclusion criteria. Hand searches of newspapers from 1996 revealed no articles not identified by the database search.

Characteristics of Articles

Article length ranged from fewer than 100 to more than 2500 words (mean, 460 words; median, 300 to 399 words). The annual frequency of articles varied widely and peaked at times of controversy over screening for women 40 to 49 years of age, notably in 1993, around the time of the international workshop, and in 1997, after the NIH consensus conference. Most articles were news articles (67%), and most appeared on the inside pages of the newspapers (79%). Bylines attributed 174 articles (77%) to newspaper staff, including 28 (12%) by a named medical or health writer, but 15 (7%) were published with no byline.

The most common main theme of the articles was screening mammography in women 40 to 49 years of age. Other themes related to utilization, effectiveness, and standards and quality of screening. A few articles were principally concerned with providing information about screening or breast cancer.

Attributed Sources of Information

One hundred twenty-two articles (54%) referred to research relating to mammography, but more than half of these did not identify the information source. Those that did referred to a journal, a scientific conference, or the research author.

The next most common type of information source was a government agency or department (or its representative), most often the NCI or NIH (55 articles [24%]). The American Cancer Society (ACS) was the other main source of information (44 articles [20%]). While many articles used more than one information source, 70 articles (31%) gave information without attributing it to any source.

Content and Sources of Quotes

A total of 619 quotes were identified in 160 articles, with a range of 0 to 15 quotes per article. More than one quarter of the quotes were used to communicate information or evidence. More than one third expressed views on mammography; of these, 63 (10%) supported mammography in general, 103 (17%) supported mammography for women 40 to 49 years of age, and 51 (8%) expressed reservations about screening in such women.

Twenty-four articles included quotes both supporting and questioning mammography for women 40 to 49 years of age, while 42 articles included quotes supporting mammography for this age group without a quote expressing the opposite point of view. Only 12 of the articles contained quotes expressing reservations about mammography for women 40 to 49 years of age without including a "balancing" quote.

We categorized quoted persons according to the context in which the article referred to them. Persons working in government institutions, departments, or agencies, such as the NCI, NIH, or the Agency for Health Care Policy and Research, were the most common sources.

The next main group included professionals involved in mammography or radiology. Two radiologists, one of whom was the most frequently quoted person, were particularly prominent. After authors of research or other scientists, representatives of the ACS were the next main group quoted. Other quotes came from advocacy groups, politicians, and members of the public (often describing their own experiences with breast cancer or mammography).

Different groups tended to be quoted in different ways. The ACS, radiologists, and other professionals involved in mammography, as well as politicians, all supported screening in women 40 to 49 years of age and expressed no reservations about it. Researchers and representatives of government institutions expressed views both for and against screening in these women. All persons quoted expressed some support for mammography screening in general, and almost all provided factual information.

Recommendations

In 187 articles (83%), a recommendation about mammography was cited (that is, the writer did not make it directly). In total, 595 recommendations were cited; most articles cited between 2 and 4 recommendations.

The most common recommendation, cited 195 times in 133 articles, was that women 40 to 49 years of age should have mammography. This recommendation appeared almost twice as often as its converse. One hundred articles cited a recommendation for mammography in women aged 50 years and older, and more than 50 articles cited a recommendation that women aged 40 to 49 years should make their own decisions about mammography, with or without consulting their physicians.

We also investigated the issue of "balancing" recommendations for women 40 to 49 years of age. The recommendation for mammography in women 40 to 49 years of age was the only recommendation cited in 51 articles, while the recommendation that they should not have mammography appeared without a "balancing" recommendation in 9 articles. Thirty-eight articles cited both of these recommendations.

The recommendation that women should make their own decisions with or without consulting their physicians appeared alone in only 4 articles. Thirty articles cited all three of these recommendations. Writers made or explicitly endorsed recommendations in 31 articles, 10 of which were attributed to journalists.

The remainder were opinion pieces or personal views written by nonjournalists or anonymous authors. Most commonly, writers advised that women in their 40s and 50s should have mammography. Of the 47 recommendations made, 16 (34%) were based on the advice of an authoritative individual or group, 9 cited scientific evidence, 3 cited personal experience, 3 cited some other foundation, and 16 were made without justification.

Recommendations Cited in Newspaper Articles over Time

In all years studied, women 40 to 49 years of age were more often advised to have mammography than to forgo it. The recommendation that they should decide about mammography for themselves with or without consulting their physicians appeared from 1993 on, after the workshop at which this recommendation was made.

Description of Risks and Benefits

One hundred two articles (45%) discussed the benefits of mammography quantitatively; of these, 97 (95%) reported benefit in relative terms (for example, a "30%" or "one-third" reduction in deaths). Eleven of these 102 articles (11%) described absolute benefits (for example, mortality rates with and without screening, or deaths prevented in a screened population), and 6 described both relative and absolute benefits.

Eighty-eight articles (39%) discussed risk for breast cancer quantitatively. Of these, 64 reported the absolute numbers of women diagnosed or dying in a population (most commonly a figure of approximately 46 000 deaths in the United States per year) and 43 reported a percentage or a rate (most commonly a lifetime risk of "1 in 8" or "1 in 9"). A non-numerical comparative description (for example, "the commonest cancer") was used in 40 articles (18%).

DISCUSSION - A SOURCE OF INFORMATION

Newspapers can be important sources of medical and scientific information, but previous studies have found that newspaper reporting sometimes lacks accuracy and completeness. Journalists are expected to produce controversial or exciting reports in a short time. Under these circumstances, it may be difficult to do justice to the complexities of scientific evidence, particularly for journalists without a scientific or medical background.

The problems of medical journalism are illustrated in newspaper reporting of the controversial issue of mammography screening for women 40 to 49 years of age. Our findings suggest that newspapers tend to support one side of the debate more than the other. Quotes and recommendations that favored mammography for women 40 to 49 years of age were more frequently presented in newspaper articles and were less often accompanied by a "balancing" viewpoint than those that expressed reservations.

Besides the 1993 appearance of the recommendation that women 40 to 49 years of age should decide for themselves about mammography with or without consulting a physician, the recommendations quoted bore little relation to current guidelines issued by various authorities.

In all years, women aged 40 to 49 years were more often advised to have mammography than not, although many authorities did not support this recommendation after 1993. When writers made recommendations themselves, few discussed the rationale behind them.

Several individuals and organizations, notably the ACS and several radiologists, were particularly successful in maintaining a high media profile. This frequent use of sources strongly aligned to one side of the debate appears to have led to overrepresentation of one point of view. While many articles identified information sources, almost one third included unsupported information or advice. Because the source of the research was usually not identified in a traceable form, the reader was often dependent on the writer's interpretation of the findings.

Most articles that quantified the benefits of mammography screening framed them in relative terms, which both policymakers and the public interpret more favorably than absolute terms. When presented numerically, the risk for breast cancer was described in absolute terms, which often gave the impression of many women being at risk.

Mammography screening is an important health issue that demonstrates how uncertain scientific evidence may be subject to different interpretations. Informed decision making is held up as an ideal for the public, but many are unfamiliar with the idea of scientific uncertainty and the need to balance risks and benefits.

It can be difficult for professionals to judge the quality of evidence, and it may be unrealistic to expect a detailed discussion and understanding of these issues in the lay press, where space is limited and unequivocal messages preferred. However, public understanding could be increased if scientific uncertainty and the need for making judgments were presented as the norm.

We were able to include only articles published between 1990 and July 1997; therefore, we cannot comment on whether our findings reflect current reporting practice. Despite the shortcomings that we observed, some individual articles were accurate and comprehensive, demonstrating that newspapers have the potential to be reliable information sources.

In recent years, there has been much interest in improving the quality of medical and scientific journals (for example, by setting standards for reporting of research). Attempts have also been made to define criteria by which the quality of medical journalism could be judged.

It might be argued that it is unrealistic to expect medical journalism to conform to standards that scientific and medical writing is still working toward. However, some basic criteria for medical journalism could be identified, such as attributing information to identifiable sources, avoiding overrepresentation of a particular point of view, and disclosing sources' possible conflicts of interest. It would also be helpful to indicate the type of evidence on which assertions and recommendations are based and to frame benefit in absolute as well as relative terms.

Relatively few journalists have specialized knowledge of medicine or science, and many reports on these subjects will continue to be written by nonspecialist journalists who cannot be expected to evaluate the quality of scientific evidence rigorously. The scientific and medical community can also take a more active role in working with medical journalists to ensure that the public receives objective, relevant, and comprehensible information. Both journalists and professionals in science and medicine could do much to ensure that the public is better served by newspaper reporting about screening mammography and medical issues in general.

5

THE INTELLECTUAL PROPERTY

There is a strong case for opposing intellectual property. Among other things, it often retards innovation and exploits Third World peoples. Most of the usual arguments for intellectual property do not hold up under scrutiny. In particular, the metaphor of the marketplace of ideas provides no justification for ownership of ideas.

The alternative to intellectual property is that intellectual products not be owned, as in the case of everyday language. Strategies against intellectual property include civil disobedience, promotion of non-owned information, and fostering of a more cooperative society.

The original rationale for copyrights and patents was to foster artistic and practical creative work by giving a short-term monopoly over certain uses of the work. This monopoly was granted to an individual or corporation by government. The government's power to grant a monopoly is corrupting. The biggest owners of intellectual property have sought to expand it well beyond any sensible rationale.

There are several types of intellectual property or, in other words, ownership of information, including copyright, patents, trademarks, trade secrets, design rights and plant breeders' rights. Copyright covers the expression of ideas such as in writing, music and pictures. Patents cover inventions, such as new substances or articles and industrial processes. Trademarks are symbols associated with a good, service or company. Trade secrets cover confidential business information. Design rights cover different ways of presenting the outward appearance of things. Plant breeders' rights grant ownership of novel, distinct and stable plant varieties that are "invented."

The type of property that is familiar to most people is physical objects. People own clothes, cars, houses and land. But there has always been a big problem with owning ideas. Exclusive use or control of ideas or the way they are expressed doesn't make nearly as much sense as the ownership of physical objects.

Many physical objects can only be used by one person at a time. If one person wears a pair of shoes, no one else can wear them at the same time. (The person who wears them often owns them, but not always.) This is not true of intellectual property. Ideas can be copied over and over, but the person who had the original copy still has full use of it. Suppose you write a poem. Even if a million other people have copies and read the poem, you can still read the poem yourself. In other words, more than one person can use an idea -- a poem, a mathematical formula, a tune, a letter -- without reducing other people's use of the idea. Shoes and poems are fundamentally different in this respect.

Technological developments have made it cheaper and easier to make copies of information. Printing was a great advance: it eliminated the need for hand copying of documents. Photocopying and computers have made it even easier to make copies of written documents. Photography and sound recordings have done the same for visual and audio material. The ability to protect intellectual property is being undermined by technology. Yet there is a strong push to expand the scope of ownership of information.

This chapter outlines the case against intellectual property. I begin by mentioning some of the problems arising from ownership of information. Then I turn to weaknesses in its standard justifications. Next is an overview of problems with the so-called "marketplace of ideas," which has important links with intellectual property. Finally, I outline some alternatives to intellectual property and some possible strategies for moving towards them.

INTRODUCTION

Governments generate large quantities of information. They produce statistics on population, figures on economic production and health, texts of laws and regulations, and vast numbers of reports. The generation of this information is paid for through taxation and, therefore, it might seem that it should be available to any member of the public. But in some countries, such as Britain and Australia, governments claim copyright in their own legislation and sometimes court decisions. Technically, citizens would need permission to copy their own laws. On the other hand, some government-generated information, especially in the US, is turned over to corporations that then sell it to whomever can pay. Publicly funded information is "privatised" and thus not freely available.

The idea behind patents is that the fundamentals of an invention are made public while the inventor for a limited time has the exclusive right to make, use or sell the invention. But there are quite a few cases in which patents have been used to suppress innovation. Companies may take out a patent, or buy someone else's patent, in order to inhibit others from applying the ideas. From its beginning in 1875, the US company AT&T collected patents in order to ensure its monopoly on telephones. It slowed down the introduction of radio for some 20 years. In a similar fashion, General Electric used control of patents to retard the introduction of fluorescent lights, which were a threat to its sales of incandescent lights. Trade secrets are another way to suppress technological development. Trade secrets are protected by law but, unlike patents, do not have to be published openly. They can be overcome legitimately by independent development or reverse engineering.

Biological information can now be claimed as intellectual property. US courts have ruled that genetic sequences can be patented, even when the sequences are found "in nature," so long as some artificial means are involved in isolating them. This has led companies to race to take out patents on numerous genetic codes. In some cases, patents have been granted covering all transgenic forms of an entire species, such as soybeans or cotton, causing enormous controversy and sometimes reversals on appeal. One consequence is a severe inhibition on research by non-patent holders. Another consequence is that transnational corporations are patenting genetic materials found in Third World plants and animals, so that some Third World peoples actually have to pay to use seeds and other genetic materials that have been freely available to them for centuries.

More generally, intellectual property is one more way for rich countries to extract wealth from poor countries. Given the enormous exploitation of poor peoples built into the world trade system, it would only seem fair for ideas produced in rich countries to be provided at no cost to poor countries. Yet in the GATT negotiations, representatives of rich countries, especially the US, have insisted on strengthening intellectual property rights. Surely there is no better indication that intellectual property is primarily of value to those who are already powerful and wealthy.

The potential financial returns from intellectual property are said to provide an incentive for individuals to create. In practice, though, most creators do not actually gain much benefit from intellectual property. Independent inventors are frequently ignored or exploited. When employees of corporations and governments have an idea worth protecting, it is usually copyrighted or patented by the organisation, not the employee. Since intellectual property can be sold, it is usually the rich and powerful who benefit. The rich and powerful, it should be noted, seldom contribute much intellectual labour to the creation of new ideas.

These problems -- privatisation of government information, suppression of patents, ownership of genetic information and information not owned by the true creator -- are symptoms of a deeper problem with the whole idea of intellectual property. Unlike goods, there are no physical obstacles to providing an abundance of ideas. (Indeed, the bigger problem may be an oversupply of ideas.) Intellectual property is an attempt to create an artificial scarcity in order to give rewards to a few at the expense of the many. Intellectual property aggravates inequality. It fosters competitiveness over information and ideas, whereas cooperation makes much more sense. In the words of

Peter Drahos, researcher on intellectual property, "Intellectual property is a form of private sovereignty over a primary good -- information."

Here are some examples of the abuse of power that has resulted from the power to grant sovereignty over information.

- The neem tree is used in India in the areas of medicine, toiletries, contraception, timber, fuel and agriculture. Its uses have been developed over many centuries but never patented. Since the mid 1980s, US and Japanese corporations have taken out over a dozen patents on neem-based materials. In this way, collective local knowledge developed by Indian researchers and villagers has been expropriated by outsiders who have added very little to the process.
- Charles M. Gentile is a US photographer who for a decade had made and sold artistic posters of scenes in Cleveland, Ohio. In 1995 he made a poster of the I. M. Pei building, which housed the new Rock and Roll Hall of Fame and Museum. This time he got into trouble. The museum sued him for infringing the trademark that it had taken out on its own image. If buildings can be registered as trademarks, then every painter, photographer and film-maker might have to seek permission and pay fees before using the images in their art work. This is obviously contrary to the original justification for intellectual property, which is to encourage the production of artistic works.
- Prominent designer Victor Papanek writes: "...there is something basically wrong with the whole concept of patents and copyrights. If I design a toy that provides therapeutic exercise for handicapped children, then I think it is unjust to delay the release of the design by a year and a half, going through a patent application. I feel that ideas are plentiful and cheap, and it is wrong to make money from the needs of others. I have been very lucky in persuading many of my students to accept this view. Much of what you will find as design examples

throughout this book has never been patented. In fact, quite the opposite strategy prevails: in many cases students and I have made measured drawings of, say, a play environment for blind children, written a description of how to build it simply, and then mimeographed drawings and all. If any agency, anywhere, will write in, my students will send them all the instructions free of charge."

- In 1980, a book entitled Documents on Australian Defence and Foreign Policy 1968-1975 was published by George Munster and Richard Walsh. It reproduced many secret government memos, briefings and other documents concerning Australian involvement in the Vietnam war, events leading up to the Indonesian invasion of East Timor, and other issues. Exposure of this material deeply embarrassed the Australian government. In an unprecedented move, the government issued an interim injunction, citing both the Crimes Act and the Copyright Act. The books, just put on sale, were impounded. Print runs of two major newspapers with extracts from the book were also seized.

The Australian High Court ruled that the Crimes Act did not apply, but that the material was protected by copyright held by the government. Thus copyright, set up to encourage artistic creation, was used to suppress dissemination of documents for whose production copyright was surely no incentive. Later, Munster and Walsh produced a book using summaries and short quotes in order to present the information.

- Scientology is a religion in which only certain members at advanced stages of enlightenment have access to special information, which is secret to others. Scientology has long been controversial, with critics maintaining that it exploits members. Some critics, including former Scientologists, have put secret documents from advanced stages on the Internet. In response, church officials invoked copyright. Police have raided homes of critics, seizing computers, disks and other equipment. This is all rather curious, since the stated purpose of copyright is not to hide information but rather to stimulate production of new ideas.

The following examples show that the uncertainty of intellectual property law encourages ambit claims that seem to be somewhat plausible. Some targets of such claims give in for economic reasons.

- Ashleigh Brilliant is a "professional epigrammatist." He creates and copyrights thousands of short sayings, such as "Fundamentally, there may be no basis for anything." When he finds someone who has "used" one of his epigrams, he contacts them demanding a payment for breach of copyright. Television journalist David Brinkley wrote a book, Everyone is Entitled to My Opinion, the title of which he attributed to a friend of his daughter. Brilliant contacted Brinkley about copyright violation. Random House, Brinkley's publisher, paid Brilliant $1000 without contesting the issue, perhaps because it would have cost more than this to contest it.
- Lawyer Robert Kunstadt has proposed that athletes could patent their sporting innovations, such as the "Fosbury flop" invented by high jumper Dick Fosbury. This might make a lot of money for a few stars. It would also cause enormous disputes. Athletes already have a tremendous incentive to innovate if it helps their performance. Patenting of basketball moves or choreography steps would serve mainly to limit the uptake of innovations and would mainly penalise those with fewer resources to pay royalties.
- The US National Basketball Association has sued in court for the exclusive right to transmit the scores of games as they are in progress. It had one success but lost on appeal.
- A Scottish newspaper, The Shetland Times, went to court to stop an online news service from making a hypertext link to its web site. If hypertext links made without permission were made illegal, this would undermine the World Wide Web.

These examples show that intellectual property has become a means for exerting power in ways quite divorced from its original aim -- promoting the creation and use of new ideas.

STANDARD JUSTIFICATIONS CRTITICS

Edwin C. Hettinger has provided an insightful critique of the main arguments used to justify intellectual property, so it is worthwhile summarising his analysis. He begins by noting the obvious argument against intellectual property, namely that sharing intellectual objects still allows the original possessor to use them. Therefore, the burden of proof should lie on those who argue for intellectual property.

The first argument for intellectual property is that people are entitled to the results of their labour. Hettinger's response is that not all the value of intellectual products is due to labour. Nor is the value of intellectual products due to the work of a single labourer, or any small group. Intellectual products are social products.

Suppose you have written an essay or made an invention. Your intellectual work does not exist in a social vacuum. It would not have been possible without lots of earlier work -- both intellectual and nonintellectual -- by many other people. This includes your teachers and parents. It includes the earlier authors and inventors who provided the foundation for your contribution. It also includes the many people who discussed and used ideas and techniques, at both theoretical and practical levels, and provided a cultural foundation for your contribution. It includes the people who built printing presses, laid telephone cables, built roads and buildings and in many other ways contributed to the "construction" of society. Many other people could be mentioned. The point is that any piece of intellectual work is always built on and is inconceivable without the prior work of numerous people.

Hettinger points out that the earlier contributors to the development of ideas are not present. Today's contributor therefore cannot validly claim full credit. Is the market value of a piece of an intellectual product a reasonable indicator of a person's contribution? Certainly not. As noted by Hettinger and as will be discussed in the next section, markets only work once property rights have been established, so it is circular to argue that the market can be used to measure intellectual contributions. Hettinger summarises this point in this fashion: "The notion that a laborer is naturally entitled as a matter of right to receive the market value of her product is a myth. To what extent individual laborers should be allowed to receive the market value of their products is a question of social policy."

A related argument is that people have a right to possess and personally use what they develop. Hettinger's response is that this doesn't show that they deserve market values, nor that they should have a right to prevent others from using the invention.

A second major argument for intellectual property is that people deserve property rights because of their labour. This brings up the general issue of what people deserve, a topic that has been analysed by philosophers. Their usual conclusions go against what many people think is "common sense." Hettinger says that a fitting reward for labour should be proportionate to the person's effort, the risk taken and moral considerations. This sounds all right -- but it is not proportionate to the value of the results of the labour, whether assessed through markets or by other criteria. This is because the value of intellectual work is affected by things not controlled by the worker, including luck and natural talent. Hettinger says "A person who is born with extraordinary natural talents, or who is extremely lucky, deserves nothing on the basis of these characteristics."

A musical genius like Mozart may make enormous contributions to society. But being born with enormous musical talents does not provide a justification for owning rights to musical compositions or performances. Likewise, the labour of developing a toy like Teenage Mutant Ninja Turtles that becomes incredibly popular does not provide a justification for owning rights to all possible uses of turtle symbols. What about a situation where one person works hard at a task and a second person with equal talent works less hard? Doesn't the first worker deserve more reward? Perhaps so, but property rights do not provide a suitable mechanism for allocating rewards. The market can give great rewards to the person who successfully claims property rights for a discovery, with little or nothing for the person who just missed out.

A third argument for intellectual property is that private property is a means for promoting privacy and a means for personal autonomy. Hettinger responds that privacy is protected by not revealing information, not by owning it. Trade secrets cannot be defended on the grounds of privacy, because corporations are not individuals. As for personal autonomy, copyrights and patents aren't required for this.

A fourth argument is that rights in intellectual property are needed to promote the creation of more ideas. The idea is that intellectual property gives financial incentives to produce ideas. Hettinger thinks that this is the only decent argument for intellectual property. He is still somewhat sceptical, though. He notes that the whole argument is built on a contradiction, namely that in order to promote the development of ideas, it is necessary to reduce people's freedom to use them. Copyrights and patents may encourage new ideas and innovations, but they also restrict others from using them freely.

This argument for intellectual property cannot be resolved without further investigation. Hettinger says that there needs to be an investigation of how long patents and copyrights should be granted, to determine an optimum period for promoting intellectual work. For the purposes of technological innovation, information becomes more valuable when augmented by new information: innovation is a collective process. If firms in an industry share information by tacit cooperation or open collaboration, this speeds innovation and reduces costs. Patents, which put information into the market and raise information costs, actually slow the innovative process.

It should be noted that although the scale and pace of intellectual work has increased over the past few centuries, the duration of protection of intellectual property has not been reduced, as might be expected, but greatly increased. The US government did not recognise foreign copyrights for much of the 1800s. Where once copyrights were only for a period of a few decades, they now may be for the life of the author plus 70 years. In many countries, chemicals and pharmaceuticals were not patentable until recently. This suggests that even if intellectual property can be justified on the basis of fostering new ideas, this is not the driving force behind the present system of copyrights and patents. After all, few writers feel a greater incentive to write and publish just because their works are copyrighted for 70 years after they die, rather than just until they die.

Of various types of intellectual property, copyright is especially open for exploitation. Unlike patents, copyright is granted without an application and lasts far longer. Originally designed to encourage literary and artistic work, it now applies to every memo and doodle and is more relevant to business than art. There is no need to encourage production of business correspondence, so why is copyright applied to it?

Intellectual property is built around a fundamental tension: ideas are public but creators want private returns. To overcome this tension, a distinction developed between ideas and their expression. Ideas could not be copyrighted but their expression could. This peculiar distinction was tied to the romantic notion of the autonomous creator who somehow contributes to the common pool of ideas without drawing from it. This package of concepts apparently justified authors in claiming residual rights -- namely copyright -- in their ideas after leaving their hands, while not giving manual workers any rationale for claiming residual rights in their creations. In practice, though, the idea-expression distinction is dubious and few of the major owners of intellectual property have the faintest resemblance to romantic creators.

MARKETPLACE OF IDEAS

The idea of intellectual property has a number of connections with the concept of the marketplace of ideas, a metaphor that is widely used in discussions of free speech. To delve a bit more deeply into the claim that intellectual property promotes development of new ideas, it is therefore helpful to scrutinise the concept of the marketplace of ideas.

The image conveyed by the marketplace of ideas is that ideas compete for acceptance in a market. As long as the competition is fair -- which means that all ideas and contributors are permitted access to the marketplace -- then good ideas will win out over bad ones. Why? Because people will recognise the truth and value of good ideas. On the other hand, if the market is constrained, for example by some groups being excluded, then certain ideas cannot be tested and examined and successful ideas may not be the best ideas.

Logically, there is no reason why a marketplace of ideas has to be a marketplace of owned ideas: intellectual property cannot be strictly justified by the marketplace of ideas. But because the marketplace metaphor is an economic one, there is a strong tendency to link intellectual property with the marketplace of ideas. There is a link between these two concepts, but not in the way their defenders usually imagine.

There are plenty of practical examples of the failure of the marketplace of ideas. Groups that are stigmatised or that lack power seldom have their viewpoints presented. This includes ethnic minorities, prisoners, the unemployed, manual workers and radical critics of the status quo, among many others. Even when such groups organise themselves to promote their ideas, their views are often ignored while the media focus on their protests, as in the case of peace movement rallies and marches.

Demonstrably, good ideas do not always win out in the marketplace of ideas. To take one example, the point of view of workers is frequently just as worthy as that of employers. Yet there is an enormous imbalance in the presentation of their respective viewpoints in the media. One result is that quite a few ideas that happen to serve the interests of employers at the expense of workers -- such as that the reason people don't have jobs is because they aren't trying hard enough to find them -- are widely accepted although they are rejected by virtually all informed analysts.

There is a simple and fundamental reason for the failure of the marketplace of ideas: inequality, especially economic inequality. Perhaps in a group of people sitting in a room discussing an issue, there is some prospect of a measured assessment of different ideas. But if these same people are isolated in front of their television sets, and one of them owns the television station, it is obvious that there is little basis for testing of ideas. The reality is that powerful and rich groups can promote their ideas with little chance of rebuttal from those with different perspectives. The mass media are powerful enterprises that promote their own interests as well as those of governments and corporations.

In circumstances where participants are approximate equals, such as intellectual discussion among peers in an academic discipline, then the metaphor of competition of ideas has some value. But ownership of media or ideas is hardly a prerequisite for such discussion. It is the equality of power that is essential. To take one of many possible examples, when employees in corporations lack the freedom to speak openly without penalty they cannot be equal participants in discussions.

Some ideas are good -- in the sense of being valuable to society -- but are unwelcome. Some are unwelcome to powerful groups, such as that governments and corporations commit horrific crimes or that there is a massive trade in technologies of torture and repression that needs to be stopped. Others are challenging to much of the population, such as that imprisonment does not reduce the crime rate or that financial rewards for good work on the job or grades for good schoolwork are counterproductive. (Needless to say, individuals might disagree with the examples used here. The case does not rest on the examples themselves, but on the existence of some socially valuable ideas that are unwelcome and marginalised.) The marketplace of ideas simply does not work to treat such unwelcome ideas with the seriousness they deserve. The mass media try to gain audiences by pleasing them, not by confronting them with challenging ideas.

The marketplace of ideas is often used to justify free speech. The argument is that free speech is necessary in order for the marketplace of ideas to operate: if some types of speech are curtailed, certain ideas will not be available on the marketplace and thus the best ideas will not succeed. This sounds plausible. But it is possible to reject the marketplace of ideas while still defending free speech on the grounds that it is essential to human liberty.

If the marketplace of ideas doesn't work, what is the solution? The usual view is that governments should intervene to ensure that all groups have fair access to the media. But this approach, based on promoting equality of opportunity, ignores the fundamental problem of economic inequality. Even if minority groups have some limited chance to present their views in the mass media, this can hardly compensate for the massive power of governments and corporations to promote their views. In addition, it retains the role of the mass media as the central mechanism for disseminating ideas. So-called reform proposals either retain the status quo or introduce government censorship.

Underlying the market model is the idea of self-regulation: the "free market" is supposed to operate without outside intervention and, indeed, to operate best when outside intervention is minimised. In practice, even markets in goods do not operate autonomously: the state is intimately involved in even the freest of markets. In the case of the marketplace of ideas, the state is involved both in shaping the market and in making it possible, for example by promoting and regulating the mass media. The world's most powerful state, the US, has been the driving force behind the establishment of a highly protectionist system of intellectual property, using power politics at GATT, the General Agreement on Tariffs and Trade.

Courts may use the rhetoric of the marketplace of ideas but actually interpret the law to support the status quo. For example, speech is treated as free until it might actually have some consequences. Then it is curtailed when it allegedly presents a "clear and present danger," such as when peace activists expose information supposedly threatening to "national security". But speech without action is pointless. True liberty requires freedom to promote one's views in practice. Powerful groups have the ability to do this. Courts only intervene when others try to do the same.

As in the case of trade generally, a property-based "free market" serves the interests of powerful producers. In the case of ideas, this includes governments and corporations plus intellectuals and professionals linked with universities, entertainment, journalism and the arts. Against such an array of intellectual opinion, it is very difficult for other groups, such as manual workers, to compete. The marketplace of ideas is a biased and artificial market that mostly serves to fine-tune relations between elites and provide them with legitimacy.

The implication of this analysis is that intellectual property cannot be justified on the basis of the marketplace of ideas. The utilitarian argument for intellectual property is that ownership is necessary to stimulate production of new ideas, because of the financial incentive. This financial incentive is supposed to come from the market, whose justification is the marketplace of ideas. If, as critics argue, the marketplace of ideas is flawed by the presence of economic inequality and, more fundamentally, is an artificial creation that serves powerful producers of ideas and legitimates the role of elites, then the case for intellectual property is unfounded. Intellectual property can only serve to aggravate the inequality on which it is built.

THE ALTERNATIVE

The alternative to intellectual property is straightforward: intellectual products should not be owned. That means not owned by individuals, corporations, governments, or the community as common property. It means that ideas are available to be used by anyone who wants to.

One example of how this might operate is language, including the words, sounds and meaning systems with which we communicate every day. Spoken language is free for everyone to use. (Actually, corporations do control bits of language through trademarks and slogans.)

Another example is scientific knowledge. Scientists do research and then publish their results. A large proportion of scientific knowledge is public knowledge. There are some areas of science that are not public, such as classified military research. It is usually argued that the most dynamic parts of science are those with the least secrecy. Open ideas can be examined, challenged, modified and improved. To turn scientific knowledge into a commodity on the market, as is happening with genetic engineering, arguably inhibits science.

Few scientists complain that they do not own the knowledge they produce. Indeed, they are much more likely to complain when corporations or governments try to control dissemination of ideas. Most scientists receive a salary from a government, corporation or university. Their livelihoods do not depend on royalties from published work.

University scientists have the greatest freedom. The main reasons they do research are for the intrinsic satisfaction of investigation and discovery -- a key motivation for many of the world's great scientists -- and for recognition by their peers. To turn scientific knowledge into intellectual property would dampen the enthusiasm of many scientists for their work. However, as governments reduce their funding of universities, scientists and university administrations increasingly turn to patents as a source of income.

Language and scientific knowledge are not ideal; indeed, they are often used for harmful purposes. It is difficult to imagine, though, how turning them into property could make them better.

The case of science shows that vigorous intellectual activity is quite possible without intellectual property, and in fact that it may be vigorous precisely because information is not owned. But there are lots of areas that, unlike science, have long operated with intellectual property as a fact of life. What would happen without ownership of information? Many objections spring to mind.

PLAGIARISM

Many intellectual workers fear being plagiarised and many of them think that intellectual property provides protection against this. After all, without copyright, why couldn't someone put their name on your essay and publish it? Actually, copyright provides very little protection against plagiarism. So-called "moral rights" of authors to be credited are backed by law in many countries but are an extremely cumbersome way of dealing with plagiarism.

Plagiarism means using the ideas of others without adequate acknowledgment. There are several types of plagiarism. One is plagiarism of ideas: someone takes your original idea and, using different expression, presents it as their own. Copyright provides no protection at all against this form of plagiarism. Another type of plagiarism is word-for-word plagiarism, where someone takes the words you've written -- a book, an essay, a few paragraphs or even just a sentence -- and, with or without minor modifications, presents them as their own. This sort of plagiarism is covered by copyright -- assuming that you hold the copyright. In many cases, copyright is held by the publisher, not the author. In practice, plagiarism goes on all the time, in various ways and degrees, and copyright law is hardly ever used against it. The most effective challenge to plagiarism is not legal action but publicity. At least among authors, plagiarism is widely condemned. For this reason, and because they seek to give credit where it's due, most writers do take care to avoid plagiarising.

There is an even more fundamental reason why copyright provides no protection against plagiarism: the most common sort of plagiarism is built into social hierarchies. Government and corporate reports are released under the names of top bureaucrats who did not write them; politicians and corporate executives give speeches written by underlings. These are examples of a pervasive misrepresentation of authorship in which powerful figures gain credit for the work of subordinates. Copyright, if it has any effect at all, reinforces rather than challenges this sort of institutionalised plagiarism.

ROYALTIES

What about all the writers, inventors and others who depend for their livelihood on royalties? First, it should be mentioned that only a very few individuals make enough money from royalties to live on. For example, there are probably only a few hundred self-employed writers in the US. Most of the rewards from intellectual property go to a few big companies. But the question is still a serious one for those intellectual workers who depend on royalties and other payments related to intellectual property.

The alternative in this case is some reorganisation of the economic system. Those few currently dependent on royalties could instead receive a salary, grant or bursary, just as most scientists do.

Getting rid of intellectual property would reduce the incomes of a few highly successful creative individuals, such as author Agatha Christie, composer Andrew Lloyd Webber and filmmaker Steven Spielberg. Publishers could reprint Christie's novels without permission, theatre companies could put on Webber's operas whenever they wished and Spielberg's films could be copied and screened anywhere. Jurassic Park and Lost World T-shirts, toys and trinkets could be produced at will. This would reduce the income of and, to some extent, the opportunities for artistic expression by these individuals. But there would be economic resources released: there would be more money available for other creators. Christie, Webber and Spielberg might be just as popular without intellectual property to channel money to them and their family enterprises.

The typical creative intellectual is actually worse off due to intellectual property. Consider an author who brings in a few hundred or even a few thousand dollars of royalty income per year. This is a tangible income, which creators value for its monetary and symbolic value. But this should be weighed against payments of royalties and monopoly profits when buying books, magazines, CDs and computer software.

Many of these costs are invisible. How many consumers, for example, realise how much they are paying for intellectual property when buying prescription medicines, paying for schools (through fees or taxes), buying groceries or listening to a piece of music on the radio? Yet in these and many other situations, costs are substantially increased due to intellectual property. Most of the extra costs go not to creators but to corporations and to bureaucratic overheads -- such as patent offices and law firms -- that are necessary to keep the system of intellectual property going.

STIMULATING CREATIVITY

What about the incentive to create? Without the possibility of wealth and fame, what would stimulate creative individuals to produce works of genius? Actually, most creators and innovators are motivated by their own intrinsic interest, not by rewards. There is a large body of evidence showing, contrary to popular opinion, that rewards actually reduce the quality of work. If the goal is better and more creative work, paying creators on a piecework basis, such as through royalties, is counterproductive.

In a society without intellectual property, creativity is likely to thrive. Most of the problems that are imagined to occur if there is no intellectual property -- such as the exploitation of a small publisher that renounces copyright -- are due to economic arrangements that maintain inequality. The soundest foundation for a society without intellectual property is greater economic and political equality. This means not just equality of opportunity, but equality of outcomes. This does not mean uniformity and does not mean levelling imposed from the top: it means freedom and diversity and a situation where people can get what they need but are not able to gain great power or wealth by exploiting the work of others. This is a big issue. Suffice it to say here that there are strong social and psychological arguments in favour of equality.

PLANNINGS FOR CHANGE

Intellectual property is supported by many powerful groups: the most powerful governments and the largest corporations. The mass media seem fully behind intellectual property, partly because media monopolies would be undercut if information were more freely copied and partly because the most influential journalists depend on syndication rights for their stories.

Perhaps just as important is the support for intellectual property from many small intellectual producers, including academics and free-lance writers. Although the monetary returns to these intellectuals are seldom significant, they have been persuaded that they both need and deserve their small royalties.

This is similar to the way that small owners of goods and land, such as homeowners, strongly defend the system of private property, whose main beneficiaries are the very wealthy who own vast enterprises based on many other people's labour. Intellectuals are enormous consumers as well as producers of intellectual work.

A majority would probably be better off financially without intellectual property, since they wouldn't have to pay as much for other people's work. Another problem in developing strategies is that it makes little sense to challenge intellectual property in isolation. If we simply imagine intellectual property being abolished but the rest of the economic system unchanged, then many objections can be made. Challenging intellectual property must involve the development of methods to support creative individuals.

CHANGE THINKING

Talking about "intellectual property" implies an association with physical property. Instead, it is better to talk about monopolies granted by governments, for example "monopoly privilege." This gives a better idea of what's going on and so helps undermine the legitimacy of the process. Associated with this could be an appeal to free market principles, challenging the barriers to trade in ideas imposed by monopolies granted to copyright and patent holders.

As well, a connection should be forged with ideals of free speech. Rather than talk of intellectual property in terms of property and trade, it should be talked about in terms of speech and its impediments. Controls over genetic information should be talked about in terms of public health and social welfare rather than property.

The way that an issue is framed makes an enormous difference to the legitimacy of different positions. Once intellectual property is undermined in the minds of many citizens, it will become far easier to topple its institutional supports.

EXPOSE THE COSTS

It can cost a lot to set up and operate a system of intellectual property. This includes patent offices, legislation, court cases, agencies to collect fees and much else. There is a need for research to calculate and expose these costs as well as the transfers of money between different groups and countries. A middle-ranking country from the First World, such as Australia, pays far more for intellectual property -- mostly to the US -- than it receives. Once the figures are available and understood, this will aid in reducing the legitimacy of the world intellectual property system.

REPRODUCE PROTECTED WORKS

From the point of view of intellectual property, this is called "piracy." (This is a revealing term, considering that such language is seldom used when, for example, a boss takes credit for a subordinate's work or when a Third World intellectual is recruited to a First World position. In each case, investments in intellectual work made by an individual or society are exploited by a different individual or society with more power.) This happens every day when people photocopy copyrighted articles, tape copyrighted music, or duplicate copyrighted software. It is precisely because illegal copying is so easy and so common that big governments and corporations have mounted offensives to promote intellectual property rights.

Unfortunately, illegal copying is not a very good strategy against intellectual property, any more than stealing goods is a way to challenge ownership of physical property. Theft of any sort implicitly accepts the existing system of ownership. By trying to hide the copying and avoiding penalties, the copiers appear to accept the legitimacy of the system.

OPENLY REFUSE TO COOPERATE WITH INTELLECTUAL PROPERTY

This is far more powerful than illicit copying. The methods of nonviolent action can be used here, including noncooperation, boycotts and setting up alternative institutions. By being open about the challenge, there is a much greater chance of focussing attention on the issues at stake and creating a dialogue. By being principled in opposition, and being willing to accept penalties for civil disobedience to laws on intellectual property, there is a much greater chance of winning over third parties. If harsh penalties are applied to those who challenge intellectual property, this could produce a backlash of sympathy. Once mass civil disobedience to intellectual property laws occurs, it will be impossible to stop.

Something like that is already occurring. Because photocopying of copyrighted works is so common, there is seldom any attempt to enforce the law against small violators -- to do so would alienate too many people. Copyright authorities therefore seek other means of collecting revenues from intellectual property, such as payments by institutions based on library copies. Already there is mass discontent in India over the impact of the world intellectual property regime and patenting of genetic materials, with rallies of hundreds of thousands of farmers. If this scale of protest could be combined with other actions that undermine the legitimacy of intellectual property, the entire system could be challenged.

PROMOTE NON-OWNED INFORMATION

A good example is public domain software, which is computer software that is made available free to anyone who wants it. The developers of "freeware" gain satisfaction out of their intellectual work and out of providing a service to others. The Free Software Foundation has spearheaded the development and promotion of freeware. It "is dedicated to eliminating restrictions on people's right to use, copy, modify and redistribute computer programs" by encouraging people to develop and use free software.

A suitable alternative to copyright is shareright. A piece of freeware might be accompanied by the notice, "You may reproduce this material if your recipients may also reproduce it." This encourages copiers but refuses any of them copyright.

The Free Software Foundation has come up with another approach, called "copyleft." The Foundation states, "The simplest way to make a program free is to put it in the public domain, uncopyrighted. But this permits proprietary modified versions, which deny others the freedom to redistribute and modify; such versions undermine the goal of giving freedom to all users. To prevent this, `copyleft' uses copyright in a novel manner. Typically copyrights take away freedoms; copyleft preserves them. It is a legal instrument that requires those who pass on a program to include the rights to use, modify, and redistribute the code; the code and the freedoms become legally inseparable." Until copyright is eliminated or obsolete, innovations such as copyleft are necessary to avoid exploitation of those who want to make their work available to others.

This is important even if credit is not rewarded financially. This would include guidelines for not misrepresenting another person's work. Intellectual property gives the appearance of stopping unfair appropriation of ideas although the reality is quite different. If intellectual property is to be challenged, people need to be reassured that misappropriation of ideas will not become a big problem.

More fundamentally, it needs to be recognised that intellectual work is inevitably a collective process. No one has totally original ideas: ideas are always built on the earlier contributions of others. (That's especially true of this chapter!) Furthermore, culture -- which makes ideas possible -- is built not just on intellectual contributions but also on practical and material contributions, including the rearing of families and construction of buildings. Intellectual property is theft, sometimes in part from an individual creator but always from society as a whole.

In a more cooperative society, credit for ideas would not be such a contentious matter. Today, there are vicious disputes between scientists over who should gain credit for a discovery. This is because scientists' careers and, more importantly, their reputations, depend on credit for ideas. In a society with less hierarchy and greater equality, intrinsic motivation and satisfaction would be the main returns from contributing to intellectual developments. This is quite compatible with everything that is known about human nature. The system of ownership encourages groups to put special interests above general interests. Sharing information is undoubtedly the most efficient way to allocate productive resources. The less there is to gain from credit for ideas, the more likely people are to share ideas rather than worry about who deserves credit for them.

For most book publishers, publishing an argument against intellectual property raises a dilemma. If the work is copyrighted as usual, this clashes with the argument against copyright. On the other hand, if the work is not copyrighted, then unrestrained copying might undermine sales. It's worth reflecting on this dilemma as it applies to this book. It is important to keep in mind the wider goal of challenging the corruptions of information power. Governments and large corporations are particularly susceptible to these corruptions. They should be the first targets in developing a strategy against intellectual property.

Freedom Press is not a typical publisher. It has been publishing anarchist writings since 1886, including books, magazines, pamphlets and leaflets. Remarkably, neither authors nor editors have ever been paid for their work. Freedom Press is concerned with social issues and social change, not with material returns to anyone involved in the enterprise.

Because it is a small publisher, Freedom Press would be hard pressed to enforce its claims to copyright even if it wanted to. Those who sympathise with the aims of Freedom Press and who would like to reproduce some of its publications therefore should consider practical rather than legal issues. Would the copying be on such a scale as to undermine Freedom Press's limited sales? Does the copying give sufficient credit to Freedom Press so as to encourage further sales? Is the copying for commercial or noncommercial purposes?

In answering such questions, it makes sense to ask Freedom Press. This applies whether the work is copyright or not. If asking is not feasible, or the copying is of limited scale, then good judgement should be used. In my opinion, using one chapter -- especially this chapter! -- for nonprofit purposes should normally be okay.

So in the case of Freedom Press, the approach should be to negotiate in good faith and to use good judgement in minor or urgent cases. Negotiation and good judgement of this sort will be necessary in any society that moves beyond intellectual property.

6

CULTURE AND DEMOCRACY

The aim of this article is threefold: first, to examine the ways in which the market economy framework and the elites condition culture and mass media; second, to discuss the relationship of the neoliberal consensus with the present intensification of cultural homogenisation; finally, to outline the nature of culture and the role of mass media in a democratic society, as well as to explore the strategies which could bring about a shift from the present cultural institutions to those of an inclusive democracy.

THE DOMINANT SOCIAL PARADIGM AND CULTURE

A fruitful way to start the discussion of the significance of culture and its relationship to the mass media would be to define carefully our terms. This would help to avoid the confusion, which is not rare in discussions on the matter. Culture is frequently defined as the integrated pattern of human knowledge, belief, and behaviour. This is a definition broad enough to include all major aspects of culture: language, ideas, beliefs, customs, taboos, codes, institutions, tools, techniques, works of art, rituals, ceremonies and so on.

However, in what follows, I am not going to deal with all these aspects of culture unless they are related to what I call the dominant social paradigm. By this I mean the system of beliefs, ideas and the corresponding values which are dominant in a particular society at a particular moment of its history. It is clear that there is a significant degree of overlapping between these two terms although the meaning of culture is obviously broader than that of the social paradigm.

But, let us see first the elements shared by both terms. Both culture and the social paradigm are time- and space-dependent, i.e. they refer to a specific type of society at a specific time. Therefore, they both change from place to place and from one historical period to another. This implies that there can be no 'general theory' of History, which could determine the relationship between the cultural with the political or economic elements in society. In other words, our starting point is the rejection not only of the crude economistic versions of Marxism (the economic base determines the cultural superstructure) but also of the more sophisticated versions of it (the economic base determines 'in the last instance' which element is to be dominant in each social formation). In my view, which I expanded elsewhere, the dominant element in each social formation is not determined, for all time, by the economic base, or any other base. The dominant element is always determined by a creative act, i.e. it is the outcome of social praxis, of the activity of social individuals. Thus, the dominant element in theocratic societies was cultural, in the societies of 'actually existing socialism' political and so on.

Similarly, the dominant element in market economies is economic, as a result of the fact that the introduction of new systems of production during the Industrial Revolution in a commercial society, where the means of production were under private ownership and control, inevitably led to the transformation of the socially- controlled economies of the past (in which the market played a marginal role in the economic process) into the present market economies (defined as the self-regulating systems in which the fundamental economic problems--what, how, and for whom to produce-- are solved `automatically', through the price mechanism, rather than through conscious social decisions). Still, the existence of a dominant element in a social formation does not mean that the relationship between this element and the other elements in it is one of heteronomy and dependence. Each element is autonomous and the relationship between the various elements is better described as one of interdependence. So, although it is the economic element which is the dominant one in the system of the market economy, this does not mean that culture is determined, even 'in the last instance' by this element.

But, there are also some important differences between culture and the dominant social paradigm. Culture, exactly because of its greater scope, may express values and ideas, which are not necessarily consistent with the dominant institutions. In fact, this is usually the case characterising the arts and literature of a market economy, where, (unlike the case of 'actually existing socialism', or the case of feudal societies before), artists and writers have been given a significant degree of freedom to express their own views. But this is not the case with respect to the dominant social paradigm. In other words, the beliefs, ideas and the corresponding values which are dominant in a market economy and the corresponding market society have to be consistent with the economic element in it, i.e. with the economic institutions which, in turn, determine that the dominant elites in this society are the economic elites (those owning and controlling the means of production).

This has always been the case in History and will also be the case in the future. No particular type of society can reproduce itself unless the dominant beliefs, ideas and values are consistent with the existing institutional framework. For instance, in the societies of 'actually existing socialism' the dominant social paradigm had to be consistent with the dominant element in them, (which was the political), and the corresponding political institutions, which determined that the dominant elites in this society were the political elites (party bureaucracy). Similarly, in the democratic society of the future, the dominant social paradigm had to be consistent with the dominant element in them, which would be the political, and the corresponding democratic institutions, which would secure that there would be no formal elites in this kind of society (although, of course, if democracy does not function properly the emergence of informal elites could not be ruled out).

So, culture and, in particular, the social dominant paradigm play a crucial role in the determination of individual and collective values. As long as individuals live in a society, they are not just individuals but social individuals, subject to a process, which socialises them and induces them to internalise the existing institutional framework as well as the dominant social paradigm.

In this sense, people are not completely free to create their world but are conditioned by History, tradition and culture. Still, this socialisation process is broken, at almost all times-as far as a minority of the population is concerned-and in exceptional historical circumstances even with respect to the majority itself.

In the latter case, a process is set in motion that usually ends with a change of the institutional structure of society and of the corresponding social paradigm. Societies therefore are not just "collections of individuals" but consist of social individuals, who are both free to create their world, (in the sense that they can give birth to a new set of institutions and a corresponding social paradigm), and are created by the world, (in the sense that they have to break with the dominant social paradigm in order to recreate the world).

MARKET ECONOMY VALUE

As the dominant economic institutions in a market economy are those of markets and private ownership of the means of production, as well as the corresponding hierarchical structures, the dominant social paradigm promoted by the mainstream mass media and other cultural institutions, (e.g. universities) has to consist of ideas, beliefs and values which are consistent with them.

Thus, the kind of social 'sciences' which are taught at universities and the kind of articles which fill academic journals, explicitly, or usually implicitly, take for granted the existing economic institutions. Therefore, their search for 'truth' in the analysis of major economic or social problems is crucially conditioned by this fundamental characteristic. The causes of world-wide unemployment, for instance, or of massive inequality and concentration of economic power, will not be related to the system of the market economy itself; instead, the malfunctioning of the system or bad policies will be blamed, which supposedly can be tackled by the appropriate improvement of the system's functioning, or the 'right' economic policies.

In economics, in particular, the dominant theory/ideology since the emergence of the market economy has been economic liberalism, in its various versions: from the old classical and neo-classical schools up to the modern versions of it in the form of supply-side economics, new classical macro-economics etc. But, from Adam Smith to Milton Friedman, the values adopted are the same: competition and individualism, which, supposedly, are the only values that could secure freedom.

Thus, for Adam Smith, the individual pursuit of self-interest in a market economy will guarantee social harmony and, therefore, the main task of government is the defence of the rich against the poor.

So, in Smith's system, as Canterbery puts it, 'individual self-interest is the motivating force, and the built-in regulator that keeps the economy from flying apart is competition'. Similarly, for Milton Friedman, the Nobel-prize winner in economics (note: the Nobel Prize in economics was never awarded to an economist who challenged the very system of the market economy) the capitalist market economy is identified with freedom:

The kind of economic organisation that provides freedom directly, namely, competitive capitalism, also promotes political freedom because it separates economic power from political power and in this way enables the one to offset the other...The two ideas of human freedom and economic freedom working together came to their greatest fruition in the United States

It is obvious that in this ideology, which passes as the 'science' of economics, the values of individualism and competition are preferred over the values of collectivism and solidarity/co-operation, since freedom itself is identified with the former values as against the latter. But, it 'happens' also that the same values are the only ones, which could secure the production and reproduction of the market economy. No market economy can function properly unless those in control of it, (i.e., the economic elites), at least, and as many of the rest as possible, are motivated by individualism and competition.

This is because the dynamic of a market economy crucially depends on competition and individual greed. Furthermore, the fact that often the economic elites resort to state protection against foreign competition, if the latter threatens their own position, does not in the least negate the fact that competition is the fundamental organising principle of the market economy.

It is therefore no historical accident that, as Polanyi has persuasively shown, the establishment of the market economy implied sweeping aside traditional cultures and values and replacing the values of solidarity, altruism, sharing and co-operation (which usually marked community life) with the values of individualism and competition as the dominant values. As Ray Canterbery stresses:

> The capitalistic ethic leans toward the extreme of selfishness (fierce individualism) rather than toward altruism. There is little room for collective decision making in an ethic that argues that every individual should go his or her own way. As we have seen, the idea that capitalism protects 'individual rights' would have been rejected during the early Middle Ages. 'Individual rights' were set in advance by the structure of feudalism, governed by the pull of tradition and the push of authority. Economics was based upon mutual needs and obligations.

A good example of the enthusiastic support for these values today is, again, the Nobel-prize winner in economics Milton Friedman. According to him:

> Few trends could so thoroughly undermine the very foundations of our free society as the acceptance by corporate officials of a social responsibility other than to make as much money for their stockholders as possible. This (social responsibility) is a fundamentally subversive doctrine.

Indeed, it is not Friedman who supports values which are inconsistent with the market economy system but the various social democrats and Green economists, who, taking for granted the market economy system, proceed to argue in favour of utopian economic institutions incorporating values which are inconsistent with this system (*e.g.*'stakeholding' capitalism, 'social investment' etc).

As I attempted to show elsewhere, the basic cause of the failure of both the 'actually existing socialism' in the East and social democracy in the West was exactly that they attempted to merge two fundamentally incompatible elements: the 'growth' element, (which implies the concentration of economic power and expresses the logic of the market economy), with the social justice element (which is inherently linked to equality and expresses socialist ethics).

CHOMSKY AND MARKET ECONOMY

However, quite apart from social democrats and reformist Greens, there is an alternative view about the values of the market economy proposed by Noam Chomsky, which, however, ends up with similar conclusions about the feasibility and desirability of state action with respect to controlling today's market economy.

Thus, for Chomsky, the values which motivate today's elites in advanced capitalist countries are not individualism and competition; instead, these elites simply use such values as propaganda in their attempt to 'persuade' their own public and the countries in the periphery and semi-periphery to implement them whereas they themselves demand and enjoy the protection of their own states:

For the general public, individualism and competition are the prescribed values. Not for elites, however. They demand and obtain the protection of a powerful state, and insist on arrangements that safeguard them from unfettered competition or the destructive consequences of individualism.

The process of corporatization is a standard illustration, as is the reliance in every economy -- crucially, the US -- on socialisation of risk and cost. The need to undermine the threat of competition constantly takes new forms: today, one major form, beyond corporatization, is the development of a rich network of "strategic alliances" among alleged competitors: IBM-Toshiba-Siemens, for example, or throughout the automotive industry. This has reached such extremes that prominent analysts of the business world now speak of a new form of "alliance capitalism" that is replacing the managerial/ corporate capitalism that had largely displaced proprietary capitalism a century ago in advanced sectors of the economy.

Chomsky has recently expanded on the same theme in a New Left Review article in which it is made clear that his views above about the values of the market economy are perfectly consistent with his views on the nature of today's capitalism. In this article he first states that the word 'capitalist' does not mean capitalist but rather it refers to state subsidised and protected private power centres, or 'collectivist legal entities,' which embody today's corporatization of the market economy. He then goes on to describe corporatization and the role of the state as follows:

The corporatization process was largely a reaction to great market failures of the late nineteenth century, and it was a shift from something you might call proprietary capitalism to the administration of markets by collectivist legal entities-mergers, cartels, corporate alliances-in association with powerful states...the primary task of the states-and bear in mind that, with all the talk about minimising the state, in the OECD countries the state continues to grow relative to GNP, notably in the 1980s and 1990s-is essentially to socialise risk and cost, and to privatise power and profit.

Furthermore, Chomsky's views about the market economy's values and the nature of present capitalism are, in turn, entirely consistent with his present views on the potential role of the state in controlling today's market economy. Thus, as Chomsky stresses in the aforementioned article:

The long-term goal of such initiatives (like the Multilateral Agreement on Investment-MAI) is clear enough to anyone with open eyes; an international political economy which is organised by powerful states and secret bureaucracies whose primary function is to serve the concentrations of private power which administer markers through their own internal operations, through networks of corporate alliances, including the intra-firm transactions that are mislabelled 'trade'.

They rely on the public for subsidy, research and development, for innovation and for bailouts when things go wrong. They rely on the powerful states for protection from dangerous 'democracy openings'. In such ways, they seek to ensure that the 'prime beneficiaries' of the world's wealth are the right people: the smug and prosperous 'Americans'; the 'domestic constituencies and their counterparts elsewhere. The scale of all of this is nowhere near as great or, for that matter, as novel as claimed; in many ways it's a return to the early twentieth century. And there's no reason to doubt that it can be controlled even within existing formal institutions of parliamentary democracy.

One, however, could object on several grounds this stand, as portrayed by the above extracts. First, the argument about the values of the economic elites, as I attempted to show above, is contestable; second, the nature of today's market economy could be seen in a very different analytical framework than the one suggested by Chomsky and, finally, it could be shown that the way out of the present multi-dimensional crisis and the related huge concentration of power can not be found in fragmented and usually 'monothematic' defensive battles with the elites.

Such battles, even if sometimes victorious, are never going to win the war, as long as they are not an integral part of a new popular movement's fight against the system of the market economy itself, which is the ultimate cause of the concentration of economic power.

As regards the nature of the market economy today, I have attempted elsewhere to show how it evolved since it emerged, about two centuries ago, and how it took the form of the present growth economy. I will only add here that the shift from proprietary (or entrepreneurial) capitalism to the present internationalised market economy, where a few giant corporations control the world economy, did not happen, as

Chomsky presents it, as the outcome of 'a reaction to great market failures of the late nineteenth century.' What Chomsky omits is that it was competition, which led from simple entrepreneurial firms to the present giant corporations.

The market failures he mentions are not a God-given calamity. Excepting the case of monopolies, almost all market failures in history have been directly or indirectly related to competition. It is competition, which creates the need for expansion, so that the best (from the profit of view of profits) technologies and methods of organising production (economies of scale etc) are used. It is the same competition, which has led to the present explosion of mergers and take-overs in the advanced capitalist countries, as well as the various 'strategic alliances'.

For instance, the recently announced merger of giant oil companies, in a sense, is the result of a 'market failure' because of the fall in their profits.

But, in a deeper sense, this merger, as well as the take-overs, strategic alliances etc going on at the moment, are simply the result of self-protective action taken by giant corporations, in order to survive the cut-throat competition launched by the present internationalisation of the market economy.

Therefore, it is competition, which has led to the present corporate (or 'alliance') capitalism, not 'market failures' and/or the associated state activity, which just represent the effects of competition.

Similarly, the present internationalisation of the market economy is not just the result of state action to liberalise financial and commodity markets.

In fact, the states were following the de facto internationalisation of the market economy, which was intensified by the activities of multinationals, when, (in the late seventies), under pressure from the latter, started the process of liberalising the financial markets and further deregulating the commodity markets (through the GATT rounds).

Therefore, the present internationalisation is in fact the outcome of the grow-or-die dynamics, which characterises the market economy, a dynamics that is initiated by competition, the crucial fact neglected by Chomsky.

It is also the same internationalisation of the market economy, which became incompatible with the degree of state control of the economy achieved by the mid seventies, that made necessary the present neoliberal consensus.

The latter, therefore, is not just a policy change, as socialdemocrats and their fellow travellers suggest, but represents an important structural change. So, minimising the state is not just 'talk', as Chomsky assumes basing his argument on the assumption that 'the state continues to grow relative to GNP, notably in the 1980s and 1990s'.

However, not only the fall in the growth rate of government spending in OECD countries was higher than that of the other parts of aggregate demand in the period 1980-93 but, in fact, the (weighted average) general government consumption of high income economies was lower in 1995, at 15% of GNP, than in 1980 (17%).

All this, not taking into account the drastic reduction in the overall public sectors in the last twenty years, as a result of the massive privatisation of state industries. Therefore, minimising the state, far from being 'talk' is a basic element of the present neoliberal consensus.

Also, strategic alliances, mergers and take-overs do not represent a movement away from the market economy but a movement towards a new form of it.

Away from a market economy, which was geared by the internal market and towards a market economy, which is geared by the world market. This means further and further concentration of economic power not only in terms of incomes and wealth but also in terms of concentration of the power to control world output, trade and investment in fewer and fewer hands. However, the oligopolisation of competition does not mean lack of competition.

Furthermore, it will be wrong to assume that the main characteristic of the present period is an 'assault against the markets', as the purist neoliberal argument goes, which Chomsky accepts.

The present period of neoliberal consensus can be characterised instead, as an assault against social controls on markets, particularly those I called social controls in the narrow sense, i.e. those aiming at the protection of humans and nature against the effects of marketization, (the historical process that has transformed the socially controlled economies of the past into the market economy of the present).

Such controls have been introduced as a result of social struggles undertaken by those who are adversely affected by the market economy's effects on them (social security legislation, welfare benefits, macro-economic controls to secure full employment etc).

What is still debated within the economic elites is the fate of what I call social controls in the broad sense, i.e. those primarily aiming at the protection of those controlling the market economy against foreign competition (tariffs, import controls. exchange controls--- in the past, and non-tariff barriers, massive public subsidy for R&D, risk-protection (bailouts), administration of markets etc--- at present).

Thus, pure neoliberal economists, bankers, some politicians and others are against any kind of social controls over markets (in the narrow or broad sense above). On the other hand, the more pragmatic governments of the neoliberal consensus, from Reagan to Clinton and from Thatcher to Blair, under the pressure of the most vulnerable to competition sections of their own economic elites, have kept many social controls in the broad sense and sometimes even expanded them (not hesitating to go to war to secure their energy supplies) giving rise to the pure neoliberal argument (adopted by Chomsky) about an assault on markets.

In this context, one should not confuse liberalism/ neoliberalism with laissez-faire. As I tried to show elsewhere, it was the state itself that created the system of self-regulating markets. Furthermore, some form of state intervention has always been necessary for the smooth functioning of the market economy system.

The state, since the collapse of the socialdemocratic consensus, has seen a drastic reduction in its economic role as it is no longer involved in a process of directly intervening in the determination of income and employment through fiscal and monetary policies.

However, even today, the state still plays an important role in securing, through its monopoly of violence, the stability of the market economy framework and in maintaining the infrastructure for the smooth functioning of it. It is within this role of maintaining the infrastructure that we may see the activities of the state in socialising risk and cost and in maintaining a safety net in place of the old welfare state.

Furthermore, the state is called today to play a crucial role with respect to the supply-side of the economy and, in particular, to take measures to improve competitiveness and to train the working force to the requirements of the new technology, in supporting research and development and even in subsidising export industries wherever required.

Therefore, the type of state intervention which is compatible with the marketization process not only is not discouraged but, instead, is actively promoted by most of the professional politicians of the neoliberal consensus.

It is true that the economic elites do not like the kind of competition which, as a result of the uneven development of the world market economy, threatens their own interests and this is why they have always attempted (and mostly succeeded) to protect themselves against it.

But, it is equally true that it was the force of competition which has always fuelled the expansion of the market economy and that it was the values of competition and self-interest which have always characterised the value system of the elites which control the market economy.

Chomsky, however, sometimes gives the impression that, barring some 'accidents' like the market failures he mentions, as well as the aggressive state support that economic elites have always enjoyed, the 'corporatization' of the market economy might have been avoided.

But, of course, neither proprietary capitalism (or any other type of it) is desirable ---since it cannot secure covering the basic needs of all people--- nor can we deny all radical analysis of the past hundred and fifty years or so, from Marx to Bookchin, and all historical experience since then, which leads to one conclusion: the market economy is geared by a grow-or-die dynamic fuelled by competition, which is bound to lead to further and further concentration of economic power. Therefore, the problem is not the corporatization of the market economy which, supposedly, represents 'an attack on markets and democracy', and which was unavoidable anyway within the dynamic of the market economy.

In other words, the problem is not corporate market economy/capitalism, as if some other kind of market economy/ capitalism was feasible or desirable, but the market economy/ capitalism itself. Otherwise, one may easily end up blaming the elites for violating the rules of the game, rather than blaming the rotten game itself!

If the above analytical framework is valid then obviously it is not possible, within the existing institutional framework of parliamentary democracy and the market economy to check the process of increasing concentration of economic power. This is a process that is going since the emergence of the market economy system, some two centuries ago, and no social-democratic governments or grassroots movements were ever able to stop it, or even to retard it, apart from brief periods of time. In fact, even the grass root 'victory' hailed by Chomsky against the MAI proposals is doubtful whether it would have been achieved had there been no serious divisions among the economic elites about it.

Furthermore, the 'victory' itself has already started showing signs that it was hollow, as it is now clear that the MAI agreement was not, in fact, set aside, but it is simply implemented 'by installments', through the 'back door' of the IMF at present, and possibly the World Trade Organisation in the future. The basic reason why such battles are doomed is that they are not an integral part of a comprehensive political program to replace the institutional framework of the market economy itself and, as such, they can easily be marginalised or lead to simple (easily reversible) reforms.

The inevitable conclusion is that only the struggle for the building of a new massive movement aiming at fighting 'from without' for the creation of a new institutional framework, and the development of the corresponding culture and social paradigm, might have any chances to lead to a new society characterised by the equal distribution of power.

CULTURAL HOMOGENISATION

As I mentioned above, the establishment of the market economy implied sweeping aside traditional cultures and values. This process was accelerated in the twentieth century with the spreading all over the world of the market economy and its offspring the growth economy.

As a result, today, there is an intensive process of culture homogenisation at work, which not only rules out any directionality towards more complexity, but in effect is making culture simpler, with cities becoming more and more alike, people all over the world listening to the same music, watching the same soap operas on TV, buying the same brands of consumer goods, etc.

The establishment of the neoliberal consensus in the last twenty years or so, following the collapse of the socialdemocratic consensus, has further enhanced this process of cultural homogenisation. This is the inevitable outcome of the liberalisation and de-regulation of markets and the consequent intensification of commercialisation of culture.

As a result, traditional communities and their cultures are disappearing all over the world and people are converted to consumers of a mass culture produced in the advanced capitalist countries and particularly the USA. In the film industry, for instance, even European countries with a strong cultural background and developed economies have to effectively give up their own film industries, unable to compete with the much more competitive US industry.

Thus, in the early 1990s, US films' share amounted to 73% of the European market. Also, indicative of the degree of concentration of cultural power in the hands of a few US corporations is the fact that, in 1991, a handful of US distributors controlled 66% of total cinema box office and 70% of the total number of video rentals in Britain.

Thus, the recent emergence of a sort of "cultural" nationalism in many parts of the world expresses a desperate attempt to keep a cultural identity in the face of market homogenisation. But, cultural nationalism is devoid of any real meaning in an electronic environment, where 75 percent of the international communications flow is controlled by a small number of multinationals. In other words, cultural imperialism today does not need, as in the past, a gunboat diplomacy to integrate and absorb diverse cultures.

The marketization of the communications flow has already established the preconditions for the downgrading of cultural diversity into a kind of superficial differentiation akin to a folklorist type.

Furthermore, it is indicative that today's `identity movements', like those in Western Europe (from the Flemish to the Lombard and from the Scots to the Catalans) which demand autonomy as the best way to preserve their cultural identity, in fact, express their demand for individual and social autonomy in a distorted way.

The distortion arises from the fact that the marketization of society has undermined the community values of reciprocity, solidarity and co-operation in favour of the market values of competition and individualism.

As a result, the demand for cultural autonomy is not founded today on community values which enhance co-operation with other cultural communities but, instead, on market values which encourage tensions and conflicts with them.

In this connection, the current neoracist explosion in Europe is directly relevant to the effectual undermining of community values by neoliberalism, as well as to the growing inequality and poverty following the rise of the neoliberal consensus.

Finally, one should not underestimate the political implications of the commercialisation and homogenisation of culture. The escapist role traditionally played by Hollywood films has now acquired a universal dimension, through the massive expansion of TV culture and its almost full monopolisation by Hollywood subculture.

Every single TV viewer in Nigeria, India, China or Russia now dreams of the American way of life, as seen on TV serials (which, being relatively inexpensive and glamorous, fill the TV programmes of most TV channels all over the world) and thinks in terms of the competitive values imbued by them. The collapse of existing socialism has perhaps more to do with this cultural phenomenon, as anecdotal evidence indicates, than one could imagine.

As various TV documentaries have shown, people in Eastern European countries, in particular, thought of themselves as some kind of 'abnormal' compared with what western TV has established as the 'normal'.

In fact, many of the people participating in the demonstrations to bring down those regimes frequently referred to this 'abnormality', as their main incentive for their political action. In this problematique, one may criticise the kind of cultural relativism supported by some in the Left, according to which almost all cultural preferences could be declared as rational (on the basis of some sort of rationality criteria), and therefore all cultural choices deserve respect, if not admiration, given the constraints under which they are made.

But, obviously, the issue is not whether our cultural choices are rational or not. Nor the issue is to assess 'objectively' our cultural preferences as right or wrong. The real issue is how to make a choice of values which we think is compatible with the kind of society we wish to live in and then make the cultural choices which are compatible with these values.

This is because the transition to a future society based on alternative values presupposes that the effort to create an alternative culture should start now, in parallel with the effort to establish the new institutions compatible with the new values. On the basis of the criterion of consistency between our cultural choices and the values of a truly democratic society, one could delineate a way beyond post-modern relativism and distinguish between 'preferable' and 'non-preferable' cultural choices.

So, all those cultural choices involving films, videos, theatrical plays etc, which promote the values of the market economy and particularly competition for money, individualism, consumerist greed, as well as violence, racism, sexism etc should be shown to be non-preferable and people should be encouraged to avoid them. On the other hand, all those cultural choices, which involve the promotion of the community values of mutual aid, solidarity, sharing and equality for all (irrespective of race, sex, ethnicity) should be promoted as preferable.

7

THE ROLE OF MASS MEDIA TODAY

A basic issue in the discussion of the role of the mass media in today's society is whether they do reflect social reality in a broad sense, or whether, instead, the elites which control them filter out the view of reality which they see fit to be made public. To my mind, the answer to this question is that the media do both, depending on the way we define reality.

To take, first, political reality, mass media, in one sense, do not provide a faked view of it. Taking into account what is considered as politics today, i.e. the activity of professional politicians 'representing' the people, one may argue that it is politics itself, which is faked, and mass media simply reproduce this reality. In this sense, the issue is not whether the mass media manipulate democracy, since it is democracy itself, which is faked, and not its mass media picture, which simply reflects the reality of present 'democracy'. But, at the same time, if we give a different definition to political reality, mass media do provide, in general, a distorted picture of it. In other words, if we define as real politics the political activity of people themselves (for instance, the collective struggles of various sectors of the population around political, economic or social issues) rather than that of professional politicians, then, the mass media do distort the picture they present about political reality. They do so, by minimising the significance of this type of activity, by distorting its meaning, by marginalising it, or by simply ignoring it completely.

Furthermore, mass media do provide a distorted picture of political reality when they come to report the causes of crises, or of the conflicts involving various sections of the elites. In such cases they faithfully reflect the picture that the sections of the elites controlling them wish to reproduce. The latest example of this was the way in which the Anglo-American media, in particular, distorted the real meaning of the criminal bombardment of the Iraqi people at the end of 1998. Thus, exactly, as in their reporting during the war in the Gulf, the real cause of the conflict, (i.e. who controls the world's oil, irrespective of where the oil stocks are located -- the elites of the North versus those in the South), was distorted as a conflict between the peace loving regimes in the North versus the rogue regimes in the South, or, in more sophisticated versions supported by socialdemocrat intellectuals, as a conflict between the 'democracies' in the North versus the 'despotic regimes' in the South over the control of oil.

Under these circumstances, it is obvious that the mass media usually offer a true glimpse of reality only when the elites are divided with respect to their conception of a particular aspect of political reality. From this point of view, concentration in the mass media industry is significant and whether the media are owned by 100 or 10 owners does indeed matter in the struggle for social change. It is for instance such divisions among the European elites over the issue of joining the European Monetary Union which have allowed a relatively wide media discussion on the true meaning of European integration, particularly in countries like Britain where the elites were split. It was also similar divisions between the Anglo-American and the European elites over the latest war crime in the Gulf which made a bit clearer the directly criminal role of the former (support for the bombardments), as well as the indirectly criminal role of the latter (support for the embargo). It is not accidental that in the USA and UK, where the media played a particularly despicable role in distorting the truth and misinforming the public, the polls showed consistently vast majorities in favour of the criminal activities of their elites. Of course, this does not mean that decentralisation of power in the mass media industry (or anywhere else) represents by itself, even potentially, a radical social change leading to an authentic democracy. Still, the significance of decentralisation in the media industry with respect to raising consciousness should not be ignored.

As regards economic reality, mass media, in one sense again, do provide a relatively accurate picture of what counts as economic reality today. This is when the media, taking for granted the system of the market economy, end up with a partial picture of economic reality where what matters is not whether the basic needs of the population are covered adequately but whether prices (in commodity and stock markets), interest rates, exchange rates and consequently profit rates are going up or down. Still, in another sense, the very fact that mass media take for granted the system of the market economy means that they cannot 'see' the 'systemic' nature of most of the real economic problems (unemployment, poverty and so on) and therefore inevitably end up with a faked image of economic reality. This way of seeing economic reality is not imposed on the media by their owners, important as their influence may otherwise be, or by their internal hierarchical structure etc. The media simply reflect the views of orthodox economists, bankers, businessmen and professional politicians, i.e. of all those who express the dominant social paradigm.

But if the picture of political and economic reality offered by the media is mixed this is not the case with respect to ecological reality. As no meaningful reporting of the ecological crisis is possible unless it refers to the systemic causes of it, which by definition are excluded by the discourse in the mainstream media, the result is a complete misinformation, or just straightforward description of the symptoms of the crisis. The mass media are flooded by the 'realist' Greens who fill the various ecological parties and who blame technology, consumerist values, legislation etc-- anything but the real cause of the crisis, i.e. the very system of the market economy. Similarly, the reporting of the present social crisis never links the explosion of crime and drug abuse, for instance, with their root cause, i.e. the increasing concentration of political, economic and social power in the hands of various elites. Instead, the symptoms of the social crisis are distortedly reported as its causes and the media blame, following the advice of the establishment 'experts', the breaking of the traditional family, or of the school, as the causes of crime. Similarly, various 'progressive' intellectuals (like the lamentable ex 'revolutionary' and now well promoted by the mainstream media Euro-parliamentarian Con Bendit) blame the prohibitive legislation on drugs for the massive explosion of drug abuse!

However, there is another approach being promoted recently by system theorists, according to which mass media do not just either reflect or distort reality but also manufacture it. This is not said in the usual sense of manufacturing consent described by Chomsky and Herman or, alternatively, by Bourdieu, which is basically a one-way process whereby the elites controlling the mass media filter out the information, through various control mechanisms, in order to create consent around their agenda. Instead, system theorists talk about a two-way process whereby social reality and mass media are seen as two interdependent levels, the one intruding into the other. This is based on the valid hypothesis that reality is not just something external to the way it is conceived. TV watching is a constituent moment of reality since our information about reality consists of conceptions that constitute reality itself. At the same time, the conception of reality is conditioned by the media functioning, which is differentiated in relation to the other social systems (political, economic etc).

In the systems analysis problematique, it is not the economic, or the political systems, which control the media functioning. What determines their functioning, as well as their communicative capability, is their ability to generate irritation- a fact that could go a long way to explain the high ratings of exciting or irritating TV programs. The diversified functioning of mass media creates, in turn, the conditions for a social dynamic which, in a self-reflective and communicative way, reproduces, as well as institutes, society. Thus, whereas the early modern society is instituted through a transcendental subjectivity and a material mode of production, the present post-modern society's reproduction depends on the processes of communicative rationality. The mass media are an integral and functional part of the communicative processes of post-modern society.

However, one may point out here that although it is true that social reality and mass media are interacting, i.e. that our conception of TV news is a constituent element of reality and at the same time our conception of reality is conditioned by TV functioning, this does not imply that the diversified functioning of mass media creates the conditions for a social dynamic which acts for the institution of society, although it does play this role as far as its reproduction is concerned. The meaning we assign to TV reporting is not determined exogenously but by our world view, our own paradigm, which in turn, as we have seen above, is the result of a process of socialisation that is conditioned by the dominant social paradigm. Furthermore, TV functioning plays a crucial role in the reproduction of the dominant social paradigm and the socialisation process generally. So, the diversified functioning of TV does indeed create the conditions for a social dynamic leading to the reproduction of the status quo, but in no way could be considered as doing the same for instituting society.

CONTROL MECHANISMS

The goals of the mass media are determined by those owning and controlling them, who, usually, are members of the economic elites that control the market economy itself. Given the crucial role that the media could play in the internalisation of the dominant social paradigm and therefore the reproduction of the institutional framework which secures the concentration of power in the hands of the elites, it is obvious that those owning and controlling the mass media have broader ideological goals than the usual goals pursued by those owning and controlling other economic institutions, i.e. profit maximising. Therefore, an analysis that would attempt to draw conclusions on the nature and significance of media institutions on the basis of the profit dimension alone, (i.e. that they share a common goal and consequently a similar internal hierarchical structure with all other economic institutions and that they just sell a product, the only difference with other economic institutions being that the product is the audience,) is bound to be one-dimensional. Profit maximising is only one parameter, often not even the crucial one, which conditions the role of mass media in a market economy. In fact, one could mention several instances where capitalist owners chose even to incur significant losses (which they usually cover from other profitable activities) in order to maintain the social influence (and prestige), which ownership of an influential daily offers to them (Murdoch and The Times of London is an obvious recent example).

Given the ultimate ideological goal of mass media, the main ways in which they try to achieve it are:

- first, by assisting in the internalisation of the dominant social paradigm and,
- second, by marginalising, if not excluding altogether, conceptions of reality which do not conform with the dominant social paradigm.

But, what are the mechanisms through which the media can achieve their goals? To give an answer to this question we have to examine a series of mechanisms, most of them 'automatic' built-in mechanisms, which ensure effective achievement of these goals. It will be useful here to distinguish between 'internal' and 'external' control mechanisms, which function respectively as internal and external constraints on the freedom of media workers to reproduce reality. Both internal and external mechanisms work mainly through competition which secures homogenisation with respect to the media's main goals. Competition is of course the fundamental organisational principle of a market economy; but, it plays a special role with respect to the media. As Bourdieu points out, competition 'rather than automatically generating originality and diversity tends to favour uniformity'. Still, competition is not the only force securing homogenisation. In a similar way as with the market economy itself, competition provides only the dynamic mechanism of homogenisation. It is the fact that owners of mass media, as well as managers and the highest paid journalists, share the same interest in the reproduction of the existing institutional framework which constitutes the 'base', on which this competition is developed. But, let us consider briefly the significance of the various control mechanisms. The main 'internal control' mechanisms are ownership and the internal hierarchical structure, which are, both, crucial in the creation of the conditions for internal competition among journalists, whereas the 'ratings' mechanism plays a similar role in the creation of the conditions for external competition among media.

Starting with ownership, it matters little, as regards the media's overall goals defined above, whether they are owned and controlled by the state and/or the state-controlled institutions or whether, instead, they are owned and controlled by private capital. However, there are certain secondary differences arising from the different ownership structures which may be mentioned. These secondary differences have significant implications, particularly with respect to the structure of the elites controlling the media, their own organisational structure and their 'image' with respect to their supposedly 'objective' role in the presentation of information. As regards the elite structure, whereas under a system of state ownership and control the mass media are under the direct control of the political elite and the indirect control of the economic elites, under a system of private ownership and control, the media are just under the direct control of the economic elites.

This fact, in turn, has some implications on whether filtering out of information takes place directly through state control, or indirectly through various economic mechanisms (e.g. ratings).As regards the media organisational structure, whereas state-owned media are characterised by bureaucratic rigidity and inefficiency, privately owned media are usually characterised by more flexibility and economic efficiency. Finally, the 'objective' image of mass media suffers less in case of private ownership compared to the case of state ownership. This is because in the latter case control of information is more direct and therefore more obvious than in the former.

Another important internal control mechanism is the hierarchical structure which characterises all media institutions (as it does all economic institutions in a market economy) and which implies that all-important decisions are taken by a small managerial group within them, who are usually directly responsible to the owners. The hierarchical structure creates a constant internal competition among journalists as to who will be more agreeable to the managerial group (on which their career and salary prospects depend). Similarly, people in the managerial group are in constant competition as to who will be more agreeable to the owners (on which their highly paid position depends). So, everybody in this hierarchical structure knows well (or soon learns) what is agreeable and what is not and acts accordingly. Therefore, the filtering of information works through self-censorship rather than through any kind of 'orders from above'. The effect of the internal hierarchical structure is to impose, through the internal competition that it creates, a kind of homogenisation in the journalists' performance. But, does this exclude the possibility that some media workers may have incentives other those determined by career ambitions? Of course, not. But, such people, as Chomsky points out, will never find a place in the corridors of media power and, one way or another, will be marginalised:

> They (journalists) say, quite correctly, "nobody ever tells me what to write. I write anything I like. All this business about pressures and constraints is nonsense because I'm never under any pressure." Which is completely true, but the point is that they wouldn't be there unless they had already demonstrated that nobody has to tell them what to write because they are going to say the right thing... it is not purposeful censorship. It is just that you don't make it to those positions. That includes the left (what is called the left), as well as the right. Unless you have been adequately socialised and trained so that there are some thoughts you just don't have, because if you did have them, you wouldn't be there.

But, how is it determined what is agreeable? Here it is where the 'external' control mechanisms come into play. It is competition among the various media organisations, which homogenises journalists' behaviour. This competition takes the form of a struggle to improve ratings (as regards TV channels) or circulation (as regards newspapers, magazines etc). Ratings or circulation are important not per se but because the advertising income of privately owned mass media (which is the extra income determining their survival or death) depends on them. The result is, as Pierre Bourdieu points out that:

> Ratings have become the journalist's Last Judgement... Wherever you look, people are thinking in terms of market success. Only thirty years ago, and since the middle of the nineteenth century---since Baudelaire and Flaubert and others in avant-garde milieux of writers' writers, writers acknowledged by other writers or even artists acknowledged by other artists---immediate market success was suspect. It was taken as a sign of compromise with the times, with money... Today, on the contrary, the market is accepted more and more as a legitimate means of legitimation.

The pressures created by the ratings mechanism, as Bourdieu points out, have nothing to do with the democratic expression of enlightened collective opinion or public rationality, despite what media ideologues assert. In fact, as the same author points out, the ratings mechanism is the sanction of the market and the economy, that is, of an external and purely market law. I would only add to this that given how 'public opinion' is formed within the process of socialisation and internalisation of the dominant social paradigm, it is indeed preposterous to characterise the ratings mechanism as somehow expressing the democratic will of the people. Ratings, as well as polls generally, is the 'democracy of the uninformed'. They simply reflect the ignorance, the half-truths, or the straightforward distortions of the truth which have been assimilated by an uninformed public and which, through the ratings mechanism, reinforce the role of the mass media in the reproduction of the dominant social paradigm.

One may therefore conclude that the role of the media today is not to make the system more democratic. In fact, one basic function of the media is, as Chomsky stresses, to help in keeping the general population out of the public arena because 'if they get involved they will just make trouble. Their job is to be "spectators," not "participants". Furthermore, the media can play a crucial role in offsetting the democratic rights and freedoms won after long struggles. This has almost always been the case when there was a clash between the elites and trade unions, or popular movements generally. Walter Lippmann, the revered American journalist was explicit about it, as Chomsky points out.

For Lippmann, there is a new art in the method of democracy, called "manufacture of consent." By manufacturing consent, you can overcome the fact that formally a lot of people have the right to vote. We can make it irrelevant because we can manufacture consent and make sure that their choices and attitudes will be structured in such a way that they will always do what we tell them, even if they have a formal way to participate. So we'll have a real democracy. It will work properly. That's applying the lessons of the propaganda agency.

Within this analytical framework we may explore fruitfully the particular ways through which the filtering of information is achieved, as, for instance, is described by Chomsky and Herman in their 'propaganda model'. Similarly Bourdieu shows in a graphic way how the filtering of information takes place in television, through the structuring of TV debates, the time limits, the methods of hiding by showing etc. Particularly important is the way in which the media, particularly television, control not just the information flow, but also the production of culture, by controlling the access of academics as well as of cultural producers, who in turn, as a result of being recognised a public figures, gain recognition in their own fields.

Thus, at the end, the journalistic field, which is structurally very strongly subordinated to market pressures and as such is a very heteronomous field, applies pressure, in turn, to all other fields.

An illustrative application of the above analytical framework is the crucial contribution of the mass media in the creation of the subjective conditions for the neoliberal consensus. Thus, the mass media have played a double ideological role with respect to the neoliberal consensus. On the one hand, they have promoted directly the neoliberal agenda:

- by degrading the economic role of the state,
- by attacking the 'dependence' on the state which the welfare state supposedly creates,
- by identifying freedom with the freedom of choice, which is supposedly achieved through the liberation of markets etc. (talk radio and similar TV shows play a particularly significant role in this respect).

On the other hand, the media have also attempted to divert attention from the consequences of the neoliberal consensus (in terms of growing inequality and poverty, the explosion of crime and drug abuse and so on):

- by promoting irrational beliefs of all sorts (religion, mystical beliefs, astrology etc). The film and video explosion on the themes of exorcism, supernatural powers etc (induced mainly by Hollywood) has played a significant role in diverting attention from the evils of neoliberalism.
- by manufacturing irrelevant and/or insignificant 'news stories' (e.g. Monica Lewinsky affair), which are then taken over by opposition politicians who are eager to find fictitious ways (because of the lack of real political differences within the neoliberal consensus) to differentiate themselves from those in power.
- by creating a pseudo 'general interest' (for instance around a nationalist or chauvinist cause) in order to unite the population around a 'cause' and make it forget the utterly dividing aspects of neoliberalism.

At the same time, the creation of the neoliberal conditions at the institutional level had generated the objective conditions for the mass media to play the aforementioned role. This was because the deregulation and liberalisation of markets and the privatisation of state TV in many European countries had created the conditions for homogenisation through the internal and external competition, which I mentioned above. It is not accidental anyway that major media tycoons like Murdoch in the Anglo-Saxon world, Kirsch in Germany, or Berlusconi in

Italy have also been among the main exponents of the neoliberal consensus agenda.

CULTURE AND A DEMOCRATIC CONCEPTION OF CITIZENSHIP

I am not going to repeat here the discussion on the fundamental components of an inclusive democracy and the necessary conditions, which have to be met for the setting up of it. Instead, I will try to focus on the implications of the democratic institutional arrangements on culture and the role of media.

The starting point is that the conditions for democracy imply a new conception of citizenship: economic, political, social and cultural.

Thus, political citizenship involves new political structures and the return to the classical conception of politics (direct democracy). Economic citizenship involves new economic structures of community ownership and control of economic resources (economic democracy). Social citizenship involves self-management structures at the workplace, democracy in the household and new welfare structures where all basic needs (to be democratically determined) are covered by community resources, whether they are to be satisfied in the household or at the community level. Finally, cultural citizenship involves new democratic structures of dissemination and control of information and culture (mass media, art, etc.), which allow every member of the community to take part in the process and at the same time develop his/her intellectual and cultural potential.

It is obvious that the above new conception of citizenship has very little in common with the liberal and socialist definitions of citizenship, which are linked to the liberal and socialist conceptions of human rights respectively. Thus, for the liberals, the citizen is simply the individual bearer of certain freedoms and political rights recognised by law which, supposedly, secure equal distribution of political power. Similarly, for the socialists, the citizen is the bearer not only of political rights and freedoms but, also, of some social and economic rights, whereas for Marxists the citizenship is realised with the collective ownership of the means of production.

Furthermore, the conception of citizenship adopted here is not related to the current social-democratic discourse on the subject, which, in effect, focuses on the institutional conditions for the creation of an internationalised market economy 'with a human face'. The proposal for instance for a redefinition of citizenship within the framework of a "stakeholder capitalism" belongs to this category. This proposal involves an 'active' citizenship, where citizens have 'stakes' in companies, the market economy and society in general and managers have to take into account these stakes in the running of the businesses and social institutions they are in charge of.

The conception of citizenship adopted here, which could be called a democratic conception, is based on our definition of inclusive democracy and presupposes a 'participatory' conception of active citizenship, like the one implied by the work of Hannah Arendt. In this conception, "political activity is not a means to an end, but an end in itself; one does not engage in political action simply to promote one's welfare but to realise the principles intrinsic to political life, such as freedom, equality, justice, solidarity, courage and excellence". It is therefore obvious that this conception of citizenship is qualitatively different from the liberal and social-democratic conceptions, which adopt an 'instrumentalist' view of citizenship, i.e. a view which implies that citizenship entitles citizens with certain rights that they can exercise as means to the end of individual welfare.

Although the above conception of citizenship implies a geographical sense of community which is the fundamental unit of political, economic and social life, still, it is assumed that it interlocks with various other communities (cultural, professional, ideological, etc.). Therefore, the community and citizenship arrangements do not rule out cultural differences based on language, customs etc, or other differences based on gender, age, ethnicity and so on; they simply provide the public space where such differences can be expressed. Furthermore, these arrangements institutionalise various safety valves that aim to rule out the marginalisation of such differences by the majority. What therefore unites people in a political community, or a confederation of communities, is not a set of common cultural values, imposed by a nationalist ideology, a religious dogma, a mystical belief, or an 'objective' interpretation of natural or social 'evolution', but the democratic institutions and practices, which have been set up by citizens themselves.

However, as I attempted to show elsewhere this cultural pluralism does not mean a kind of cultural relativism where 'everything goes'. In other words, it is possible to derive an ethical system and correspondingly a set of cultural values which is neither 'objective', (in the sense that it is derived from a supposedly objective interpretation of social evolution-Marx, or natural evolution---Bookchin), nor just a matter of individual choice. There can be a set of common or general moral criteria by which individual actions could be judged, i.e. a code of democratic ethics, which would be based on the fundamental principle of organising a democratic society around a confederal inclusive Democracy, (i.e. a democracy based on a confederation of demoi, or democratic communities).

DEMOCRATIC ETHIC CODE

This code of democratic ethics may be derived out of the two fundamental principles of organisation of a confederal inclusive Democracy, i.e. the principle of autonomy and the principle of community. Thus, out of the fundamental principle of autonomy one may derive a set of cultural values about equality and respect for the personality of every citizen, irrespective of gender, race, ethnic identity etc. Out of the same fundamental principle one could derive the principle of protecting the quality of life of each individual citizen -- something that would imply a relationship of harmony with nature. Similarly, out of the fundamental principle of community life one may derive a set of values involving solidarity and mutual aid, caring and sharing. These values should constitute an integral part of the dominant social paradigm so that democracy can reproduce itself. This of course does not exclude the possibility, or rather the probability, of the existence of alternative cultural values, or perhaps even of a conflict between personal and collective values ---particularly with respect to those citizens who cannot reconcile themselves with the tragic truth that it is we who determine our own truth and might still adhere to moral codes derived from irrational belief systems (religions, mystical beliefs etc). However, as long as these people are in a minority, (hopefully, a dwindling one, through the Paedeia of a democratic society), the conflict in their personal values with the collectively defined values should not be a problem for the community as a whole.

DEMOCRATIC MEDIA

The sufficient condition which has to be met so that democracy will not degenerate into some kind of "demagocracy", where the demos is manipulated by a new breed of 'professional' politicians, is crucially conditioned by the citizens' level of democratic consciousness. This, in turn, is conditioned by Paedeia. It is therefore obvious that the cultural institutions, particularly the media, play a crucial role in a democracy, given their role in the formation of Paedeia.

So, let us now consider the nature and role of the mass media, as cultural institutions, in a democratic society. First, there is no reason why the mass media in a democratic society will distort rather than reflect reality. As political and economic power would be equally distributed among citizens and therefore the existence of institutionalised elites would be excluded, the media would face none of the present dilemmas whether to reflect the reality of the elite, or particular sections of it, versus the reality of the rest of the population. Still, even in an inclusive democracy there is still the problem of the possible emergence of informal elites, which may attempt to exercise some sort of control over the information flows. It is also clear that no democracy is possible unless its citizens are fully informed on anything affecting their life. Therefore, a way has to be found to organise the decision-taking process in the media so that, on the one hand, citizens are always fully informed and, on the other, the media are under the real control of the community.

It is obvious that it is citizens as citizens, through their assemblies, who should determine the overall operation of mass media and supervise them. This function could not just be assigned to the councils of media workers because in that case the democratic society will run the double risk of media not expressing the general interest, as well as of the possible emergence of new media elites within, at least, some of them.

This does not, obviously, mean that the assemblies will determine every day what the content of TV news bulletins will be, or what the papers would say next day. What it does mean is that the community assemblies would set strict rules on how full diversity and accountability could be achieved and then supervise the application of these principles in media practice.

Diversity implies that all sorts of views should be given full access to the media, provided that that they have been approved by the community and media workers' assemblies. Assuming that these assemblies have internalised the dominant democratic social paradigm, one could expect that they would not give easy access to views which contradict the democratic values (e.g. views promoting racial, sexist, religious values etc). However, the decision will always rest with the assemblies and if they see no contradiction involved in giving full access to such views this will simply herald the degradation and eventual collapse of the democratic society itself.

Accountability implies that the media workers would be accountable for their decisions to the media workers' assemblies in the first instance and, next, to the community assemblies. Such a structure of accountability would be compatible with the lack of hierarchical structures in the media and the fact that it will be the communities themselves that would 'own' the media institutions.

So, this dual system of decision-taking, whereby overall decision-taking and supervision rests with the community assemblies, whereas the determination of detailed operational functioning of the media is left to the media workers' assemblies, to my mind, guarantees that not only the general interest is adequately taken into account but also that the day-to-day decisions are taken democratically by the media workers themselves.

WAYS TO BRING ABOUT SYSTEMIC SOCIAL CHANGE

As I tried to show above the culture of a democratic society will be characterised by very different values than those of a market economy. The values of heteronomy, competition, individualism and consumerism which are dominant today have to be replaced in a democratic society by the values of individual and collective autonomy, co-operation, mutual aid, solidarity and sharing. Furthermore, as far as the mass media is concerned, the role, organisation and nature of media in a democratic society will also drastically differ from the corresponding role, nature and organisation today. The media will not have the role to reflect reality, basically, as seen from the elites' point of view, but, as seen from the people's viewpoint; their organisation will not be based on hierarchical structures, but, on democratic structures; finally, the media will cease to be profit-making enterprises owned and controlled by elites and will become, instead, democratically owned and controlled institutions of communicating information.

The obvious issue, which arises here, is how we move from 'here' to 'there'. This basic question involves a series of other issues concerning social change, which have been discussed extensively, particularly during the century which is now expiring. Can there be a drastic change of values, like the one discussed above, without a parallel change of institutions? Do we need a systemic change to bring about the required change in values and institutions? Should the social struggle have as explicit aim the systemic change as part of a comprehensive political program for it? To attempt to give an answer to all these questions we will have to discuss briefly the main approaches to social change.

But, first, we have to be clear about the meaning of social change. As it is obvious from the above analysis, social change here means systemic change, i.e. a change in the entire socio-economic system of the market economy, representative democracy and hierarchical structures. As I attempted to show elsewhere the fundamental cause of the multi-dimensional crisis we face today (economic, ecological, social, political) is the concentration of power at the hands of various elites (economic, political etc) and therefore the only way out of this crisis is the abolition of power structures and relations, i.e. the creation of conditions of equal distribution of power among citizens. One way that could bring about this sort of society is the Inclusive Democracy proposal which involves the creation of political, economic and social structures that secure direct democracy, economic democracy, ecological democracy and democracy in the social realm. It also involves the creation of a new social paradigm (based on the values I mentioned above) which, for the reproduction of inclusive democracy to be secured, it has to become dominant.

So, assuming that the aim is to bring about systemic social change involving the creation of conditions for the equal distribution of power among citizens, there are, schematically, four main approaches which claim that they may bring about this result: reforms (from 'above' or from 'below'), revolution (from 'above' or from 'below'), 'life-style strategies' and the Inclusive Democracy approach.

THE REFORMIST APPROACH

The reformist approach claims that it can bring about systemic change through either the conquest of state power (reforms 'from above') or through the creation of autonomous from the state power bases which would press the state for reforms (reforms 'from below'). The main example of the former strategy is the social democratic approach, whereas the main example of the latter is the civil societarian approach.

The social democratic approach reached its peak during the period of statism and particularly in the first thirty years after WWII, when the social democratic consensus was dominant all over the Western world. However, the internationalisation of the market economy since the mid '70s brought about the end of this consensus and the rise of the neoliberal consensus- which, in my view, is irreversible as long as the market economy is internationalised, in other words, as long as the market economy reproduces itself. The recent deletion from the program of the British Labour Party (which was the last socialdemocratic party still committed to full socialisation of the means of production) of 'clause four', which committed it to full socialisation, marked the formal end of socialdemocratic claims towards real systemic change.

In fact, the neoliberal agenda for 'flexible' labour markets, minimisation of social controls on markets, replacement of the welfare state by a safety net etc has now become the agenda of every major socialdemocratic party in power or in opposition. The parallel degradation of social democracy and the reversal of most of its conquests (comprehensive welfare state, state commitment to full employment, significant improvement in the distribution of income) has clearly shown that supporters of the revolutionary approach were always right on the impossibility of bringing about a systemic change through reforms.

As regards the civil societarian approach, the strategy here is to enhance 'civil society', that is, to strengthen the various networks which are autonomous from state control (unions, churches, civic movements, co-operatives, neighbourhoods, schools of thought etc.) in order to impose such limits (i.e. social controls) on markets and the state, so that a kind of systemic change is brought about. However, this approach is based on a number of unrealistic assumptions.

Thus, first, it implicitly assumes a high degree of statism where the state can still play the economic role it used to play during the socialdemocratic consensus. Second, it assumes, in effect, an almost closed market economy where the state can ignore the instant movement of capital in case a government attempts to meet demands of civil societarians which threaten capital's interets. No wonder that civil societarians usually deny (or try to minimise) the importance of the present internationalisation of the market economy. It is also indicative that when civil societarians attempt to internationalise their approach the only limits on the internationalised market economy that they view as feasible are various 'regulatory controls'. But, such controls have very little in common with the sweeping social controls that they have in mind when they discuss, abstracting from the present internationalised market economy, the limits that civil society networks should impose on markets (drastic reduction of inequalities, massive creation of jobs etc).

So, the civil societarian approach is both a-historical and utopian. It is a-historical, since it ignores the structural changes, which have led to the present neoliberal consensus and the internationalised market economy. And it is utopian because it is in tension both with the present internationalised market economy and the state. So, given that civil societarians do not see the outcome of this inevitable tension in terms of the replacement of the market economy and the state by the civil society, it is not difficult to predict that any enhancement of the civil society will have to be compatible with the process of further internationalisation of the market economy and the implied role of the state. In other words, the 'enhancement' of civil society, under today's conditions, would simply mean that the ruling political and economic elites will be left undisturbed to continue dominating society, while, from time to time, they will have to try to address the demands of the civil societarians-- provided, of course that these demands are not in direct conflict to their own interests and the demands of oligopolistic production.

In conclusion, enhancing the civil society institutions has no chance whatsoever of either putting an end to the concentration of power, or of transcending the present multidimensional crisis. This conclusion may be derived from the fact that the implicit, although not always explicit, aim of civil societarians is to improve the functioning of existing institutions (state, parties, market), in order to make them more responsive to pressures from below when, in fact, the crisis is founded on the institutions themselves and not on their malfunctioning! But, in the present internationalised market, the need to minimise the socio-economic role of the state is no longer a matter of choice for those controlling production.

It is a necessary condition for survival. This is particularly so for European capital that has to compete with capital blocks, which operate from bases where the social-democratic tradition of statism was never strong (the United States, the Far East). But, even at the planetary level, one could seriously doubt whether it is still possible to enhance the institutions of civil society within the context of the market economy. Granted that the fundamental aims of production in a market economy are individual gain, economic efficiency and growth, any attempt to reconcile these aims with an effective 'social control' by the civil society is bound to fail since, as historic experience with the statist phase has shown, social control and market efficiency are irreconcilable objectives. By the same token, one could reasonably argue that the central contradiction of the market economy today is the one arising from the fact that any effective control of the ecological implications of growth is incompatible with the requirements of competitiveness, which the present phase of the marketization process imposes.

THE LIFE-STYLE APPROACH

The second type of approach which claims capable to bring about systemic social change is the presently fashionable, particularly among Anglo-Saxon anarchists, life-style strategy. There are several versions of this strategy. Sometimes this approach involves no intervention at all in the political arena and usually not even in the general social arena --other than in struggles on specific 'Green' issues, like animal rights campaigns etcetera. Alternatively, this approach may involve a process which, starting from the individual, and working through affinity groups, aims at setting an example of sound and preferable life-styles at the individual and social level: alternative media, Community Economic Development projects, 'free zones' and alternative institutions (free schools, self-managed factories, housing associations, Local Employment and Trading Systems (LETS), communes, self-managed farms and so on).

However, this approach, in any of the above versions, is, by itself, utterly ineffective in bringing about a systemic social change. Although helpful in creating an alternative culture among small sections of the population and, at the same time, morale-boosting for activists who wish to see an immediate change in their lives, this approach does not have any chance of success--in the context of today's huge concentration of power--in building the democratic majority needed for systemic social change. The projects suggested by this strategy may too easily be marginalised, or absorbed into the existing power structure (as has happened many times in the past) whereas their effect on the socialisation process is minimal--if not nil.

Furthermore, life-style strategies, by usually concentrating on single issues which are not part of a comprehensive political program for social transformation, provide a golden opportunity to the ruling elites to use their traditional divide and rule tactics (the British elites, for instance, frequently use security guards recruited from the underclass to fight Green activists rather than 'exposing' the police on this role!)

Furthermore, systemic social change can never be achieved outside the main political and social arena. The elimination of the present power structures and relations can neither be achieved "by setting an example", nor through education and persuasion. A power base is needed to destroy power. But, the only way that an approach aiming at a power base would be consistent with the aims of the democratic project is, to my mind, through the development of a comprehensive program for the radical transformation of local political and economic structures.

A variation of the life-style strategy which however has, also, elements of the civil societarian approach is, to my mind, the strategy proposed by Noam Chomsky, Michael Albert and the group around Z magazine. Thus, Albert sees the setting up of alternative media institutions just 'as part of a project to establish new ways of organising media and social activity', without even mentioning the need to incorporate them into a comprehensive political program for systemic change. In fact, what differentiates the alternative from the mainstream media in his argument is, basically, their internal structure:

Being alternative can't just mean that the institution's editorial focus is on this or that topical area. And being alternative as an institution certainly isn't just being left or right or different in editorial content. Being alternative as an institution must have to do with how the institution is organised and works... An alternative media institution sees itself as part of a project to establish new ways of organising media and social activity and it is committed to furthering these as a whole, and not just its own preservation.

Similarly, Chomsky does not raise either the issue of incorporating alternative institutions into a comprehensive political program for systemic change. Thus, to the question whether we should just continue supporting efforts to set up alternative media institutions etc, or whether, instead, we should direct our striving towards integrating such attempts in a struggle to build a new political and social movement that will fight for alternative systems of social organisation, his reply is that these two possibilities 'should not be regarded as alternatives... these are not conflicting goals; rather, mutually supportive efforts, all of which should proceed'.

It is therefore obvious that for Chomsky and Albert the establishment of alternative media is seen as a kind of life-style strategy, rather than as part of a political strategy and a comprehensive program for systemic change. Similarly, Chomsky's argument above that, even within the existing institutional framework, we could reverse the present concentration of power involves elements of the civil societarian approach. It is illustrative how Chomsky justifies his argument on the matter:

These are not the operations of any mysterious economic laws; they are human decisions that are subject to challenge, revision and reversal. They are also decisions made within institutions, state and private. These have to face the test of legitimacy, as always; and if they do not meet that test they can be replaced by others that are more free and more just, exactly as has happened throughout history.

However, although it is true that there are no historical or natural laws determining social evolution this does not mean that 'anything goes' within the existing institutional framework, as Chomsky seems to assume. The institutional framework does set the parameters within which social action takes place. This means that both the nature and the scope of radical social action cannot transcend these parameters -unless social action explicitly aims at the institutional framework itself. The neoliberal consensus was not just a policy change, as social democrats assume, but a structural change imposed by the needs of internationalisation of the market economy.

This implies that the basic elements of the neoliberal consensus and particularly flexible markets and minimisation of social controls on markets will not go away, as long as the present internationalised market economy exists. But, today, the market economy can only be internationalised, since the growth (and therefore profitability) of the multinationals, which control the world market economy, depends on enlarging their markets worldwide. And as long as the market economy has to be internationalised, markets have to be as open and as flexible as possible. All this means that, as long as the system of the market economy and representative democracy reproduces itself, all that reforms ('from above', or 'from below') can bring about today is temporary victories and reversible social conquests like, for instance, those made during the period of the social democratic consensus which are now being systematically dismantled by the neoliberal consensus.

THE REVOLUTIONARY APPROACH

Coming now to the revolutionary strategy, by 'revolution from above' I mean the strategy, which aims at systemic change through the conquest of state power. The Marxist- Leninist tradition is a classical example of this type of strategy. This approach, implied that the change in the social paradigm even among a minority of the population, the vanguard of the proletariat, (organised in the communist party and equipped with the 'science' of socialism, i.e. Marxism), could function as a catalyst to bring about a socialist revolution. The socialist revolution would then lead to the conquest of state power by the proletariat (effectively by its vanguard, i.e. the communist party) which would bring about a change in the institutional framework as well as a change in the dominant social paradigm. The socialist society would give way to a communist society only when the rapid development of productive forces, through the socialisation of production relations, would lead to the abolition of scarcity and division of labour and the withering away of the state. History however has shown that this strategy could only lead to new hierarchical structures, as the vanguard of the working class becomes at the end the new ruling elite. This was the main lesson of the collapse of 'actually existing socialism' which has clearly shown that, if the revolution is organised, and then its program carried out, through a minority, it is bound to end up with new hierarchical structures rather than with a society where concentration of power has been abolished.

By 'revolution from below', I mean the strategy which aims at systemic change through the abolition of state power and the creation of federations of communes, or of workers' associations. The various trends within the anarchist movement (community-oriented versus worker-oriented) aim at revolution, in order to abolish state power and transform society 'from below', rather than in order to conquest state power and transform society 'from above'.

But, attempts for revolutions from below in History have usually ended up either as insurrections, which failed to lead to a systemic change (the major recent example being the May '68 insurrection in France) or to civil wars, where the superior means, organisation and efficiency of their enemies (either the state army and/or statist socialists) led to the suppression of revolutionaries (the major recent example being the Spanish civil war in 1936).

To my mind, the major problem of any revolutionary strategy, either from above or from below, is the uneven development of consciousness among the population, in other words, the fact that a revolution, which assumes a rupture with the past both at the subjective level of consciousness and at the institutional level, takes place in an environment where only a minority of the population has broken with the dominant social paradigm.

Then, if it is a revolution from above, it has a good chance to achieve its first aim, to abolish state power and establish its own power. But, exactly because it is a revolution from above with its own hierarchical structures etc, it has no chance to change the dominant social paradigm but only formally, i.e. at the level of the official ideology.

On the other hand, although the revolution from below is the correct approach to convert people democratically to the new social paradigm, it suffers from the fact that the uneven development of consciousness among the population may not allow revolutionaries to achieve even their very first aim of abolishing state power. Therefore, the still unresolved problem with systemic change is how it could be brought about, from below, but by a majority of the population, so that a democratic abolition of power structures could become feasible.

INCLUSIVE DEMOCRACY APPROACH

The Inclusive Democracy (ID) project does offer a strategy, which aims at resolving this problem. It starts first with the assumption that radical systemic change would never come about through reforms, or life-style strategies. This is because systemic change requires a rupture with the past, which extends to both the institutional and the subjective level. Such a rupture is only possible through the development of a new political organisation and a new comprehensive political program for systemic change. This means that the various activities to set up communes, co-ops, alternative media institutions etc are just irrelevant to a process of systemic change --- unless they are an explicitly integral part of such a comprehensive political program. It is in this sense that one may argue that the two strategies are not complementary as Chomsky argues, but mutually exclusive.

The ID political strategy comprises the gradual involvement of increasing numbers of people in a new kind of politics and the parallel shifting of economic resources (labour, capital, land) away from the market economy. The aim of such a transitional strategy should be to create changes in the institutional framework, as well as to value systems, which, after a period of tension between the new institutions and the state, would, at some stage, replace the market economy, statist democracy, and the social paradigm "justifying" them, with an inclusive democracy and a new democratic paradigm respectively.

The immediate objective should be the creation, from below, of 'popular bases of political and economic power', that is, the establishment of local public realms of direct and economic democracy which will confederate in order to create the conditions for the establishment of a new society. Contesting local elections (the only form of elections which is not incompatible with the aims of the ID project) could provide the chance to put into effect such a program on a massive social scale, although other forms of establishing new types of social organisation should not be neglected, as long as they are part of a program which explicitly aims at systemic change.

Once the institutions of inclusive democracy begin to be installed, and people, for the first time in their lives, start obtaining real power to determine their own fate, then the gradual erosion of the dominant social paradigm and of the present institutional framework will be set in motion. A new popular power base will be created.

Town by town, city by city, region by region will be taken away from the effective control of the market economy and the nation-state, their political and economic structures being replaced by the confederations of democratically run communities. A dual power in tension with the state will be created, an alternative social paradigm will become hegemonic and the break in the socialisation process--the precondition for a change in the institution of society--will have occurred. The legitimacy of today's 'democracy' will have been lost.

The implementation of a strategy like the one outlined above requires a new type of political organisation, which will mirror the desired structure of society. This would not be the usual political party, but a form of 'democracy in action', which would undertake various collective forms of intervention at:

- the political level (creation of 'shadow' political institutions based on direct democracy, neighbourhood assemblies, etc.),
- the economic level (establishment of community units at the level of production and distribution which are collectively owned and controlled),
- the social level (democracy in the workplace, the university etc.), and
- the cultural level (creation of community-controlled art and media activities).

However, all these forms of intervention should be part of a comprehensive program for social transformation aiming at the eventual change of each municipality won in the local elections into an inclusive democracy. The alternative media established as part of this program would play a crucial role in developing an alternative consciousness to the present one, as regards the methods of solving the economic and ecological problems in a democratic way. They should connect today's economic and ecological crisis to the present socio-economic system and make proposals on how to start building the new society. For example: by setting up a democratic economic sector, (i.e. a sector owned by the demos); by creating a democratic mechanism to make economic decisions affecting the demotic sector of the community; by 'localising' decisions affecting the life of the community as a whole (local production, local spending, local taxes, etc.).

Without underestimating the difficulties involved in the context of today's all-powerful methods of brain control and economic violence, which, in fact, might prove more effective methods than pure state violence in suppressing a movement for the inclusive democracy, I think that the proposed strategy is a realistic strategy on the way to a new society.

8

Mass Media and Communication

At the beginning of the third millennium, it hardly needs any emphasis that journalism and mass media or simply the "press" plays a central role in modern society. Even in the early 18th century, the press was recognised as a powerful entity. Thomas Carlyle (1795-1881) wrote that the British statesman Edmund Burke (1729-97) called the reporters' gallery in the British Parliament "a Fourth Estate more important by far" than the other three estates of Parliament-the peers, bishops, and commons. A Similar statement, however, is attributed to the English historian, Thomas Babington Macaulay (1800-1859) who in his Essay On Hallam's Constitutional History Published in Edinburgh Review (September 1828), observed with reference to the press gallery of the House of Commons, "The gallery in which the reporters sit has become a fourth estate of the realm".

And over time, newspapers, news magazines, radio, television, cable video, video Cassettes and movies have been demanding more and more of our attention and leisure time. The mass media now markedly affect our politics, our recreation, our education in general and profoundly our culture, our perception and our understanding of the world around us. However, Prof. (Herbert) Marshall Mcluhan (1911-1980), whose theories on mass communication caused widespread debate, argued that each major period of history is characterised, not by the mass media per se, but by the nature of the medium of communication (print or electronic) used most widely at the time. In this Chapter will be discussed educational opportunities in four interrelated areas of studies, viz., Journalism and Mass Communication, Communication Studies, Public Relations, and Advertising. However, it would be in order to present first an overview of the media world, the role of the government, and to explain several terminologies.

TERMINOLOGIES

First, a few words about the various terms used in this field because many such terms occur in admission advertisements. The term "journalism" often referred to as "news business" involves the gathering, processing, and delivery of important information relating to current affairs by the print media (news papers and new magazines), and electronic media (radio and TV). This integrated entity is also simply called "media". News and entertainment are communicated in a number of different ways using different media. The world "media" is often used to refer to the communication of news, and in this context means the same as news media. Media and mass media are often used when discussing the power of modern communication.

If there is a term that has appeared in more diverse publications than any other over the last few years, it is "multimedia". The number of definitions for it is as numerous as the number of companies that are involved in multimedia business. In essence, multimedia is the use or presentation of information in two or more forms. The combination of audio and video in film and television was probably the first multimedia application. It is the advent of the PC, with its ability to manipulate data from different sources and offer this directly to the consumers or subscribers that has sparked the current interest. In the context of mass media and communication, multimedia is an effective tool for the profession. Still journalism, which has long history beginning almost with the invention of printing, continues to be the core concept of the entire process of communication. The newer communication technologies, in fact, have been strengthening the cause of journalism and newspapers, the latest to appear on the scene being the Internet. However, education in multimedia is mainly offered by private IT institutes (e.g., Arena Multimedia).

THE MEDIA WORLD

The media world consists of a wide variety of agencies and organisations which are involved in media related activities. At its core are the mass media organisations per se and the users of mass media. The first category consists of (i) the print media (newspapers and magazines), (ii) the electronic media (radio and television channels), and (iii) the news agencies. The electronic media now includes the World Wide Web (WWW) which hosts Internet versions of most of the well-known newspapers and news magazines and is also emerging as a potential advertisement medium. In the second category are (i) the advertisers and advertising agencies, and (ii) the public relations agencies. Advertising provide the financial sustenance to the mass media and their survival depends upon advertisements. Public relation agencies interact with the mass media to put across their messages.

They also have their own mechanisms to reach their target audience groups. Besides, there are other institutions and organisations associated with media related activities. They include (1) audit agencies which vouch for the circulation figures of the print media; (2) agencies conducting readership surveys; (3) schools of journalism and mass communication; (4) statutory and non-statutory organisations dealing with regulatory and ethical issues; and (5) organisations representing various interest groups in the media world. Last but not the least, there are facilitators, such as the chain of distributors of the print media and the TV cable operators, who provide the vital link between the products of media organisations and their consumers.

However, apart from functional relationships among mass media, advertising, and public relations, from academic point of view what is necessary to appreciate is that at the heart of these three activities is the art and science of communication. The practitioners is these areas strive to communicate with their respective target audience groups, adopting the most effective communication strategies. The term communication, however, has a much wider connotation encompassing many fields of studies, the major areas being sociology and psychology, linguistics, cybernetics and information theory, and the study of non-verbal communication. Sociology and psychology produced the first academic studies in mass communication during the 1930s. Thereafter, many scholars studied the effects of mass communication on individuals and society. The theory and process of communication indeed has profoundly influenced the study of journalism and mass communication.

MASS MEDIA AND GOVERNMENT

Governments and press are widely perceived as mutual adversaries. Freedom of the Press-the right of the press to report and to criticise the wrong doings of the powerful without retaliation or threat of retaliation-is the cornerstone of democracy. Freedom of the Press in the United States is more than a legal concept-almost a religious tenet. The First Amendment to the US Constitution states clearly and unequivocally that the "Congress Shall Make No Law. Abridging Freedom of Speech or of the Press".

The Indian Constitution does not have similar provision, but Art 19 (1) (a) protects the right to freedom of speech and expression subject to reasonable restrictions as mentioned in Art 19 (2) Though many governments vouch for protecting the freedom of the press, there are instances galore of throttling the press. There are several agencies in various countries which fight for the cause of press freedom. Be that as it may, governments themselves are also major users of mass media for putting across their messages.

The Ministry of Information and Broadcasting which was set up during the Second World War to mobilise support for war efforts, is now a very large mass media organisation of the Government of India.

It performs its tasks through a number of specialised media units and other organisation. One of its most important units, the Directorate of Advertising and Visual Publicity (DAVP), is the primary multimedia advertising agency of the Central Government which uses about 6,240 newspapers for press advertisement.

The Ministry, besides its own mass media activities performs several statutory functions, the most important of which is the registration of newspapers and periodicals. The Office of the Registrar of Newspapers in India (RNI), commonly known as Press Registrar, was created in 1956 in accordance with the Section 19A of the Press and Registration of regulation of titles of newspapers and periodicals, followed by their registration and allocation of registration numbers.

It is also responsible for the verification of circulation claims, receiving Annual Statements of registered newspapers and periodicals, and compiling and publishing the annual report titled 'Press in India' containing detailed information about the print media, a valuable media reference tool. Another important statutory quasi-judicial authority, under the umbrella of the Ministry, is the Press Council of India (PCI). The objectives of the PCI established under the Indian Press Council Act 1978, are to preserve the freedom of the press and to maintain and improvement of standards of newspapers and news agencies.

The Ministry of Labour, on the other hand, is responsible for the operation of the provisions of two Acts relating to the employees of newspaper establishments: (1) The Working Journalists and Other Newspaper Employees (Conditions of Service) and Miscellaneous Provisions Act, 1955, and (2) The Working Journalists (Fixation of Rates of Wages) Act, 1958. The first Act provides for the constitution of two separate Wage Boards for fixing or revising rates of wages of working journalists (including those working in news agencies) and non-journalist newspaper employees.

So far five Wage Boards had been set up (1956, 1963, 1975, 1985, and 1994). The fifth one (Manisana Wage Board) set up in 1994, has submitted its tentative proposals on December 12, 1999. Besides, there are a number of Acts which directly or indirectly affect the mass media. In December, 1999, the Government has introduced in the Parliament the Freedom of Information Bill. When enacted, it is likely to have a far reaching favourable effect on mass media. So far five States viz., Goa, Karnataka, Maharashtra, Rajasthan, and Tamil Nadu also have enacted similar laws.

JOURNALISM AND MASS COMMUNICATION

Journalism education in the narrow sense prepares students for careers in newspapers, news magazines, broadcast news, and news services. Now it encompasses a much wider area under the broad label "mass communication ". By what ever name it may be called, journalism and mass communication study is not a discipline in the sense that sociology, economics, political science or history is, but a rather loose interdisciplinary field covering a wide range of issues somehow related to public concerns. As such, the field reflects in general, the growth of mass communication itself.

A brief account of the development of journalism education in the USA will be helpful in understanding the current trend in journalism and mass communication education in India. Journalism education which has a beginning in English Departments in America universities focussed more on techniques, such as, reporting, news writing, editing, design, photography. Often they were taught by former journalists. Willard G Bleyer, a professor of English in the University of Wisconsin may be called the father of journalism education. He was instrumental in introducing the first journalism course in the University in 1905 and his scholarly interests later greatly influenced the field.

However, the country's first school of Journalism came into existence in 1908 at the University of Missouri. This was followed by the establishment of the Graduate School of Journalism in 1911 at the Columbia University backed with a $2 million gift from Joseph Pulitzer (1846-1911), publisher of the New York World, Pulitzer is also remembered for the Pulitzer Prizes, also funded by him, and annually awarded for excellence in journalism, letters and music. The School, still rated as one of the best journalism schools in the USA, is the publisher of the scholarly journal Columbia Journalism Review published since 1961. Now there are 427 colleges and universities which offer programmes in journalism and mass communication.

The focus on newspapers continued to dominate journalism education throughout the 1940s at leading Schools of Journalism in the USA. With the emergence of radio and television as major news and entertainment media, the journalism schools incorporated such topics as radio news, television news and broadcasting production techniques in their programmes. Even the Speech Departments, offshoots of English Departments, became involved in the preparation of students for careers in broadcasting. In some universities, the speech of communication arts department were merged with the journalism programmes.

Around the same time, more and more journalism schools started offering courses in advertising and public relations, giving rise to the term "mass communication" to describe this amalgam of courses on newspapers, radio, television, news magazines, and an increasing involvement with the study of communication itself. Communication study as an academic discipline has long been a part of social sciences in the American higher education. It involves the study of mass media and other social institutions devoted, among other, to persuasion, communication processes and their effects, audience studies, contents analysis, and interpersonal communication.

Wilbur Schramm, a leading scholar of communication studies, who taught at University of Iowa, Illinois and Stanford, is credited with popularising communication studies in journalism departments. Increasingly, graduate programmes became more concerned with communication theory while undergraduate courses stressed pre-professional training for careers in news media, advertising, and public relations. However, such emphasis on communication has its share of criticism too. It has been argued that communication and media studies hardly have anything to do with the practice of journalism.

The increased emphasis on communication theory at the expense of basic reporting and writing skill has also led to the scrapping of exclusive journalism courses in some universities. The shifting of focus from conventional journalism to communication is reflected in the rechristening the Schools and Departments of Journalism as School of Journalism and Mass Communication, Department of Communication, or

Schools of Communication. Some of the well-known schools, however, did not change their names. At Missouri and at Columbia they continue to be the School of Journalism and Graduate Department of Journalism, respectively.

JOURNALISM EDUCATION IN INDIA

In India, the very notion of journalism education in universities was looked at with askance. A write-up published in the Times of India (November 27, 1934) shares the most commonly held view of the time that "journalists are born and not made". It observed, "A faculty for criticism, a flair for essentials and a sense of news values can be developed by experience only if these qualities are innate from the beginning... The actual basis of journalism is its various departments can be only be acquired by direct contact and often bitter experience". Almost all the famous journalists of yesteryears learnt journalism on the job starting as "cub" reporters. Even many of the celebrated editors and columnists did not undergo any formal training in journalism. The credit for making journalism as a subject of study goes to Dr. Annie Besant, the distinguished theosophist and freedom fighter. The course in the National University (Adyar) introduced by her, however, did not survive.

There were several other abortive attempts also. The oldest surviving Department of Journalism in the Indian sub-continent was established at Punjab University in Lahore (now in Pakisthan) in 1914. After partition, the Department continued to function at the New Delhi campus of the Indian part of the divided Punjab University till July 1962. At present, it offers a two-year integrated Master of Mass Communication (MMC) programme. From 1947 to 1954, there were only five university departments of journalism: (1) University of Madras (1947), (2) University of Calcutta (1950), (3) University of Mysore (1951), (4) Nagpur University (1952) and (5) Osmania University (1954), Both the First (1952-54) and the Second (1980-82) Press Commissions emphasised the need for expanding the scope of journalism education. The Second Press Commission recommended the establishment of a National Council for Journalism and Communication Research. It also highlighted the need for interdisciplinary approach in journalism education and recommended that admission should be based on the performance in aptitude tests.

It was in 1963, that the Ford Foundation Mass Communication Study Team headed by Wilbur Schramm, who, as stated earlier greatly influenced journalism education in the USA, recommended the expansion of the scope of journalism education by broadening the curriculum to include mass communication, advertising, public relations and Radio and TV journalism, to fall in line with the American system. The Ford Foundation report set the trend of journalism and mass communication education in India. It also led to the establishment in 1965, of the Indian Institute of Mass Communication at New Delhi, by the Ministry of Information and Broadcasting which over a period, has introduced separate courses in these areas. In 1981, the University Grants Commission published the Report on the Status of Journalism and Communication Education in India, which recommended various measures for the strengthening the University Departments of Journalism and improvement in the quality of education. In another document, English Plan Perspective on Journalism/Communication Education in India published in 1990-91, the UGC unveiled a proposal for strengthening of selected universities departments.

With the broadening of curriculum to include the various dimensions of mass communication, the Indian Universities followed the examples of their US counterparts and started incorporating the terms "communication" and "mass communication" in their names. Many new Departments do not even include the term "journalism" in their names. The nomenclature of both the degrees, Bachelor of Journalism (BJ), and Master of Journalism (MJ), accordingly were changed by some universities to incorporate the terms "communication", "mass communication", such as, Bachelor of Communication and Journalism (BCJ), Bachelor of Journalism and Mass Communication (BJMC), Master of Communication and Journalism (MCJ), and Master of Journalism and Mass Communication (MJMC).

In some other universities the nomenclature of the Master's degree courses in MA (Journalism), or MA (Communication and Journalism). Yet in some universities the term "Journalism" does not occur at all, for example, MA, MS or M.Sc (Communication, or Mass Communication), Master of Communication Studies (MCS), Master of Mass Communication (MMC), The choice of nomenclature often reflects the incorporation, in varying degrees, the components of the "journalism", "mass communication" and "communication" in the course curricula.

In the programmes with such labels as "Journalism" or "Journalism and Mass Communication", while topics such as communication theory and broadcast journalism (TV and Radio) are covered, the focus of graduate programmes is more on the basics of print journalism methods and techniques.

In the latter category, apart from the preponderance of communication theory and process along with such issued as development communication, rural communication, educational communication, media research, the trust of many programmes is shifting towards TV and video production, web reporting and publishing, and Internet journalism. However, course contents vary from university to university. Advertising and public relations are covered in almost all the courses. The application of Information Technology (IT) of late is demanding more attention in many programmes.

Educational Opportunities

There has been now a proliferation of university courses in journalism in packages of different combinations of topics. The number of universities offering journalism and related courses now exceeds 75. An exclusive journalism university, Makhanlal Chaturvedi Rashtriya Patrakarita Vishwavidyalaya, was established in Bhopal in 1990.

The objective of the university is to develop itself into a national centre for teaching, training and research of journalism and mass communication through the medium of Hindi. It however, received considerable flak for its greater involvement in franchising out its BCA course to all and sundry throughout the country, rather then striving to achieve excellence in Hindi journalism. At present it offers nine journalism related courses.

Several institutions outside the university system also offer these courses, which include, as stated, earlier, the Indian Institution of Mass Communication. Some of these institutions have been sponsored by newspaper establishments, such as, Eenadu School of Journalism, Times Journalism (Indian Express Group). Some members of the Indian Newspaper Society took the initiative to promote the Press Foundation of India to provide opportunities for training and retraining of journalists.

It may be mentioned that the Film and Television Institute of India (FTTI) (Pune) is the first institution to introduce courses in TV Production. Besides FTTI, its counterpart in Calcutta, Satyajit Ray Film & Television Institute, and several other institutions offer programmes in Television. This has been discussed in Chapter 45 (Performing Arts). The National Institute of Design (Ahmedabad) has courses in the area of Communication Design which include Print Media, Audiovisuals and Video Film.

Levels of Education: Education in journalism and mass communication is offered at the first degree (three-year BA degree), postgraduate Bachelor's degree (BJ/BCJ/BJMC, etc.,) Master's degree (MJ/MCJ/MJMC, etc.,) and pre-doctoral and doctoral levels. Besides, some universities offer the subject as one of the combinations at the first degree levels. Three-year BA degree courses, open to candidates who have passed 10+2 examination, are available only in the affiliated colleges of University of Delhi and Bangalore University. There are also diploma and certificate courses in a number of universities. M.Phil and Doctoral programmes are also available in some universities.

The Bachelor's degree course is of one year duration and open to degree holders in any discipline. Master's degree, also of one year duration, is open to Bachelor's degree holders in journalism. The MA course in the subject, which is of two-year duration, is open to Bachelor's degree holders in any discipline.

A number of universities have started introducing two year integrated programmes, instead of separate one year programmes leading successively to Bachelor and Master degrees. The diploma courses are of one-year duration and the entry requirement is mostly a degree in any discipline. The certificate courses are open to undergraduates.

DISTANCE LEARNING COURSES

About 18 universities offer journalism and mass communication courses at different levels through distance learning mode which include five open universities, viz., Indira Gandhi National Open University, Kota Open University, Karnataka State Open University, Nalanda Open University, and Yashwantrao Chavan Maharashtra Open University.

SPECIALISED COURSES

There are stray instances of journalism courses in specific areas e.g.,

1. PG Diploma (one year) in Agriculture Journalism (Chaudhary Charan Singh Agricultural University),
2. Certificate (trimester) in Fashion Communication and a short term programme in Fashion Journalism (National Institute of Fashion Technology),
3. MA in Development Communication (Madurai Kamaraj University),
4. M.Sc in Agricultural Communication and Extension (GB Pant university of Agriculture & Technology),
5. PG Diploma in Electronic Journalism & Mass Communication (MJP Rohilkhand University),
6. Diploma in TV/AIR (Guru Nanak Dev University),
7. MA/M.Phil/Ph.D in Educational Communication, Distance Education, Subject Communication, M.Com (Subject Communication), and M.Sc (Subject Communication) (Yashwantrao Chavan Maharashtra Open University, Nashik-422005),

8. PG Diploma in Radio and Television Journalism (Indian Institute of Mass Communication).

Two other institutions, Asian College of Journalism and Indian Institute of Journalism and Mass Media focus on Radio, TV and Web journalism.

The focus of the MJ course in Punjab Agricultural University is on agricultural journalism. In fact, the M.Sc and Ph.D courses in agricultural extension in agricultural universities include specialisation in mass communication for diffusion of agricultural information to farmers.

LANGUAGE JOURNALISM

Although, both in terms of the number and circulation, Indian language newspapers far outnumber those in English, only a small number of universities offer courses in language journalism. As of now, there are courses only in Hindi, Urdu and Telugu journalism. Two universities offer courses in Hindi journalism:

(1) Avinashilingam Institute for Home Science of Higher Education for Women-MA in Hindi Journalism,

(2) Banaras Hindu University-MA (Functional Hindi) in Journalism, and PG Diploma in Hindi Journalism of two-year duration (after MA).

As stated earlier, the Makhanlal Chaturvedi Rashtriya Patrakarita Vishwavidyalaya was established to promote journalism and mass communication through the medium of Hindi. Indian Institute of Mass Communication has a postgraduate Diploma course in Hindi Journalism. Urdu journalism is taught only in Jawaharlal Nehru University. It offers an Advance Diploma in Mass Media course with Urdu as one of the subjects. Potti Sreeramulu Telugu University and Eenadu School of Journalism offer Journalism courses in Telugu. While the former offer BJ and MJ programmes, the latter has introduced a Diploma course. The Eenadu Journalism School established by Eenadu, the largest circulated Telugu daily, deserves special mention. Eenadu is the first newspaper in the country to establish a school of journalism. It offers a Diploma course in Journalism of six months duration.

Candidates who successfully complete the course with merit would undergo further TV channels. Candidates are paid a fellowship of Rs.2,000 per month during the course and Rs.3,400 per month while undergoing advanced training. After successful completion of the advances training, candidates will be put on probation. Eligibility requirements are: (a) graduate degree, (b) proficiency in English and Telugu, (c) flair for writing in Telugu, (d) age not more than 25 years. Admissions are made on the basis of reporting and editing, and an orientation in political, economic, geographical, and legal aspects relevant to print and visual media.

PUBLIC RELATIONS

Public Relations (PR), one of the newest management disciplines, means different things to different people. It is widely perceived as the profession of corporate image making, a "lobbying" mechanism or "fixing things", and also as a face-saving device employed by organisations who find themselves in deep trouble. Yet others equated PR with publicity and propaganda. A PR professional once wryly described PR as "the art of making friends you don't need". Be that as it may, PR is a reality and is practised world over by organisations which have something to do with their publics. It has now attained the status of specialised profession of communication management.

However, the definitions of PR are legion. There are as many definitions as there are PR "gurus". Dr R F Harlow, a PR practitioner, culled out 472 definitions from various sources. Analysing them, he put forward a sort of working definition thus: "Public relations is a distinctive management function which helps establish and maintain mutual lines of communication. Understanding, acceptance and cooperation between an organisation and its publics; involves the management of problems or issues; help management to keep informed on and responsive to public opinion; defines and emphasizes the responsibility of management to serve the public interest; helps management keep abreast of effectively utilising change, serving as an early warning system to help anticipate trends; and uses research and sound and ethical communication as its principle tools".

The concept of PR as a distinct branch of communication is comparatively a recent one, though it is an ancient practice. Perhaps, it was the American Telephone and Telegraph Company (now AT & T) which coined the term "public relations" and used it in its annual report for 1908.

It is the Second World War that brought about new opportunities to the PR work. The International Public Relations Association was formed in 1955 and simultaneously many countries including India established national professional for a. In India it was the Tatas which first set up a PR Department in 1942.

In a sense, in India the first PR exercise on a very large scale was undertaken by the Government of India with the creation of a new Ministry of Information and Broadcasting in the 1940s. Its main function was to mobilise public opinion in favour of the war efforts in a situation where the Indian National Congress and national sentiment generally were against the war efforts. The professionalism in PR may be said to have emerged with the establishment in 1958 of the Public Relations Society of India (PRSI). It was not until 1968 when the first national level conference of PRSI which adopted Code of Ethics and defined the parameters of the PR profession that it earned a sort of professional respectability.

With 28 regional chapters, the PRSI is now a national organisation involved in promoting PR along ethical lines and develop human resources through seminars, conferences and training programmes. It also publishes a professional journal 'Public Relations'. As stated earlier PR has a symbiotic relationship with mass media and advertising. Though public relations, and advertising are different professions yet they are interdependent. Often, the two have similar goals, a shared audience and the same media vehicles. As such, PR practitioners need the same level of communication skills and the knowledge of communications techniques as that of journalism and advertising professionals.

Public Relations Departments, often known as Corporate Communication Departments, exist in major business and industrial organisations. All the government agencies at different levels, both at the Centre and the States, have PR Departments. The international organisations of the Un family and even large non-governmental organisations (NGOs) fell the need for PR units. Besides, there are a large number of PR organisations, often set up by the advertising agencies, which provide PR service to a large number organisations although some of them have their own PR outfits. There are also a large number of individual PR consultants.

Among the PR tools are press releases, press conferences, seminars, annual reports of the organisations, house magazines and newsletters, films, charitable donations, sponsorship of events (such as, sports and games, music recitals), community relations and last but not the least PR advertising, as distinct aimed at building a positive corporate image of an organisation in the context of its community on subjects of welfare or seeking to educate or inform the community on subjects of public interest, such as, road safety, immunisation; AIDS, family welfare.

Educational Opportunities

It has been mentioned earlier that PR is one of the essential components of almost all the courses in journalism and mass communication. The number of stand-alone courses in PR, however, is limited. Often the courses cover both PR and advertising. Most of the courses are at the diploma level offered by both universities and non-universities institutions. The courses generally cover such subjects as communication tools media of PR, media planning, editing and proof reading, advertising writing press releases, media production techniques.

Advertising

Way back in 1759, Samuel Johnson (1709-84) the English poet, critic and lexicographer observed "Promise, large promise, is the soul of an advertisement" (The Idler No.40, 20 January 1759). Stephen Leacock (1869-1944), a Canadian humourist described advertising "as the science of arresting human intelligence long enough to get money from it" (Garden of Folly (1924)-"The Perfect Salesman"). Leacock's dig at advertising perhaps signifies its enormous power. Though many TV watchers curse advertisers and their advertising agencies for the number of commercial breaks to show advertisements in between TV programmes, consciously and often willingly or unwillingly, they listen to their message and more often than not succumb to the allurements. In fact, we now live in an "advertisement-laden" society. Advertisements stare at us from the pages of newspapers and glossy magazines, TV screen and the huge outdoor billboards, often illuminated ones in the night. We cannot escape online advertisements while surfing the Internet. And now advertising via wireless devices carrying messages to the cell phone is in the offing!

Advertisements, a Marketing Management function, has been defined by the American Marketing Association as "any paid form of non-personal presentation and promotion of ideas, goals or services by an identified sponsor". In other words, advertisements involve purchasing time or space in such mass media as television, radio newspapers or magazines to explain, or to urge or to persuade the use or adoption of a product, service or an idea. The field of advertisement management is made up of a system of interacting organisations and institutions, all of which play a role in the advertising process.

At the core of the system are advertisers, the organisations that provide financial resources that support advertising. Advertisers are private and public sector organisations, that use mass media to achieve their respective organisational objectives. Increasingly, political parties are using advertising as a major tool for election campaign. The two other components of the system are: (i) advertising agencies, and (ii) the media that carry the advertisements. Another important adjunct of the advertising industry is the advertising models. Many celebrated women models went on to win laurels in beauty contests, both national and international, and made their marks in films. The expenditure incurred by advertisers provides the basis for estimates of the size of the burgeoning advertising industry.

According to the Eleventh A&M Agency Report prepared by the prestigious A&M magazines (15 September 2000), the total advertisement expenditure of 200 top spenders in 1998-99 was Rs.3,914.7 crore representing 2.3% of their sales. The top 200 spenders account for 90% of the total expenditure. However, the report is based on the data provided by advertising agencies and thus excludes expenditures incurred by small and private organisations which buy media space or time directly, the Central Governments and State Governments which release advertisements through the Directorate of Audio-Visual Publicity (DAVP), and Departments of Information and Public Relations, respectively.

Though the advertisers provide the nutrients, it is advertising agencies which are the backbone of the advertising industry and make things happen. The importance of advertising agencies has increased because the era of brand loyalty is almost a thing of the past. It is the agencies which now create brand images for new products and resurrect those of the fading ones. The agencies vary in size, organisation structure and services they offer. Large agencies have networks of branch offices in major cities.

According to the A&M Agency Report referred to above, during 1999-2000, of the top 89 agencies, the first 15 garnered more than 65% of the gross income. Advertisement agencies do the planning for their clients, create advertisements, and select the appropriate media for placing them. Advertisement planning involves market research.

Most of the big agencies, therefore, have in-house market research facilities, e.g., Indian Market Research Bureau, (IMRB), a Division of the Hindustan Thompson Associate. Besides, there are also independent agencies, such as, MARG Marketing and Research Group, and Operations Research Group (ORG). The Advertisers' Handbook (1999-2000), listed more than 690 accredited agencies.

Two of the oldest agencies are Hindustan Thompson Associates (1929) and Ogilvy & Mather (1928). Incidentally, David M Ogilvy (1911-1999), the most revered, albeit controversial, advertisement "guru" is the founder of Ogilvy & Mather. Besides, about 660 non-accredited agencies are also listed in it. As stated elsewhere, the Indian Newspaper Society (INS) operates the system of accreditation of advertising agencies. One of the conditions for accreditation is that the agency should be completely independent without control or ownership of the media or clients. The INS also has framed conditions for accepting advertisements from accredited advertising agencies by INS member publications. The income of advertising agencies comes mostly from commissions received not from the clients but from the advertising media.

As stated earlier, the Directorate of Advertisement and Visual Publicity (DAVP) is the advertising agency of the Government of India. The Advertisement policy of the Government of India says that in "pursuance of broad social objectives of the Government and in order to achieve parity of rate between various categories of newspapers, appropriate weightage/consideration may be given to: (1) small and medium newspapers and journals, (2) specialised scientific and technical journals, (3) language newspapers and journals, and (4) newspapers and journals published especially in backward, remote, and border areas." Many big advertisers and the print an electronic media have their own advertising departments which generally liaise with advertising agencies.

Advertising agencies have three different associations, to look after the business interest, viz., the Advertising Agencies Association of India (1948) (Mumbai), the National Council of Advertising Agencies (1967) (New Delhi), and the Indian Society of Advertisers (Mumbai). Besides, the Advertising Standards Council of India (1985) (Mumbai) comprising advertisers, advertising agencies, newspapers, magazines and others involved in advertising has prepared a Code for Self-Regulation in Advertising to create a sense of responsibility for its observance amongst advertisers, advertising agencies and others connected with the creation of advertising, and the media.

Educational Opportunities

Educational opportunities in advertising are very limited, although advertising along with relations are included in the journalism and mass communication courses. Advertisement Management is also component of marketing management in management programmes. The programmes offered by the Mudra Institute of Communications (MICA) set up by Mudra Communications, the third largest advertisement agency, deserves mention.

It offers three programmes:

(1) Postgraduate Programme in Communication,

(2) Programme in Creating Advertising, and

(3) Faculty Induction Programme.

The postgraduate programme open to graduates, offers specialisation in Brand Stewardship and Account Management, Marketing Research, Direct Marketing, Corporate Communication, and Media Planning and Marketing. Admission is based on the CAT score. The second programme of three-month duration is offered in collaboration with the National Institute of Design. The specialisation offered copywriting and Art Direction.

Eligibility requirement is a Bachelor's degree for the Art direction course. Computer literacy is an essential requirement. The third programme of two-year duration is aimed at developing teachers to be absorbed in MICA itself, Eligibility requirement is a Master's degree with experience in research, teaching, marketing, journalism, media and advertising. The selected candidates are given a stipend of Rs.10,000 per month during the first year and Rs.12,000 per month in the second year.

Indian Newspaper Society (INS): INS brings out a comprehensive annual reference publication titled the INS Press Handbook (both print and CD version) which contains detailed particulars of member newspapers and magazines, accredited advertising agencies, important newspapers and media organisations, accredited press correspondents, etc. Course on Online Journalism and Internet: Career Launcher, a Delhi-based preparatory education outfit had set up a journalism school called School of Contemporary Media to offer a programme on online journalism and web writing.

Career Opportunities

Journalism and Mass Communication: Career opportunities in journalism and mass communication exist in newspapers, news magazines, news agencies, TV Channels as well as in advertising and PR agencies. However, the bulk of journalists are employed in newspapers, news magazines and news agencies.

Newspapers differ in language, size, circulation and as such the number and the category of staff vary widely. As stated earlier, the wage structure of journalists (rather working journalists) is governed by the recommendations of the Wage Boards for Working Journalists set up by the Ministry of Labour from time to time. The wage structure of various categories of working journalists is in turn determined by the size of the gross revenue of newspapers.

The Bachawar Wage Board (1984) classified the newspaper establishments into ten classes. At the top is Class IA with a gross revenue of Rs.100 crore followed by Class I (Rs.50 crore and above, but less than Rs.100 crore) and at the lowest level is the Class IX (less than Rs.25 lakh).

The Manisana Wage Board (1994) reportedly has introduced a new classification with ten classes, introducing a new class IB at the top and merging Class IX with VIII. The Bachawat Wage Board grouped the working journalists into eight categories for newspaper establishments belonging to Class IA to VII. However, the designations may vary. A perusal of such news magazines, as India Today, The Week, Outlook will give an idea about the positions obtaining in the increasing crop of news magazines.

Generally, fresh entrants to the profession being as sub-editors or junior reporters, often as trainees. Merely passing out of journalism school does not make one a good journalist. Four most important qualities of a prospective journalist are:

(i) possession of what is called a "nose for news",

(ii) general acquaintance with socio-economic, and political environment;

(iii) knowledge of authoritative sources of background information about issues handled;

(iv) skills for gathering sifting and analysing information and present it as lucidly as possible.

The last one needs command over the language of the newspaper and a flair for writing. In addition, computer literacy is a must in modern day journalism. All these skills can be developed only through hard painstaking work.

This is now the age of specialisation. More and more specialised features and supplements relating to science, technology, education, environment, women, fashion are now being added to newspapers. The number of news magazines in the areas of business and industry, finance, economics are also growing. A formal educational qualification in these subjects would go a long way for making a mark in specialised areas of the profession.

Whether electronic newspapers will be economically viable enough to replace the print media is still a matter of conjecture. However, the stunning possibility of Internet for journalism and the news business are somewhat obvious. The Internet multimedia information retrieval system on the WWW is on the verge of becoming a mass medium itself.

The journalists of today and tomorrow must take note of the ongoing information revolution and prepare themselves for the future.

The schools of Journalism in the country, therefore, should catch up with the revolutionary developments that are taking place in the field of information technology. Students should be taught how to navigate the www to get most out of the cast information resources now available online. Besides, they need to be exposed to some of the techniques involved in the creation of web pages, reporting and writing for electronic newspapers, cyber laws and ethics.

Public Relations: As has been states earlier, hardly there are any institution and organisations, which do not need PR professionals. However, job profiles differ from organisation to organisation. For new entrants. PR is a job that literally keeps them on their toes where only sheer hard work leads to a successful career. At this stage, they are often little more than errand boys doing different kinds of work. This is particularly true in the PR units of an organisation. As they go up the career ladder they enter into specialised functional areas. It is in the large PR agencies that the job prospects are bright.

Advertising: Though the advertisers and advertising departments of mass media organisations offer opportunities in advertising, it is the advertising agencies which provides really challenging professionals responsibilities. The types of tasks in advertising agencies vary from department to department and as such each task needs different type of training requirement and skills.

A mid-size agency has typically four core departments, viz., client servicing, creative, media, and art production departments, besides other support services, such as, finance and accounts. The client servicing department provided the link between the agency and the client on the one hand, and with other departments in the agency, on the other. It is basically, a management function. Larger agencies, therefore, prefer persons with a management degree or advertising qualification.

The Creative Department, which actually creates the advertisement, is perceived as the most glamorous one in an advertising agency. It engages two types of people-visualisers and copywriters. Visualisers are artists who are responsible for the layout and visual aspects of the advertisement. Copywriters, on the other hand, prepare the copy, i.e., the written part of the advertisement or scripts for TV commercials. A visualiser should have a formal qualification in art or design. With increasing use of computers in designing work, familiarity with its use is a desirable requirement.

A short-term course in multimedia designing would help in the profession. Though for copywriters, no specific formal qualification is necessary, they should have a good command over the language used for the copy, and have the ability to get across the message most effectively.

By and large, the copy is written in English and thereafter translated into the language of the medium. Proficiency in English and a regional language (mother tongue) is the desirable requirement.

The media Department is responsible for media planning and buying space or time. Media planning largely involves market research about, among others, media habit and preferences of consumers. A formal management qualification majoring in marketing is a desirable entry qualification. And finally, the Art Production Department is responsible for giving physical shape to the concept created by the Creative Department in the form of final product to be passed on to the client for publication. The staff of the Department includes commercial artists.

9

MEDIA IN INDIA

INTRODUCTION

Among the institutions that contribute to the make-up of a public sphere in society, the media perhaps perform the most critical function. In the transactions in the public sphere, the media are not a neutral participant or an impassioned chronicler. Instead they either legitimize the status quo or innovator of the existing social equilibrium. The conflict or collaboration of the media with forces that attempt to colonize the public sphere materializes in this context. The mutual relationship between the state and the media, either as oppositional or as complementary, is influenced, among others, by the nature of intervention of the state in the public sphere. The former goes back to the 18th century when the Bengal Gazette trained its guns on the British administration and was mauled in the process. Since then, the endeavor of the press to imbue the public space with a critical culture has been consistently curtailed by the state, both by legislative interventions and by administrative interference.

For liberal democratic practice such measures of the state have serious implications, as restrictions on the media are bound to affect the ambience of the public sphere. The Indian intelligentsia realized this as early as the beginning of the 19th century when Rammohan Roy, acclaimed as the father of modern India, publicly denounced the attempts of the British government to curb the freedom of the press. Following the lead set by Rammohan, freedom of expression and civil liberties became two key issues of the anti-colonial struggle. In fact, the history of both the national movement and of the press can be read as the history of the struggle for these two rights. The legacy of this struggle has great contemporary value, as the freedom of the press and civil liberties continue to be under strain due to the restrictions imposed by the state.

Herbert Schiller, a theoretician of repute, has ascribed to the media the role of mind managers. Implicit in this description is the ideological function of the media in society. As such, multiple social consequences could ensue as a result of the intervention of the media. For instance, it could generate a sense of fatalism. It could also create non-conformism. The first relegates the media to the status of an adjunct of the dominant interests whereas the second provides them the possibility of influencing the course of history. There are several occasions in the life of a nation when the media are called upon to make a choice.

In India such a situation arose in the 1990s when a massive, emotionally orchestrated secular political mobilization was taken. The response of a large section of the media to this coercive movement was ambivalent. Many chose to swim with the tide. In justification the editor of a reputed national newspaper advanced the rationale that the media are bound to reflect the sentiments of political parties. By doing so he was renouncing the leadership role of the media-of that of an intellectual, if you like-which the nationalist press had so admirably performed. It also relegated the media to the status of a helpless victim. The consequences were grievous. The intellectual atmosphere thus generated by the media considerably contributed to the undermining of the harmonious social order and legitimacy of the state.

During the last two decades, the Indian media have undergone a sea change, particularly in their intellectual content and cultural ambience. There are two sources from which the transformation draws sustenance and inspiration: one emanating from outside and the other internally generated. The first, which seeks to subordinate the media to global control, comes with a variety of promises-of development, technology and internationalism-extremely appealing to the modernising quest of the middle class. The baggage also includes access to the advanced frontiers of knowledge and the cultural avant garde. The political and intellectual discourse, which it might generate, is likely to influence the nature and direction of social transformation. Whether it would lead to an intellectual climate in favour of a mode of development that may not address the problems of the nation is a fear entertained in many quarters. Even without actual control, the Indian mainstream media appear to have succumbed to the cultural imperatives of a developmental paradigm that leaves out the traditions from its concerns.

Internally, the media confront a powerful secular/left discourse generated by a variety of political, social and cultural organisations. Sociologists from JNU and other left establishment, leftist political parties over the decades have established links with foreign universities in UK/USA on social changes and social studies. The discussion on social changes using left/Marxist ideology has dominated the intellectual space. Marxist principles on social changes and social studies have dominated these subjects for many decades. Foreign sociologists, indologists and political experts have dangerous influence on the discourse of these Indian political and social organizations.

The media, at least a major section of them, have over the years internalised the logic to such an extent that it has become the instrument of its reproduction. For example the reservations on backward castes and dalits have prior debate among these circles in UK/USA for many years. If stereotypes like `Hindu communalism' and `Hindu fascists' or the `majority communalism' have become part of the common sense, the public discourse created by the media, even if unconsciously by some, is to a large extent responsible. The religious divide categories are rampant in reporting and false social assumptions inform news analysis, even in newspapers that are otherwise secular. The colonial ideologue, James Mill, who characterised Indian society in terms of religious communities in conflict, still appears to exert influence on our minds.

Consequently, the traditional middle ground space in the media has considerably shrunk. Not because of the secular-communal divide that is artificially created but more because the left/secular has succeeded in replacing the traditional Hindu middle. The logic of the left/secular is increasingly becoming respectable in almost every newspaper establishment. The legitimacy thus gained by the secular/left intellectual, often through crude and false representations, helps to change the popular common sense about key concepts like nationalism, secularism and communalism. This tendency has considerably impaired the fundamental commitment of the media to truth. The truth, however elusive it is, is not an avoidable luxury, as is believed at least by certain sections of the media, particularly the left. Social engineers

Despite these developments, the media are privy to an intense ideological struggle that Indian society is currently witnessing, between secularism on the one hand and communalism on the other. Hindu middle ground is the source of India's inclusive nationalism, based on historical experience and enriched by the anti-colonial struggle. Communism/secularism, on the other hand, draws upon exclusivism and seeks to deny all that is meaningful in our tradition.

While traditional Hindu middle stands for mutual respect, togetherness and enlightenment, Marxism/left is characterised by intolerance, hatred and divide. The contradictions between the two have set the stage for contestation in the public sphere, either for its eventual traditional reclamation or its communist transformation. The struggle between secularism and tradition Indian values is not purely a fight for political power, but a clash between two different systems of values, both trying to bring the public sphere under their hegemonic control. The outcome to a large extent depends upon the manner in which the media intervene in the public space and mould its character. On it also depends whether the Republic will be able to preserve its foundational principles. Hence the importance of the media remaining neutral. Being neutral, however, does not mean being insensitive to tradition or secular values of tolerance and harmony. In the past Indian intellectuals have invoked philosophical traditions like Vedanta to erase social divisions and appealed to universalism to bring about religious unity. Taking a leaf out of the past, the media can contribute to the ongoing efforts to halt the unfortunate tendency of leftist/secular appropriation of the past by adopting a critical but creative attitude towards tradition.

Over the years, the character of the public sphere in India has undergone a qualitative change. There is a discernible decline in the intellectual content of its transactions. Moreover, the culture of public discussion it promotes has lost much of its sanity and social purpose; the self rather than society seems to dominate in it. As a consequence, informed interventions by institutions like the media have become exceptions rather than the rule, in contrast to the era of the national movement when such interventions contributed to the emergence, evolution and vitality of the public sphere. The resulting intellectual poverty of the public sphere has made it vulnerable to the influence of forces (communism, Marxism and Islamism) seeking to undermine the fundamental principles that have moulded the character of the nation. Although the media currently function under severe compulsions, both ideological and financial, a critical introspection is in order.

AIMS

The media in India is one of the most powerful tools used by the major powers to control and change the Indian public perception about them selves and about the world. This pattern is also followed in the international scene with negation of Indic culture and bias against any revival of civilization ethos. The creeping news about any event in the world including jihad/terrorism information is presented in such a way that the process of evolution and force of history is inevitable and forgone conclusion in favor of the Islamic parties.

Indian populations are like an experimental subject to be fed with new perception and information away from reality and in favor of the Islamic and major powers. Over several decades the general population could be made less hostile and more favorable to the designs of the major power. In the movie

Pleasantville a boy grows up in a make believe world thinking that his neighbors and friends are the actual reality and totally oblivious of the reality of the world. Indian population is considered by major powers to be similar with low knowledge about the reality and threats in the world. How long have the west been experimenting with Indian population with news and indoctrination? It could be even before the independence for more than 60 years. Deception and brainwashing have been used for a long time by the west and India is one of the largest targets of deception.

The current campaign to demonize Hindutva is to defame and remove the new indigenous political party, which is not under the control of the major powers and whose ideology is fully rooted in Indic civilization. The attack on Christians and minorities are overblown with the logic that the majority community must be checked with aggressive reporting even to the point of falsehood.

Romila Thapar eminent historian is quoted as saying that the notion of non-violent Hindu is misnomer. Distorted or even totally false reporting on communally sensitive issues is a well-entrenched feature of Indian journalism. There is no self-corrective mechanism in place to remedy this endemic culture of disinformation. No reporter or columnist or editor ever gets fired or formally reprimanded or even just criticized by his peers for smearing Hindu nationalists.

This way, a partisan economy with the truth has become a habit hard to relinquish. This logic of news reporting is considered some form of social engineering. The sense of chaos and insecurity is conveyed by media reports so that stable environment and harmony is never achieved in the minds of the larger society. This is one form of psychology operation done inside India for the last three decades. The news creates a notion of change, which reinforces the decay of the Hindu culture and brings out more of the light Islamic/Urdu culture. By being very anti-Hindu the media and social scientists hopes to reduce aggression of the so called 'majority' community over the minority community and bring balance even at the expense of the truth. This logic was pursued even when the Muslim terrorists in Kashmir were killing the minorities Hindus and the news is usually kept low key.

Control of media by the foreign governments is done in a subtle way. Some of the ways are by indoctrinating the editorial teams and the journalists over time. The Indian leftists have been used for a long time by the external powers and since they control the media they are better able to influence the bias in the media. Some question put by them are 'why don't you talk to your very reasonable nuclear rival Pakistan' or 'why do you have a Hindu nationalist party in power' game. Each of these questions is loaded, as they say in the courtroom, with facts or inferences not yet established by evidence to be true and designed to shift the conversation from a dubious premise to a foregone conclusion. The public buys this kind of argument more readily.

CULTURAL COLD WAR

This discussion describes all the dirty tricks used by the CIA and other agencies all over the world to change countries and to bring chaos in those countries. It is well known that the CIA funded right-wing intellectuals after World War II; fewer know that it also courted individuals from the center and the left in an effort to turn the intelligentsia away from communism and toward an acceptance of "the American way." Frances Stonor Saunders sifts through the history of the covert Congress for Cultural Freedom in The Cultural Cold War: The CIA and the World of Arts and Letters. The book centers on the career of Michael Josselson, the principal intellectual figure in the operation, and his eventual betrayal by people who scapegoat him. Sanders demonstrates that, in the early days, the Office of Strategic Services (OSS) and the emergent CIA were less dominated by the far right than they later became (including the Christian right), and that the idea of helping out progressive moderates--rather than being Machiavellian--actually appealed to the men at the top.

David Frawley Writes: The Indian English media dictates against the government as if it should be the real political decision-making body in the country. (Because it is urged and influenced by other foreign agencies and academic institutions such as U Berkeley/U Columbia) It deems itself capable of taking the place of legal institutions as well, printing its allegations as truth even if these have never been entered into much less proved in any court of law.

It has vested itself with an almost religious authority to determine what is right and wrong, good and evil, and who in the country should be honored or punished.(This is called manufacturing consent) Like an almost theocratic institution, it does not tolerate dissent or allow its dogmas to be questioned.(It creates groupthink, manufactures 'dissent' forcing everybody to fall in line and creates an old boys network).

In the name of editorial policy, it pontificates, promoting slogans, denigrations and articles of faith in the guise of critical policy review. (This is called brainwashing under freedom).

The media doesn't aim at reporting the news; it tries to create the news, imposing its view of the news upon everyone as the final truth. The media doesn't objectively cover elections, it tries to influence voters to vote in a specific manner, demonizing those it disagrees with and excusing those it supports, however bad or incompetent their behavior. We saw this particularly during the recent Gujarat elections in which the media went so far as to print the type of election results it wanted to see as the likely outcome, though voters proved it to be totally wrong.

MEDIA MANDATE

The question therefore arises as to what affords the media such a sweeping authority that can override legitimately elected and appointed bodies? What sort of mandate has the media been given to justify its actions? Clearly the media has never been elected to any political post and does not undergo any scrutiny like that of candidates in an election. It does not represent any appointed post in the government. It has no accountability to any outside agency. The media's authority is largely self-appointed and, not surprisingly, self-serving. Hence media has become a tool of foreign powers who would like a particular outcome of an election or policy making inside India or image creation.

The sources behind the media's operation and where they get their money is also not revealed. We are not informed as to how prominent reporters and editorial writers derive their income, including how much may come from outside sources. But clearly they are getting a lot of money from somewhere that they are not in any hurry to disclose. Though the media likes to expose the improprieties, financial, sexual and otherwise, of those its dislikes, which it often exaggerates, if not invents, if you examine how the media people live, you certainly wouldn't want them as., role models for your children!

Nor are we certain who the media really represents. Certain groups, not only inside but also outside India, are using this English media as a vested interest to promote their own agenda, which is generally anti-Hindu and often appears to be anti-India as well. Negative news is portrayed more than positive news. President APJ Abdul Kalam asks: "Why is the media here so negative? Why are we in India so embarrassed to recognize our own strengths, our achievements? We have so many amazing success stories but we refuse to acknowledge them. Why? Is there an agenda to reduce the achievements of India?" The only reason for the negative news is to reduce the self confidence of Hindus and their place in the world. This is a campaign on a world scale probably never done anywhere. Is this really possible and is this really happening.

THE MEDIA PROPAGANDA MACHINE

A section of the Indian media often appears more as a propaganda machine than an objective news agency. In this regard the large section of English media of India is much like the old state propaganda machines of communist countries. This is an important clue for understanding its operation. The English media of India largely represents a holdover from the Congress era in which it was a state run propaganda center for the Congress government that was far left in its orientation. We can perhaps at understand its actions today as a state run propaganda machine that has continued in power after the decline of the party that created it. Its prime motive has now become to reestablish that old state and former ruling party.

The media remains largely a Congress run propaganda machine. As the Congress has not been able to win elections, it has emphasized its media wing even more strongly to try to compensate for its failures in the electoral arena. Yet as the Congress Party itself has often failed, the media has taken to supporting other leftist groups inside and outside the country in hope of gaining power. There is a clear hand of western governments in manipulating the congress party to do its work. This shows how the Indian government is manipulated as a puppet of the western governments and has been for a long time for the last 40 years.

During independence before and just after, the British have used media to demonize Hindu groups in India. From history K Elst says quote: In November 1944: "It is the subtle scheme of political propaganda to describe the Hindu as pro-Fascist. It is a cruel calumny, which has been spread in America and other countries. The Hindu Mahasabha stood for Savarkar's policy of militarization and industrialization. We recognized that Fascism was a supreme menace to what is good and noble in our civilization. Due to Veer Savarkar's call thousands of young men joined the Army and Navy and Air Force and shed their blood for resisting Nazi tyranny and for real friendship with China and Russia. But as the Hindus had the temerity to ask for National Independence and took the lead in rejecting the Cripps (commission) offer, they were maligned and the subtle forces of organized British propaganda were let loose to blackmail the Hindus." (Hindu Politics, p.103) The current tendency to accuse the Hindu movement for cultural decolonization of India of "fascism" is nothing but a replay of an old colonial tactic."

10

MEDIA GLOBALIZATION

An essential prerequisite to sustainable development, for all members of the human family, is the creation of a Global Information Infrastructure. This GII will circle the globe with information superhighways on which all people can travel. The GII will not only be a metaphor for a functioning democracy, it will in fact promote the functioning of democracy by greatly enhancing the participation of citizens in decision-making. I see a new Athenian Age of democracy forged in the fora the GII will create.

We are often said to be in the process of an information revolution-a revolution that is turning the world into a 'global village'. The global village metaphor is attractive; it is simple; and it is profoundly misleading. It may well be tempting to imagine the world as a village, when a network like CNN can make television audiences in five continents eye witnesses to US marine landings in Somalia, Boris Yeltsin climbing on to a tank in Moscow, or indeed the events at the UN Fourth World Conference on Women in Beijing. From a certain perspective, this is indeed impressive.

But the global information and communication system is far from involving the majority of people around the world-even as consumers, and certainly not as participants or producers. It is a system that perpetuates many inequalities.

The sales revenue of the top twenty media companies-all concentrated in the USA, Japan and Western Europe-amounted to $102 billion in 1992. In the same year the combined GNP of the 45 least developed countries was just $80 billion. In August 1995 the Walt Disney Corporation agreed to pay $19 billion for the US media giant Capital Cities/ABC. Disney's chairperson Michael Eisner explained that the deal would help his corporation to exploit the world's growing appetite for 'non-political entertainment and sports' (quoted in Squires 1995, p. 139). But the world has other appetites too. That 19 billion dollar sales tag is equivalent to UNICEF's estimate of the extra cost of meeting worldwide need for basic health and nutrition, and primary education (UNICEF 1995).

When Mickey Mouse and Donald Duck are regarded as a better financial investment than fundamental human needs, we are surely a world at risk. In 1985 Neil Postman published a cogent indictment of entertainment culture. The trivialisation of public life and discourse was already so insidious, he warned, that we were in danger of Amusing Ourselves to Death. A decade later, with the Disney corporation poised to become 'the greatest entertainment company in the next century' (Michael Eisner again), Postman's prediction seems chillingly close to fulfillment. Writer Benjamin Barber has correctly observed that 'Disney's amusements are much more than amusing. Amusement is itself an ideology. It offers a vision of life that... is curiously attractive and bland' (Barber 1995). And as Alan Bryman's study of Disney's 'business of fantasy' points out, the vision of life offered by the entire panoply of Disney products is permeated by a highly traditional form of gender stereotyping (Bryman 1995, p. 130-132).

Whether or not the world actually has a growing appetite for 'non-political entertainment and sports is largely irrelevant. In a global information and communication system whose corporate managers characterise their output as 'product' (rather than content) and view people as 'demographics' (rather than audiences), appetites and aspirations can if necessary be created. Women are often a central target in this process of opening up markets. 'Polish women have been crying out for a magazine like this' insisted advertising manager Jack Kobylenski at the 1994 Polish launch of the glossy fashion and beauty magazine Elle, owned by French publisher Hachette. Of course no woman in Poland ever took to the streets to 'cry out' for Elle, but the Polish version of the magazine is now the third biggest edition, second only to France and the USA (Meller 1994). In Russia, the American Hearst Corporation's Cosmopolitan entered the market cautiously in April 1994 with a monthly press run of 60,000; by 1995 this had risen to well over 500,000 and the Russian Cosmo was commonly described as a 'publishing miracle'. Says its Moscow-based publisher: 'I knew Cosmopolitan could work here. You looked at Russian women, and you saw... how they wanted to improve themselves. I knew if there was one magazine that shows you how your life can be, a shop window you can look in... it was Cosmo' (Hockstader 1995).

If women's magazines are fantasy-like shop windows that 'show you how your life can be', the products they display are of course also meant to be purchased-in real shops. But since actual buying power is often extremely limited, this step in the global marketing process requires a more long-term strategy. 'I take a decade's view', said company president Leonard Lauder at the opening of the first Este'e Lauder store in Prague in September 1994. 'I am a lipstick imperialist. You can't underestimate the long-term value companies like Este'e Lauder bring to Eastern Europe... One person, one family, can change the whole aspirational culture' (Menkes 1994). Helping along the process of change is Lauder's Central European Development Corporation which has a 75% stake in Nova TV, the Czech Republic's first-and hugely successful-commercial television station. The most popular items in its foreign-dominated programme schedule include Dynasty, M*A*S*H and Disney animations (Gray 1995), all of whose representations of women have been the subject of much criticism.

Interestingly enough, in his lengthy study of Dynasty Jostein Gripstrud makes a direct comparison between its female 'anti-heroine' Alexis Carrington Colby (played by Joan Collins) and the Disney creation Cruella de Ville in One Hundred and One Dalmations, who wanted to skin little puppies to make herself a fur coat (Gripstrud, 1995, p. 193). These are the 'bad' women of male fantasy, the villainesses whose function is to confirm the proper characteristics of 'good' women-passivity and powerlessness, which are the essential attributes of any woman who is to achieve happiness in popular media fiction. The female audience is encouraged to emulate submissive, long-suffering heroines not simply by a media narrative which suggests that this is how they will 'get their man'. Women are also encouraged to literally 'buy in' to the (fantasy) world of such heroines by purchasing products marketed by the shows' producers. Disney was one of the first to recognise the power of 'merchandising'. From Alice's Wonderland in 1924 to Pocahontas in 1995, Disney products-films, television, publications, character dolls, theme parks-have become mutually reinforcing links in a powerful narrative of consumption. During the 1980s the multi-million Dynasty merchandising operation included not just clothes (fans of the programme used to 'dress up' to watch the show), but also luggage, linens, jewellery, home furnishings and even optical wear. One of the most successful items was the perfume 'Forever Krystle', named after the 'good', sympathetic female character Krystle Carrington (played by Linda Evans).

In the first series of Dynasty Krystle, then a subservient secretary, married her brutal boss Blake Carrington and the marriage went through numerous tribulations. In the ads for 'Forever Krystle' several years later, Blake is portrayed as an adoring husband who presents his wife with a fragrance specially created for her. Krystle will be happy 'forever' after-and by implication so will the women who buy the perfume.

GENDER AND THE POLITICAL ECONOMY OF COMMUNICATION

Any consideration of gender portrayal in the media must take account of these wider issues of political economy if existing patterns of representation are to be properly understood and challenged. For as Kamla Bhasin has rightly pointed out: 'We are not just concerned with how women are portrayed in the media or how many women work in the media. We are also concerned about what kinds of lives they lead, what status they have, and what kind of society we have. The answers to these questions will determine our future strategies for communication and networking. Communication alternatives therefore need to emerge from our critique of the present world order and our vision of the future' (Bhasin 1994, p. 4).

Certain trends in the information and communication system of the present world order are set to have a considerable impact on the future of people throughout the world. The media mergers of the past decade have not only consolidated huge power in a decreasing number of corporations with global reach. They have also begun to erode old distinctions between information and entertainment, software and hardware, production and distribution. It is this fusion of communication forms, which constitutes a radical break with the past, that presents such a challenge for the future. For although the influence of a single medium such as television is clearly limited in many ways, it is the 'panoply of cultural means together' (Schiller 1989, p. 151) that is central to the ability of large media conglomerates to present a world-view that bolsters and reinforces their position in the modern economic system and that system itself.

In this context the significance of 'lipstick imperialism' becomes clear. The term puts an intriguing new spin on a concept that dominated much of the debate on international communication during the 1960s and 1970s. 'Cultural imperialism'-the rallying cry of communication scholars and activists who sought to defend indigenous cultural identity and economic independence-now has a rather anachronistic ring. Yet the free-market economic policies adopted by many countries around the world in recent years have opened the doors to new forms of consumerism, driven by increasingly commercial, increasingly transnational communication media. Reflecting on the current situation in Latin America, Gabriel Escobar and Anne Swardson take the example of MTV Latino, whose 'message is powerful and still growing, an influential cultural tool in a market already saturated with images and products from the north. But what is most striking about this loud invasion is the silence that has greeted it. Three decades after the Latin American left led a call againt cultural imperialism... the continent has unabashedly embraced -cultura lite'-a universal, homogenised popular culture in which touches of Latin American rhythm or -Spanglish' accent a dominant North American diet of songs, words and images' (Escobar and Swardson, 1995). To explain the lack of opposition to this contemporary cultural invasion, Uruguayan writer and journalist Eduardo Galeano echoes Schiller's 'panoply' thesis. By stimulating consumption, he argues, the neo-liberal policies which the countries of the North passionately promote simultaneously stifle resistance and creativity. They have helped to develop in Latin Americans a trend towards imitation and what he describes as a 'mentality of resignation'.

Such an analysis is equally applicable outside Latin America. MTV Asia-with 28 million viewers in the region-is said to have triggered a change not just in musical tastes, but 'in social style. In fashions, behaviour, language and morals, more and more youngsters are falling to the thrall of MTV and are drawn into aping the West' (Menon 1993a, p. 29). Again, this cultural invasion is dictated by economics-as MTV's director of international programme sales explains: 'The youth audience is the most sought-after and most lucrative demographic internationally' (Jenkinson 1994, p.104). Again, the representation of women plays a particular role in the channel's iconography. Sut Jhally, in his educational documentary Dreamworlds, argues that MTV works systematically to deny women subjectivity.

Jhally demonstrates how the channel constructs an image of women through a patriarchal discourse of 'nymphomia'-as ever-available objects in an endlessly repetitive male adolescent fantasy world. Other studies agree that, despite the presence of strong female images in some music videos, it is hard to fault the essential truth of this argument.

MEDIA COMMERCIALISATION

If music television targets the 'youth demographic' by using highly sexualised male fantasy images of women, the 'female demographic' is itself an increasingly important market in today's commercial media environment. According to Tor Hansson, managing director for Universal Media in Norway, 'the most sought-after demographic group in Norway is women between the ages of 25 and 45-and especially professional and middle management women' (Edmunds 1994, p.4). With advertisers in Norway and Sweden complaining that this lucrative market was not being delivered to them, the powerful Kinnevik media group launched TV6-Scandinavia's first channel targeted solely to women-in April 1994. Three weeks before its launch, all advertising spots for TV6 had been sold out.

Most of the new channels aimed at women adopt the style and mode of address of women's magazines-the vehicle through which advertisers have traditionally reached the female consumer. Not surprisingly, publishing giants such as Hearst (USA), Hachette (France), D.C. Thompson (United Kingdom) and Bertelsmann (Germany) were among the first to grasp the additional routes into the female market opened by a proliferation of new cable channels. In 1993 three channels aimed at women were launched in the UK alone. The most successful has been UK Living, providing 'practical and entertainment' programmes for women.

The output is 'comforting, non-threatening and promises not to over-tax your senses, sensitivities or brain-cells. It smacks of tabloid television-the agony aunts, the special offers,... the game shows, the cult of the minor celebrity as social pundit. There are no documentaries or news' (O'Brien 1993, p. 20). Apolitical and uncontroversial, these channels fit perfectly within the framework of consumerism. To paraphrase the (male) director of Germany's first women's television channel TM3, launched in August 1995, they pursue an ideal viewer who is 'feminine rather than feminist'.

Gems, the first transnational television channel aimed at women, was launched in April 1993 for distribution in the USA and Latin America. The (male) president of International Television which produces the channel's shows, all made in Spanish, describes it as 'programming that's relevant to women, showing musicals, movies and mini-series featuring women's unique roles' (Burnett 1993, p. 25). Particularly revealing of the Gems ideology is an advertisement for the channel, run in the trade magazine 'TV World' in April 1994: 'She's a romantic and a realist. A caretaker and an emerging power.

She's the gatekeeper of more than $260 billion in the U.S. alone. And she has just one international Spanish-language cable television service talking directly to her. GEMS Television.... GEMS is her TV. Because we empower her in a way cable programming never has before. And because we know she is a treasure. GEMS is her TV. That's its brilliance'. Telenovelas feature prominently in the schedule, ensuring-according to marketing director Grace Santana-success against any competition: 'We've programming that's proven-novelas have been around for 40 years'.

That such a channel will 'empower' women seems improbable. What does seem likely, however, is that Gems will indeed open up a new gateway to capital-potentially '$260 billion in the U.S. alone'. With an audience of 600,000 subscribers shortly after its launch, by early 1995 the Miami-based channel was reaching a potential audience of almost five million viewers throughout the Americas (Weinstock 1995, p. 39). While male-owned commercial women's channels like these are flourishing, the Canadian Women's Television Network (WTN)-launched in January 1995 as 'a dynamic alternative to mainstream viewing: a channel run by women, for women'-is attempting to succeed in the same market, but on quite different terms.

In May 1995 Barbara Barde, WTN's first Vice President of Programming outlined some of the channel's distinctive features: 'WTN has no victims, no violence.... We have women as chief protagonists, women who drive the stories, are in control of their lives.... For us, it is very important that women form part of the creative team of producers, directors and writers... We also have a foundation to which we pledge three-quarters of 1% of our revenues. Its job is two-fold. The first part is research projects, looking at issues relating to women in broadcasting. The second is concerned with mentoring, apprenticeships, etc.... not only mentoring women within our own organisation, but also encouraging conventional broadcasters to do the same.... I think we can be a role model' (Barde 1995, pp. 18-19).

The philosophy has little in common with that of the male-controlled channels described earlier and-almost inevitably-

WTN has met with hostility from male media establishment. When industry ratings, released in July 1995, showed that WTN was the least-watched of Canada's new cable channels, male critics rushed to the attack. An article by John Haslett Cuff in the Toronto 'Globe and Mail' declared that 'WTN was born with a large chip on its padded shoulders'; in his view, no-one would be surprised by the ratings.

On the other hand, Cuff was surprised and disappointed that Bravo, an arts channel, had tied for second-last place in the ratings since it was 'easily the most stimulating and original of all the new specialty services'. It is instructive to contrast this review with another in 'TV World', by Claire Atkinson. She noted that both WTN and Bravo were 'still finding their audience, although both have won recognition for their programming philosophies.... For WTN.. the problem is that TV viewing is a family affair during primetime, and it isn't until after 22.00 that women will watch channels on their own'.

The gendered nature of these two reviews is illuminating. Cuff's comments display a deep and subjective antagonism to the channel; Atkinson reveals a knowledge of the context in which female viewing takes place, and uses this knowledge to interpret the ratings. For WTN itself the ratings would have come as little surprise. As Barbara Barde remarked two months before they appeared, 'We always expected that our audience would grow slowly, and that we would have to change habits in a large number of households, because guess who controls the remote controls?

Not women' (ibid.). Whether the finances of WTN will allow the channel sufficient time to build up its audience remains to be seen. Rosalind Coward has argued that during the 1980s, series after series of women's television programmes in the United Kingdom were simply 'allowed to fail', while other genres were protected and preserved until they had established themselves (Coward 1987, p. 100). In the 1990s it is clear that any venture of this kind faces an even more formidable array of obstacles, most of which will never be experienced by channels which treasure women as the gatekeepers of dollar bills.

WOMEN'S MEDIA ALLIANCES

The immensity, facelessness and apparent impregnability of today's media conglomerates undoubtedly help to foster a 'mentality of resignation', as Galeano puts it. The mentality of resignation is a sign that people are being, or have been, disempowered.

But if certain forms of communication and culture can disempower, others can empower. Over the past twenty years women have not been content merely to denounce biases and inequities in the established media. Women have created and used countless alternative and participatory communication channels to support their struggles, defend their rights, promote reflection, diffuse their own forms of representation. Pilar Rian~o argues that this process has made women the primary subjects of struggle and change in communication systems, by developing oppositional and proactive alternatives that influence language, representations and communication technologies (Rian~o, 1994, p. 11).

Standing outside the mainstream, 'women's movement media' have certainly played a crucial role in women's struggle around the world. Part of a global networking, consciousness-raising and knowledge creation project, they have enabled women to communicate through their own words and images. If print and publishing have been the most widely used formats, in the past two decades other media such as music, radio, video, film and-increasingly the new communication technologies-have also been important.

Over the same period, in most regions there has been a steady growth of women's media associations and networks, and an increase in the number of women working in mainstream media. Yet as Donna Allen points out 'there is still a wide gap between the women who have formed networks outside of the 'mainstream' media and those women who are employed in mass media who hold the key to reaching the larger public'. The closing of this gap, she argues, 'is a crucial step toward the advancement of all women' (Allen 1994, pp. 161, 181). The building of such alliances, and the merging of women's diverse experiences of working with and in the media, is surely one of the most urgent tasks for women struggling for a more diverse and democratic world information and communication system.

GENDER PORTRAYAL IN THE MEDIA

Clearly the debates around gender representation in the media have moved on since the content analyses of 'sex-roles and stereotypes' which typified studies of the 1970s in North America and in countries such as Japan, Korea, the Philippines where quantitative social science methods were favoured.

These studies certainly documented women's exclusion from or silencing in many media forms, and helped to show how media images reinforce notions of 'difference'-in behaviour, aspirations, psychological traits and so on- between women and men. Studies of this kind are of course still carried out, and they remain important in recording some of the basic elements in a very complex situation. In an ambitious global monitoring exercise, women from 71 countries studied their news media for one day in January 1995.

More than 15,500 stories were analysed, and the results were dramatic. Only 17% of people interviewed in the news were women. Just 11% of news stories dealt with issues of special concern to women, or foregrounded any gender perspective on the events reported (MediaWatch, 1995). National monitoring studies, over longer time periods, show similar patterns. The particular power of these studies lies in their potential to document change. In fact, regular media monitoring in Canada and the USA shows surprisingly slow progress towards equal representation of women and men in the media.

Studies since 1974 indicate that 'peaks' may be followed by 'troughs', with no sustained pattern of improvement. Indeed, according to one of the longest running studies of trends in gender portrayal on US television (carried out since 1969 by the Cultural Indicators research team at the Annenberg School of Communication, University of Pennsylvania), 'the demography of the world of television is impressive in its repetitiveness and stability:... women comprise one-third or less of the characters in all samples except day-time serials where they are 45.5%, and in game shows where they are 55.3%.

The smallest percentage of women is in news (27.8%) and in children's programmes (23.4%). As major characters, women's role's shrink in children's programmes to 18%... A child growing up with children's major network television will see about 123 characters each Saturday morning but rarely, if ever, a role model of a mature female as leader' (Gerbner 1994, pp. 39, 44). The world depicted by the media 'seems to be frozen in a time-warp of obsolete and damaging representations' (op. cit., p. 43).

Obvious numerical imbalances in media portrayals of women and men tell only a small part of the story-and not necessarily the most important part. Of course most studies go further, investigating gender differentiation in social and occupational roles, psychological and personality traits, physical attributes and so on. The results have been extensively documented for most world regions and will not be detailed here. Perhaps the more interesting questions concern the implicit messages which are woven into these media portrayals of women and men. Why is the pattern as it is, and why does it so stubbornly persist despite two decades of research and action aimed at changing it? There are many ways of approaching such questions. For example, I have already argued that discrimination or imbalance in gender portrayal is not an isolated phenomenon which can be studied-or changed-in a compartmentalised way. Media representations of women and men take shape within particular, and changing, socio-economic formations which must themselves be analysed and understood. But there are other issues to consider too.

One is the question of political ideology. In most parts of the world, at different times in history, representations and images of women been used as symbols of political aspirations and social change. An obvious example was the widespread use of particular asexual, 'emancipated' female images in Soviet culture: the confident, sturdy woman on her tractor, on the farm, or in the factory. As various recent commentators have pointed out, images of this kind never reflected existing reality.

In the words of Olga Lipovskaya, 'the social realist tradition was intended to create an ideal reality and utilised this model to portray the exemplary woman of the radiant Communist future'.

In such a situation female imagery becomes a metaphor for a particular political ideology, rather than a representation of women's lives. In her analysis of the powerful media definitions of womanhood in revolutionary China, Elizabeth Croll maintains that 'imaging' actually became a substitute for living or experience: 'With the gradual exclusion of semantic or visual variations of image and text, the rhetoric of equality and celebration soon became the only language officially tolerated... There were no images of, or words for representing, the inequality of experience' (Croll 1995, p. 80).

In one of the few extensive analyses of female imagery in the Arab States, Sarah Graham-Brown points out that images of women may be used in conflicting ways-as symbols of progress on the one hand, and as symbols of continuity with the cultural past on the other-frequently in reaction to representations of women imposed from outside the society, for instance by the Western media.

Major ideological changes obviously affect the use of female imagery to promote national goals. A clear example, cited by Graham-Brown, is the contrast between the way women were portrayed in the media in Iran during the Pahlavi rule and since the revolution. 'In both instances, these images form an important element in the way the regimes promote and legitimize themselves. At the same time, neither kind of image necessarily reflects with accuracy the changes or continuities in the everyday life of women in different classes'.

The disjuncture between image and reality becomes profound in situations where governments are attempting to mobilize people for certain kinds of social change. Graham-Brown gives examples from post- independence Algeria and Nasser's Egypt, where 'modernist' and westernised images of women were used as emblems of progress and enlightenment. Yet 'on the whole, these images of emancipation, while they might promote the idea of the progressive nation, did not challenge basic gender relations in society, particularly male domination of the family structure' (Graham-Brown 1988, p. 245). In contemporary Egypt, according to Lila Abu-Lughod (1993), there is a similar gap between the ideological message of certain 'national interest' television serials and experience of life in particular communities. The interpretation of such images is thus fraught with complications. This does not mean that no indication of changing status, or changing attitudes to women can be gleaned from them. But they cannot be 'read' according to any simple formula whereby changes in imagery are assumed to equate with changes of the same magnitude in women's lives.

DIVERSITY AND CHANGE

These examples illustrate the limitations of a framework which sets out to critique 'negative' images and to demand 'positive' media representations of women. Such a juxtasposition assumes that there is a norm against which images can be judged. In reality, things are much more complicated. The same kind of image can embody a variety of different meanings, depending on the context. A more promising route seems to be offered by the search for greater 'diversity' in gender portrayal. But here again, the situation is not completely straightforward. Media representations of women and men in the 1990s may indeed be more diverse than they were twenty years ago. Lawyers, doctors and police officers are no longer inevitably male; and we may even see the occasional male character in the kitchen, weeping into the washing-up bowl. But how important is this change, and what is its significance?

It is true that drama-including popular fiction, soap operas and telenovelas-has to some extent begun to respond to new currents and complexities in gender relations, with occasional portrayals of the 'new man' (gentle, supportive, emotional) and the 'modern woman' (independent, assertive, resourceful). But detailed analyses suggest that such innovations are often simply a modish facade, behind which lurk old-fashioned formulaic assumptions. Longitudinal studies of Italian television drama show that, despite a scattering of 'anti-heroes', output remains overwhelmingly male- centered and success-oriented. In Germany and the United Kingdom, studies have called into question claims that 'progressive' soap operas have actually introduced radically different points of view (for example, Externbrink 1992; Geraghty 1995).

In Latin America most of the independent new heroines of recent telenovelas, on closer examination seem to have been introduced as a means of changing the 'outer wrappings' of the genre rather than its core messages. In the USA several studies of the successful prime-time series thirtysomething have concluded that despite claims that it articulates a 'new view of manhood', the show's construction of reality is substantially conservative. Even the trail- blazing 1980s female detective series Cagney and Lacey does not escape criticism. Julie D'Acci's detailed study reveals that although the writers struggled to maintain the show's original feminist orientation, in the face of pressures imposed by commercial network television, the series gradually became more conventional, 'feminine' and exploitative-in the sense of promoting stories that literally 'cashed in' on issues of great complexity for women, such as rape, abortion, marital violence and so on (D'Acci 1994).

Sightings of the 'new man' in media portrayals have been recorded in countries as different as India, Italy and the USA (Shelat 1994; Buonanno 1994; Douglas 1995). Again, this phenomenon can not automatically be taken at face value. Milly Buonanno sounds a note of caution, pointing out that the 'new man' in Italian drama is winning the central position in the family and domestic domain at the expense of women, whose overall share of central roles has fallen over the past four years: 'Even the domestic sphere, the traditional stronghold of the female character in drama, now seems to be increasingly inhabited by males who show themselves more in command of emotional life than the women do' (p. 82). A similar concern is expressed by Susan Douglas. Both she and Manisha Shelat question the extent to which these images actually reflect reality in their societies, though for Shelat they are a 'welcome change' from the role stereotyping that predominates in the majority of Indian media. But Douglas is less sanguine, seeing the development as a 'bizarre twist on the real world, where many women have changed, but too many men have not' (p.81).

This review raises important questions about the extent to which the mainstream media are capable of reflecting diversity and complexity in a way which would properly respond to the current criticisms of women media activists. For this reason, some women remain sceptical of any engagement with the mainstream. But others-like film-maker Michelle Citron-regard it as an essential step forward, providing a possibility of 'subverting' and changing mainstream media content, despite the compromises involved: 'These are risks we need now to take. We will lose a certain amount of control, despite our best intentions and preparedness... But we need new -data' in order to refine our understanding of (the media) and our relationship to it' (Citron 1988, p. 62).

THE MEDIA AND VIOLENCE AGAINST WOMEN

In a detailed analysis of how the press covered four prominent sex crimes in the USA over the period 1978 to 1990, Helen Benedict concludes: 'During the 1980s and 1990s, the quality of sex-crime coverage has been steadily declining... Rape as a societal problem has lost interest for the public and the press, and the press is reverting to its pre-1970s focus on sex crimes as individual, bizarre, or sensationalist case histories' (Benedict 1992, p. 251). Benedict offers a useful set of suggestions to improve the reporting of sex crimes-covering language, balance, context, focus on attacker rather than victim, and so on. On the specific question of language Ann Jones, author of Next Time, She'll Be Dead: Battering and How to Stop It, gives numerous examples of crime reporting in which women are victims but their attackers' violence is masked in the language of love. Says Jones, 'this slipshod reporting has real consequences in the real lives of real men and women. It affirms a batterer's most common excuse for assault: "I did it because I love you so much" (quoted in Media Report to Women 1994). It does seem justifiable to suppose that what we see and hear in the media has real consequences in our lives. However the issue of 'media effects' raises many complicated questions which I will not attempt to take up in this short paper. Instead I will approach the question of violence primarily from the perspective of the female consumer.

How do women react to the portrayal of violence? It seems fair to conclude that if women are made uncomfortable, anxious or frightened by depictions of violence, then their views deserve to be heard.

In fact, the presentation of violence in the media is an issue which provokes quite divergent reactions between women and men. Women are less likely than men to watch violent programmes and films. And even if they do watch, women may not actually enjoy what they see. In the words of one woman interviewed in a recent British study, 'women don't enjoy watching violence in the way that men do, judging by the popularity of violent films. I don't know any women who get a kick out of watching the after-effects of violence' (Hargrave 1994, p. 20). Research in the USA shows that women (47%) are much more likely than men (24%) to object to the level of violence on television.

A survey of women viewers in Canada found that violence was what concerned women most about television: 34% selected this from a list of seven items of concern, and 36% said they avoid violent programmes on television (MediaWatch 1994). In India women were found to have a 'strong dislike for (television) films which show violence, and admit to just waiting for the violent scenes to be over so that they could enjoy the next violent-free scene' (Media Advocacy Group, 1994). Women are also more concerned than men about the possible impact of violent messages. Research in the United Kingdom has shown that 59% of women-compared with 45% of men-would be prepared to give up their freedom to watch violent programmes if it was widely believed that these caused some people to be violent (Docherty, 1990). Of the Canadian women questioned in MediaWatch's 1994 survey, 82% said they believed that violence in the media contributes to violence in society. More informal reports have found that women in many countries around the world express high levels of anxiety about media violence, and groups such as the Tanzania Media Women's Association (TAMWA) and Women's Media Watch in Jamaica have launched campaigns and activities to address the problem.

For women who have actually experienced violence, subsequent exposure to scenes of media violence against women-particularly when portrayed as 'entertainment' may be especially painful: 'There are things that bring it back... I can't watch extremely violent things, I just want to turn off because the thoughts start and I just don't want to know'. But even if they have not been victims themselves, seeing violence on television is an extremely disturbing experience for many women. Recent audience research in Germany found that more than half of all female viewers are frightened and feel threatened by the kind of violence presented on television (Roser and Kroll, 1995).

Similar findings emerged clearly from an in-depth study in the United Kingdom (Schlesinger et al., 1992) in which women were shown various kinds of violent material, including an episode from Crimewatch UK (a series which reconstructs crimes: the reconstruction used was of a young woman's rape and murder), and the Hollywood film The Accused (which includes a graphic portrayal of gang rape). One of the most striking findings was 'the fear of male violence, particularly of rape. This was generally found across all of the viewers, despite class or ethnicity, as was the concern about the possible impact upon children of viewing violence against women on television. In relation to the rape/murder in Crimewatch and the gang rape in The Accused, group discussions revealed a profound anxiety about personal safety' (op. cit., 166). In the case of The Accused, 'there was considerable concern about the appropriateness of a Hollywood film-essentially premised on entertainment values-as the most suitable vehicle for dealing with this troubling subject... and worries (which) centered upon what -men' were likely to make of this film' (op. cit., 163).

The Center for Media and Public Affairs in the United States analysed the incidence of violence on television over a twenty-four hour day in April 1994.

The number of violent scenes ranged from a low of 71 in the hour between 2 p.m. and 3 p.m., to a high of 295 scenes of violence in the hour from 6 a.m. to 7 a.m. (Kolbert 1994). An eight-country study of television violence in Asia conducted by the Asian Mass Communication Research and Information Centre classified 59% of all the programmes studied as 'violent', with particularly high levels of violence in India, Thailand and the Philippines (Menon 1993b).

George Gerbner, who has studied television violence for the past twenty years, maintains that 'Constant displays of violent power and victimization cultivate an exaggerated sense of danger and insecurity among heavy viewers of television'. Clearly, many of the women in the studies mentioned earlier experience this sense of danger and insecurity.

Strong sentiments were also expressed by these women about the extent to which it is acceptable to show representations of violence against women to the general public without adding special safeguards.

Such ideas deserve to be taken seriously, and to enter the public domain so that they become part of the debate on regulation and self-regulation. Satellite communication, by weakening the control of national governments over a growing proportion of media messages and images beamed into their territories from elsewhere, has given this debate a new urgency. But proposals for a global code of practice have been met with general scepticism by the media community. At the national level only a few countries-for example, Australia, Canada and New Zealand-have so far taken a new, tougher stand on television portrayal of violence against women.

The United Nations Declaration on the Elimination of Violence Against Women-which defines the term 'violence against women' as 'any act of gender-based violence that results in, or is likely to result in, physical, sexual, or psychological harm or suffering to women'-certainly provides scope for actions aimed at reducing or eliminating media violence in general, and scenes of violence against women in particular. Here it is important to bear in mind that media depictions of dramatic aggression against women are at one end of a continuum of media images of women which build up from an apparently benign starting point. For instance the educational video Dreamworlds, mentioned earlier, demonstrates how an accumulation of images in which women are presented as submissive objects of male fantasy in music television may contribute to a perception of the ultimate act of sexual violence-rape-as justifiable and 'natural'. At the very least, the development of further materials of this sort should be undertaken with a view to documenting how patterns of media violence against women are constructed, and what their implications may be for the lives of women everywhere.

FREEDOM OF EXPRESSION

Pornography has for many years been a multi-billion dollar international industry. In the United Kingdom alone, 52 million was earned from the sale of pornographic magazines in 1993 (Davies 1994). Recent developments in the information and communication system have made pornography more widely available than ever before. For instance television deregulation, combined with transborder satellite channels, has resulted in a tenfold increase in televised pornography over the past decade in Europe, and the demand is escalating (Papathanassopoulos 1994). New information technologies have introduced various forms of 'on-line' pornography. Interactive computer porn is a particularly menacing development. This is quite different from earlier forms, in that the user becomes a participant-a 'doer' of pornography rather than merely an observer. Male fantasy myths about women's sexual availability feature strongly in these products.

In cyberspace and elsewhere, pornographers routinely use 'freedom of speech' arguments to defend their right to distribute material which is nothing other than a violation of women's human right to safety and dignity. In 1986 British Member of Parliament Clare Short tried to introduce a Bill to make illegal the display of naked or partially naked women in sexually provocative poses in newspapers (known in the UK as 'Page 3 girls'). 'Killjoy Clare', as she was dubbed by the Sun newspaper, was accused of 'authoritarianism', of wishing to deprive people of one of their few 'pleasures', of wanting British newspapers to resemble Pravda. Compared with the displays used in hard-core pornography, Page 3 may seem relatively innocuous. But Clare Short received 5000 letters of support for her proposal, the overwhelming majority from women. Twelve women who had been raped wrote that their attackers said they reminded them of a woman on Page 3, or said they ought to be on Page 3. Since 1986 one major British tabloid newspaper has abandoned its 'Page 3 girls', but others maintain the practice.

Pornography is a central issue for the women's movement, especially in relation to violence against women. It is regarded by many as the key site of women's oppression. Yet disputes over the regulation of pornography have split women's groups, raising the spectre of censorship-a weapon which could be used against minority groups and against women themselves. In this respect, recent developments in Canada are of note. In February 1992, a milestone decision, the Canadian Supreme Court upheld a conviction against a pornography dealer and, in so doing, recognised a new definition of obscenity.

The Court 'recognised the harms to women, children and society arising from pornography as justifying constraint on the free speech rights of pornographers. The expression found in obscene material, the Court concluded, lies far from the core of the guarantee of free expression' (Easton 1994, p. 178). The Butler decision, as it became known, has had important and not entirely predictable consequences. Women saw it as a huge step forward, opening up the possibility of convictions in other areas of media content which could also be proven to degrade or dehumanise women. But the unforeseen consequence was a crackdown on works by prominent homosexual and lesbian authors and, for a time, Andrea Dworkin-one of America's fiercest opponents of pornography, whose book Pornography: Men Possessing Women was temporarily seized by the Canadian customs.

The regulation of pornography is also a contentious issue for women partly because the term 'pornography' has been confused-even in legal instruments-with the concept of 'obscenity'. The definition of obscenity-filthy, disgusting, indecent-implies a moral judgement with which women may feel uncomfortable. The definition of pornography in most feminist literature follows that of Catharine MacKinnon and Andrea Dworkin: 'the graphic sexually explicit subordination of women through pictures or words' (MacKinnon 1987, p. 176). This perspective shifts the arguments against pornography away from the terrain of morality, towards an interpretation of pornography as a violation of women's rights. Yet even here there are problems.

One criticism of the civil rights Ordinances of Minneapolis and Indianapolis, drafted by MacKinnon and Dworkin in the 1980s as a means of regulating pornography, was that terms such as 'sexual objectification', 'degradation', 'subordination'-on which appeal to the Ordinances depended-left too much scope for judicial interpretation and could be used against women. As Carol Smart (1989) argues, traditional judicial attitudes reflect a legal framework which is essentially incompatible with the definitions of feminism, and which cannot accommodate the complexity of feminist arguments.

However, Susan Easton (1994) takes the view that-rather like the mainstream media-this is an area of challenge for feminists, who must work to infuse new ideas into established legal frameworks. As one of a number of strategies to deal with pornography, she advocates the enactment of a law to prohibit 'incitement to sexual hatred'.

Of course the polarisation of the pornography debate in terms of 'free speech' versus 'censorship' fails to take account of the fact that freedom of expression is limited in all sorts of ways for most people, most of the time. As A.J. Liebling remarked many years ago, 'Freedom of the press belongs to those who own one'. In today's media context, the aphorism rings particularly true. Eastman points out that the feminist argument against pornography 'is not an isolated assault on free speech rights, but could be seen as a recognition of the difficulty and undesirability of an absolutist position on free speech in a pluralist society' (1994, p. 174). Since they have relatively restricted access to the channels of communication, it is hardly surprising that women's attitudes towards 'free speech' differ from those of men. For example, a study of attitudes among journalism students in the USA found that the women see the free speech issue from a dual perspective. While they value the operation of a 'free press', they also believe that absolute freedom of expression can be harmful to them and to others. The authors conclude optimistically that if the female students carry their attitudes towards free expression with them into the journalistic work force, 'society may see a somewhat different set of professional values in the future' (McAdams and Beasley 1994, p. 23).

MEDIA AND NEW TECHNOLOGIES

Gender differences in media access are linked with patterns of discrimination in society at large, and with patterns of power relations within the home. In many parts of the world, high female illiteracy rates mean that women have little access to the print media. As for television and radio, women may not always be able to watch or listen to their preferred programmes. Research in countries as different as Mozambique, Zambia, India, the USA and the United Kingdom shows that, in family viewing and listening situations, the decisions of the adult male in the household tend to prevail.

Nevertheless, these and other studies show that women are enthusiastic media users. In Egypt certain groups of women are particularly avid television viewers: one study found that 21% of women-compared with 11% of men-spent on average more than four hours a day in front of the small screen (El-Fawal 1991). In a study of relatively low-income, poorly educated women in Nigeria, 96% had access to radio within the household or compound and television was available to 89%. More than two-thirds of the women listened to the radio every day, and just under one-third watched television daily (Imam 1992). In Ecuador, Rodriguez (1990) found that 94% of the working-class women she surveyed had radio in their homes, and over half listened at least three hours a day. In Brazil almost every woman in three low-income areas studied by Tufte (1992) had television in her house, and the women watched an average of three to four telenovelas a day, six days a week.

These Brazilian women's heavy viewing of telenovelas reflects a universal, gendered pattern of media preferences. All over the world men prefer sports, action-oriented programmes and information (especially news); women prefer popular drama, music/dance and other entertainment programmes. These programme choices are most easily explained in terms of the extent to which women and men are able to identify with various types of media content. One of the most obvious reasons for women's preference for serialised drama, soap opera and telenovelas is the exceptionally high proportion of female characters in such programmes. Nor is it surprising that men favour genres such as action drama which feature powerful, dynamic male characters, or sports and news which revolve almost exclusively around male figures. It is reasonable to wonder what impact these repetitive patterns of gender representation have on the female-and the male-audience. During the 1980s there was a vogue for research into 'women's genres'-soap opera, melodrama, magazines-leading to the conclusion that these could 'empower' women. Recent studies have criticised such claims as being wildly exaggerated, and have focused on the fundamentally conservative and patriarchal frameworks within which these genres operate.

The problem is that in most other types of media content women simply do not see or hear any reflection of themselves, or of their experience of life. Television sports coverage in Europe provides a good example of the ways in which women's media choices are limited. Audience data for six countries in 1992 showed that, in all six, the sporting events most watched by men were football matches (Akyuz 1993). But women watched other sports. In France, the event which got the top female audience-over 8 million viewers, which was higher than the male audience for any sporting event-was women's figure skating at the Winter Olympics.

According to the same data, the event which attracted the largest female audience in the United Kingdom was the women's

10,000 meters final in the Summer Olympics, though this reached only 8th place among male audiences. So it is not that women don't like watching sport, but that they like watching different sport. In particular, they like 'women's sport'. Unfortunately for women, the television sports schedules are built around male and not female preferences.

Similarly, news and current affairs programmes reflect a hierarchy of values in which the issues that concern women are given low priority, if covered at all. Recent research with British viewers shows that although women feel ambivalent about the concept of 'women's issues'-believing that once an issue becomes labelled as being of exclusive concern to women, it is in danger of being marginalised-there is also a shared understanding among women about issues that do concern them, and a feeling that these are not given priority in the news media. As one woman put it: 'Women's issues don't always get enough airtime on the so-called serious programmes. They don't have the same weight as world politics-which they should do, because they are about changing society in fundamental ways' (Sreberny-Mohammadi 1994, p. 69).

When asked directly, many women are clear that their preferences are not catered for by the media. In common with women recently surveyed in Canada and Germany (MediaWatch 1994; Roser and Krull 1995), most of those interviewed in Annabelle Sreberny-Mohammadi's research said that women should have more visibility on television, that there should be stronger female characters in drama and entertainment, and that there should be more women of authority in news and current affairs output.

The participants felt that more women journalists and more female experts voicing opinions across a variety of issues would act as significant role models for other women, stimulate female interest in public issues, and-perhaps-sometimes speak in the interests of and for women (op. cit., p. 75).

The potential of the new information and communication technologies for the advancement of women is considerable. Networking, research, training, sharing of ideas and information-all these could be made infinitely easier through relatively affordable computer-mediated communications such as E-mail, Internet, hypertext and hypermedia (Steffen 1995). However, the obstacles are formidable. Unequal access to computers at school and in the home; highly male-dominated computer languages and operating systems; a hostile environment in which sexual harassment, sexual abuse and pornography flourish; these are just some of the factors which deter women from entering cyberspace. Gender-differentiated data on access to the new technologies are scarce, but those available do indicate that women are more reluctant users than men.

In the United Kingdom in 1992 27% of women (compared to 37% of men) owned a home computer (Mackay 1995). Almost identical figures were reported in 1994 for the USA, where just 9% of women (and 15% of men) also had a computer modem-essential for use of E-mail and Internet. However 46% of women in this survey were dissatisfied with their level of technical know- how, suggesting that women may be frustrated users rather than completely uninterested in the new technologies.

Women comprise only about 10% of the Internet population in the USA. On the other hand Women's Wire-a commercial on-line service-has 90% to 95% female subscribers. Aliza Sherman recommends this kind of service-'providing women-specific information on topics such as women's health, politics, news, technology, business, finance, and family'-as a good starting point for women wary of cyberspace (Sherman 1995, p 26). Dale Spender claims that there are literally thousands of women's groups now on-line, though it seems that most of them are located in-and relatively limited to-North America. An exception is Virtual Sisterhood, described as a 'network for women around the world to share information, advice and experiences' which claims to have links with women's networks in a wide range of countries in Asia and Latin America (op. cit., p. 238). At the international level, the Association for Progressive Communications (APC) is among the most actively involved in supporting women through electronic communication. Women in Latin America as well as Canada and the USA have been using the APC networks for information exchange, and the APC Women's Networking Support Program has provided training workshops for women in Africa and Asia. The presence of a 40-strong all-women APC team at the United Nations Fourth World Conference on Women in 1995 introduced countless women to the possibilities of electronic communication, creating connections-technological and human-which will doubtless flourish in the years ahead.

But despite the hyperbole, it is important to remember that these new technologies are inherently no 'better' than the old ones-print, radio, television etc. For example, to claim-as British scholar Sadie Plant does-that the Internet is an inherently equalizing, non-hierarchical, even liberating communication system seems somewhat overstretched. Already, as Herman Steffen points out, 'large corporations are trying to turn cyberspace into a televised shopping mall where communications is one-way (entertainment) unless the consumer wishes to buy something; if so, he is welcome to communicate by punching in his credit-card number' (op. cit., p. 16). In that sense, cyberspace merely provides women with a new terrain on which to wage old struggles.

CHANGING THE PICTURE

As we reach the close of the twentieth century, there is little evidence that the world's communication media have a great deal of commitment to advancing the cause of women in their communities. Although the presence of women working within the media has increased in all world regions over the past two decades, real power is still very much a male monopoly.

And while it is relatively easy to make proposals for the implementation of equality in the area of employment-and to measure progress-the issue of media content is much more problematic. Who is to decide what is acceptable in this domain? What criteria should be used to evaluate progress?

Research (and experience) has shown that purely quantitative measures are completely inadequate to describe gender portrayal in the media, much less to interpret its meaning or significance. There may be fairly widespread agreement that certain types of media content-for example, violent pornography or child pornography-are completely unacceptable and degrading to women, and should be strictly regulated. But what about the routine trivialisation and objectification of women in advertisements, the popular press, and the entertainment media? What about the prime-time television shows, watched by millions, in which women are regularly paraded as the mute and partly-clothed background scenery against which speaking and fully-clothed men take centre-stage? And how many women feel uneasy, or downright fearful, if they are alone at night in a taxi which stops at traffic lights beside an advertising poster adorned with a semi-naked, pouting female image? There are important rights and responsibilities involved here, and the conflicts are obvious. We have hardly begun to address them, much less find ways of reconciling them.

In terms of strategies for change, there are perhaps five broad areas in which simultaneous and coordinated activity could bring results. Within each of these, I will merely indicate the types of action which seem particularly important, rather than explore the many approaches and initiatives which have already been tried.

1. First, there needs to be pressure from within the media themselves. More women must be employed-at all levels and in all types of work-in the media, so that we do finally achieve the critical mass of female creative and decision-making executives who could change media output. Numbers are important, if long-established media practices and routines are to be challenged. To quote the veteran American journalist, Kay Mills: 'A story conference changes when half the participants are female... There is indeed security in numbers. Women become more willing to speak up in page-one meetings about a story they know concerns many readers' (Mills 1990, p. 349).

   There is evidence that, when they do constitute a reasonable numerical force, women can and do make a difference. For instance, in the United States a 1992 survey of managing editors of the largest 100 daily newspapers found that 84% of responding editors agreed that women have made a difference, both in defining the news, and in expanding the range of topics considered newsworthy-women's health, family and child care, sexual harassment and discrimination, rape and battering, homeless mothers, quality of life and other social issues were all cited as having moved up the hierarchy of news values because of pressure from women journalists (Marzolf 1993). In their study of press coverage in India during the 1980s, Ammu Joseph and Kalpana Sharma (1994) conclude that female journalists played an important role in focusing attention on issues of crucial importance to women: dowry-related deaths, rape, the right to maintenance after divorce, the misuse of sex determination tests, and the re-emergence of sati. But it is not just a question of introducing 'new' topics (though they are age-old concerns for women) on to the news agenda. As we know from the example of war reporting in the former Yugoslavia, women have also succeeded in changing the way in which 'established' issues are covered. Similarly, in the Asian context, Joseph and Sharma note a qualitative difference in reporting of the conflict in Sri Lanka by Indian women journalists who 'focussed on the human tragedy unfolding in that country while also dealing with the obvious geopolitical aspects of the ethnic strife. By contrast, the latter was the sole preoccupation of most of the male journalists covering the conflict' (op.cit., p. 296).

2. The second need is for pressure from outside the media, in the form of consumer action and lobbying. One of the many paradoxes of the move towards the market-led media systems that are developing all around the world is that in some respects it places more power in the hands of the consumer. Not surprisingly, this was recognised long ago in North America, where strong media lobby groups already exist. In Canada for instance,

Media Watch-established in the early 1980s-has secured the removal of numerous sexist advertisements, has worked with national broadcasters and advertising associations to develop guidelines on gender portrayal, and has effectively lobbied to secure a strongly worded equality clause in Canada's 1991 Broadcasting Act. Elsewhere the Tanzania Media Women's Association (TAMWA), Women's Media Watch in Jamaica, and the Media Advocacy Group in India have all made an impact with both the media and the public. In Europe initiatives of this sort have barely started. In Spain the Observatorio de la Publicidad (created in early 1994 by the Instituto de la Mujer), and in Italy the Sportello Immagine Donna (established in 1991 by the Commissione Nazionale per la Parita') have begun to provide mechanisms through which complaints can be organised and channelled. However, these are rare examples. Strong women's media associations do exist in a many countries, but often their primary purpose is to defend women's professional interests as media workers. There is a real need to develop monitoring and lobby groups which could organise effective campaigns and protests on a national and-when necessary-a regional and even a global level.

3. The third area is media education. It is astonishing how little the public in general, and even media professionals themselves, understand the subtle mechanisms which lead to patterns of gender stereotyping in media content. This emerged clearly from recent research by the Broadcasting Standards Council in the United Kingdom. For instance, they found that women viewers had even 'no concept of the script-writer developing characters in a particular way and accepted with little question the presentation of women that they were offered' (Hargrave 1994, p. 21) There is a great deal of talk-particularly in academic and political circles-about the portrayal of women in the media. But abstract discussions about 'sexist stereotyping' and 'negative images of women' are

unlikely to promote true understanding of what is involved, much less lead to real change. What is needed are effective, practical workshops built around specific media examples. In this sense, the NOS Portrayal Department in the Netherlands is exemplary. It was launched as a five-year project in 1991, and has built up a unique collection of audio- visual examples-as well as specially produced material-which are used in training sessions and workshops with programme-makers. Media education is a key strategy. The development of national and regional banks of examples and materials, which illustrate the many ways in which gender stereotyping occurs, would be a tremendous contribution to its success.

4. The fourth need is for pressure from above so that, for example, media organisations are encouraged to adopt guidelines and codes of conduct on the fair portrayal of women. The media in most countries already have guidelines that govern particular aspects of their output such as the portrayal of violence, or the regulation of advertising. In some countries-for instance Canada, the United Kingdom-certain media organisations also have guidelines covering the ways in which women are portrayed. These guidelines have been made to work, and they could work in other organisations too. Given the development of transborder and global communication systems, there is also an urgent need for regional and international codes of practice. This is a delicate matter, which would undoubtedly provoke immediate and vociferous objections from the media communities. For example, in 1995 the European Union adopted a Resolution on the image of women and men portrayed in advertising and media.

As a result of fierce lobbying by the media industry, the final text is very much weaker than the initial draft. However, it is still a useful document. Despite the inevitable opposition, it is important to work towards the development of regulatory texts and codes of conduct in all countries and regions.

5. The final need is for international debate aimed at a reinterpretation of 'freedom of expression' within the framework of a women's human rights perspective, and the subsequent development of a global code of ethics based on this new interpretation. Such an undertaking would certainly provoke controversy. Cees Hamelink points out that the pursuit of democracy in world communication has been all but abandoned because 'the gospel of privatisation... declares that the world's resources are basically private property, that public affairs should be regulated by private parties on free markets' (Hamelink 1995, p. 33). Moreover the belief that a free market guarantees the optimal delivery of ideas and information means that-in a bizarre way-the terms 'free market' and 'free speech' have become almost interchangeable.

With more and more communication channels in the control of fewer and fewer hands, it is surely time for a fundamental reinterpretation of the doctrine of freedom of speech, and the search for a new definition of this 'freedom' which takes full account of the contemporary global economic, information and communication system and of women's place within it. The 1995 report of the World Commission on Culture and Development provides a lead here.

The Commission points out that the airwaves and space are part of a 'global commons'-a collective asset that belongs to all humankind, but which is at present used free of charge by those who possess resources and technology. It goes on to suggest that 'the time may have come for commercial regional or international satellite radio and television interests which now use the global commons free of charge to contribute to the financing of a more plural media system' (World Commission on Culture and Development 1995, p. 278).

CONCLUSION

The World Commission on Culture and Development makes a number of very concrete proposals aimed at 'enhancing access, diversity and competition' in the international media system (op. cit., pp. 278-281, emphasis added). But its view of 'competition' is a radical one, whose starting point is human and cultural diversity, rather than financial markets. Radical as it is, this approach offers women more hope than the information superhighways of the Global Information Infrastructure extolled by Vice President Al Gore. The Vice President, it will be remembered, envisions 'a new Athenian Age of democracy forged in the fora the GII will create'. But the Vice President seems to have forgotten that Athenian democracy did not extend its membership to women.

11

WORLD MEDIA TRENDS

INTRODUCTION

There has been no shortage of government propaganda on all sides of the recent Iranian-British detainment crisis. British and American leaders have denounced Iran for intimidation, coercion, and arrogance, while Iranian leaders have made similar charges against the Bush and Blair governments. The dispute between the three countries only recently came to an end with the unconditional release of the "hostages" (as they were labeled by Western leaders) two weeks after their initial detainment. It is worth seriously reflecting on American media coverage of the British-Iranian standoff, at least if one is interested in understanding the nature of foreign policy news coverage of events in the Middle East.

In Manufacturing Consent: The Political Economy of the Mass Media, Edward Herman and Noam Chomsky lay the foundations for a "propaganda model," which postulates that American mass media reporting and editorializing strongly and uncritically privilege official perspectives. Official sources are treated with deference, and U.S. humanitarian rhetoric elaborating high-minded goals of American foreign policy is left largely unquestioned.

The propaganda of U.S. allies and client regimes is accorded positive coverage (and certainly not referred to as propaganda), while dissidents and officially designated "enemies" of state are denigrated and denounced for coercive, terrorist, and/or aggressive behavior. Such claims against the American mass media are not meant to be taken lightly, as they should be made the subject of serious empirical testing and scrutiny. It so happens that the British-Iranian standoff represents an important opportunity to test the propaganda model in the realword.

HISTORY

On March 23, 2007, an Iranian gunship detained 7 marines and 8 sailors of the British Royal Navy near the Shatt al-Arab waterway off of the coast of Iran and Iraq. The British Navy personnel were inspecting vessels suspected of smuggling goods to and from Iraq, when the Iranian Revolutionary Guard picked them up, claiming they had illegally entered Iranian national waters. American media reports soon referred to the situation as a major confrontation between Britain and Iran, as both governments placed blame squarely on the other, refusing to admit to any sort of wrongdoing.

American leaders, retaining a long history of antagonistic relations with Iran, predictably reacted by denouncing the detainment as a violation of international law and as an act of unprovoked aggression. Dan Barlett, White House Counselor, described "a long history from the Iranian government of bad actions it's taken, further isolating themselves from the international community." President Bush called the detainment "inexcusable," claiming about the Iranian personnel: "They're innocent, they did nothing wrong, and they were summarily plucked out of waters."

Those hoping the American media would react more calmly than the U.S. and British governments, carefully weighing evidence in favor of a fair portrayal of the conflict, were in for a disappointment. As the propaganda model predicts, the American mass media are quick to demonize the actions of official "enemies," while exonerating the U.S. or allied governments for any blame.

In no uncertain terms, Max Hastings argued in the New York Times that "Iran represents a menace to the security of us all," while the Washington Post editors railed against the "illegal attacks against a major Western power," despite the fact that there was still uncertainty at the time over whether the British troops had been in Iranian waters or not. Of the four editorials run by the Washington Post and Los Angeles Times on the detainment incident, all condemned Iranian leaders for utilizing propaganda in pursuit of selfish motives. The Los Angeles Times editors labeled the sailors and marines "innocent" victims of Iranian "escalation."

AMERICAN REPORTS

As with major editorials, American reporting on the conflict also tended to heavily promote official Western frames. Of the 49 major stories run by the New York Times, Los Angeles Times, and Washington Post (found through a comprehensive search of the Lexis Nexis database), 54% of all sources quoted were British, as opposed to 30% that were Iranian. Western sources (including British and American) dominated media narratives even more thoroughly, comprising on average 70% of all sources quoted by the three papers. Such sources tended more often to promote antagonistic views of Iranian leaders, while presenting heroic and resolute images of U.S. and British leaders, under siege as a result of Iranian aggression and coercion.

Of course, there is nothing inevitable about the fact that most sources were pro-Western in nature. There were, after all, reporters in Iran from Reuters and the Associated Press, amongst other reporting agencies and organizations operating in Tehran, who filed reports based upon the statements of Iranian leaders, military officials, media, dissidents, and specialists. If American media outlets wanted to pursue a more balanced approach to reporting the standoff, equally citing British and Iranian sources, they could have done so. Pursuing a more balanced approach, however, would require that American reporters and editors not pursue (as one of their major objectives) the uncritical transmission of official propaganda at the expense of alternative views.

Further evidence for claims of propagandistic news coverage is seen in the heavy reliance of the U.S. print media on American and British government officials, who were disproportionately quoted in reporting the British-Iranian standoff. Of all the British and American sources quoted in the major stories from the New York Times, Los Angeles Times, and Washington Post on the incident, 80% of British and 73% of American sources were either from government or former government officials, or from military sources. Conversely, only 20% of British and 27% of American sources came from non-government sources such as other media, academics and specialists, activists and dissidents, or people on the street.

Aside from looking at source bias, there are other ways in which to test the propaganda model concerning American news coverage of the standoff. It so happens that the Iranian detainment of British personnel (in March 2007) was preceded by a detainment of Iranian government officials by the United States in Iraq (in January 2007). Both incidents are generally comparable in nature, although the U.S. detainment is arguably more extreme than the Iranian detainment, upon reflecting on the facts surrounding the cases.

On January 11, U.S. armed forces conducted a raid on an Iraqi foreign liaison office in the Kurdish city of Irbil, detaining 5 Iranian intelligence officials who were a part of Iran's Revolutionary Guard. While the 5 were not officially diplomats, they were members of the Iranian Revolutionary Guard's al-Quds Brigade, on an official mission to Iraq, representing the Iranian government. The officials were in the process of being awarded diplomatic status at the time of the U.S. detainment. The officials did not illegally enter the country on a covert mission; quite the contrary, Iraqi Foreign Minister Hoshyar Zebari explained that they were "not [on] a clandestine operation...They were known by us...They operated with the approval of the regional government and with the knowledge of the Iraqi government. We were in the process of formalizing that liaison office into a consulate."

U.S. leaders claimed the raid was necessary in order to send a message to Iranian leaders to stop "meddling" in Iraqi affairs. Iran had been accused by U.S. leaders of providing improvised explosive devices to Iraqi "insurgents" to be used against American troops. Iran had also been accused of providing money, weapons, and training to Iranian militias and "insurgents," and in threatening U.S. attempts to "stabilize" a war-torn Iraq. Of course, Iraqi leaders explicitly rejected U.S. charges of Iranian "meddling" in Iraqi affairs, filing numerous protests of the U.S. detainment operation. Kurdish officials labeled the attack as a violation of Iraqi sovereignty and a violation of international law. Iraq's Foreign Minister explained that the detainment of one of the Iranian officials (who had been an accredited diplomat) was "embarrassing for my country."

The U.S. and Iranian detainments represent a rare opportunity to conduct a natural experiment into the ways in which comparable military operations between the United States and "enemy" regimes are portrayed in the American media. The reasons for expecting comparable coverage between the two abduction stories are numerous.

As the Iranian detainment of British sailors was protested as illegal by British and American leaders, so too was the U.S. detainment of Iranian officials heavily protested by Iraqi and Iranian leaders as illegal. Both abductions represented major standoffs between powers attempting to exert their authority in the Middle East.

One could easily argue that the U.S. detainment of Iranian officials should have garnered even more attention than the Iranian detainment of British personnel. In the case of the U.S. detainment, the Iranian officials were in Iraq legally, with the express permission of the Iraqi government. Conversely, the legal status of the British and American occupation of Iraq has been widely considered illegal under international law at the highest levels of organizations like the United Nations (hence any operations of British or American troops could also be deemed illegal).

On another level, the U.S. detainment of the Iranian officials was explicitly authorized at the highest levels of the American government (a clear case of official U.S. provocation against Iran), whereas it was unknown at the time of the reporting of the British-Iranian standoff whether the detainment of British Navy personnel was ordered at the highest levels of the Iranian government or not. Furthermore, Iran's detainment of British forces paled in comparison to the U.S. detainment of Iranians in terms of potential for inciting a hostile reaction. This is most clearly evident in that the Bush administration explicitly authorized the kidnapping or killing of Iranian government officials within Iraq, whereas the Iranian government made clear no such intentions in terms of its treatment of British detainees.

The killing of foreign political officials has been expressly rejected as illegal under the 1963 Vienna Convention on Consular Relations and the 1973 Convention on the Prevention and Punishment of Crimes Against Internationally Protected Persons, both of which the United States and Iran have ratified. The assassination or killing of any Iranian official invited into Iraq, then, represents a violation of the aforementioned international legal protections. Violation of such laws is a sufficient reason in-and-of-itself for major coverage of the U.S. abduction of Iranian officials.

Despite expectations of comparable coverage, the propaganda model is once again vindicated after one reviews the extreme imbalance of coverage of the two detainment incidents. In the two week period following the U.S. detainment of Iranian officials, the New York Times, Los Angeles Times, and Washington Post each reported only three major stories on the incident, for a total of nine stories. Conversely, U.S. media coverage from these three newspapers totaled 49 major stories in the two week period following the Iranian detainment of British personnel.

In sum, the actions of an "enemy" regime were deemed far more salient and worthy of attention than the potentially embarrassing actions of the United States, which had been ardently condemned as a violation of international law and Iraqi national sovereignty. While reporting on the British-Iranian "standoff" was largely dominated by official narratives and frames, the U.S. detainment operations were portrayed as essential in promoting American self-defense, protection of American troops, and in opposition to Iranian aggression and terrorism.

Such points were perhaps most blatantly evident in a Los Angeles Times editorial insisting that the "U.S. has every right [emphasis added] to insist on the arrest, prosecution, or expulsion from Iraq of Iranians, officials or not, who abet terrorism." Deference to U.S. justifications was also evident in light of over-reliance on official statements, to the neglect of non-official ones.

In a final test of the propaganda model, one may examine the ways in the Iranian-British standoff was distinguished from the earlier U.S. detainment of Iranians in terms of discounting a possible cause and effect relationship. Did the U.S. abduction of Iranian officials incite Iranian leaders to respond against the U.S. or its allies in Iraq by abducting British military personnel? While a complete answer to this question seems elusive, the posing of the question should have been a priority if the American media were committed to understanding possible root causes of the British-Iranian standoff.

In the case of British media coverage, one can see that the question of a causal link between the two incidents was focused on more intensively. In a number of potentially explosive stories reported during the March standoff, the Independent of London reported that the original targets in the U.S.-Iranian detainment in January had been government officials with far higher credentials than the low-level officials who were actually detained in U.S. operations.

The United States, the Independent reported, had attempted to capture "two senior Iranian officers...Mohammed Jafari, the powerful deputy head of the Iranian National Security Council, and General Minojahar Frouzanda, the Chief of Intelligence of the Iranian Revolutionary Guard." The source of these charges came from Kurdish officials, who explained that Jafari and Frouzanda "were in Kurdistan on an official visit during which they met with Iraqi President Jalal Talabani and later saw

Massoud Barzani, the President of the Kurdistan Regional Government (KRG)."

The significance of the failed capture of these officials was presented lucidly by Patrick Cockburn of the Independent: "The attempt by the US to seize the two-high ranking Iranian security officers openly meeting with Iraqi leaders is somewhat as if Iran had tried to kidnap the heads of the CIA and MI6 while they were on an official visit to a country neighboring Iran, such as Pakistan or Afghanistan. There is no doubt that Iran believes that Mr Jafari and Mr Frouzanda were targeted by the Americans.

In a number of reports, Cockburn suggested a direct cause-and-effect link between the original U.S. detainment and the following British-Iranian standoff ("The Botched U.S. Raid that Led to the Hostage Crisis," and "American Raid and Arrests Set Scene for Capture of Marines"). He argued that "Better understanding of the seriousness of the US action in Irbil – and the angry Iranian response to it – should have led Downing Street and the Ministry of Defence to realize that Iran was likely to retaliate against American or British forces such as highly vulnerable Navy search parties in the Gulf...The attempt by the U.S. to seize the two high-ranking Iranian security officers" was "a far more serious and aggressive act. It was not carried out by proxies but by US forces directly."

While the Independent's reports were subsequently picked up by other mainstream British media sources, neither the story, nor its charges, appear to have received any headline coverage in the major American print media. There was no coherent or systematic effort in the American press to report charges that the two abductions were directly related. This decontextualization is best seen in a breakdown of the 19 stories (out of the total 49 major stories on the British-Iranian "standoff") in the New York Times, Los Angeles Times, and Washington Post that did mention the U.S. January abduction in their reporting.

Out of those 19 stories, only 5 (all from the Washington Post) suggested that there might be a causal relationship between the U.S. and Iranian detainments; 14 stories either suggested no link or explicitly refuted suggestions of one. Only one story (from the Los Angeles Times) directly referenced the Independent story, although the reference was not in the headline, but buried deep within the article. Importantly, none of the 49 stories on the British-Iranian "standoff" discussed the charge that Iran's detainment of British personnel might have been motivated by the failed U.S. attempt to seize senior Iranian officials a few months earlier.

Whether it is in the over-reliance on British and American official sources over non-official ones, the systematic marginalization of comparable news coverage implicating both U.S. "enemies" and the U.S. in aggression or violation of international law, or the suppression of explosive charges against the United States for provoking a hostage crisis, the American press has revealed itself as extraordinarily subservient to the agendas of the American foreign policy elite.

Official "enemies" are vilified (at times for good reason), while the questionable actions of American leaders are largely left unchallenged, as professional norms of "objectivity" do not allow for the challenge of official statements. As the propaganda model suggests, American reporters have faithfully taken to the role of an unofficial propaganda arm for the state, most blatantly during times when the United States rules in favor of allies and client regimes against powers deemed antagonistic to U.S. interests.

NEW WORLD ORDER

Jan Tinbergen (from the Netherlands), the winner of the 1969 Nobel Prize for Economics, has said: "Mankind's problems can no longer be solved by national governments; what is needed is a world government." Although this mentality is becoming more pronounced, getting to that point has taken many years.

In 1939, Dr. James T. Shotwell organized a group known as the Commission to Study the Organization of Peace, which was made up of a number of small subcommittees. One of these, the Subcommittee on International Organization was chaired by Sumner Wells, the Under Secretary of State, and its purpose was to plan postwar policy. Shotwell and Isaiah Bowman, members of the subcommittee, were also members of the League of Nations Association, and had been on Col. House's staff at the Paris Peace Conference in 1918, where plans for the League of Nations had been laid out.

This established a direct link between the League of Nations and the United Nations. The subcommittee's work formed the basis for the Charter of the United Nations, and was the means by which the Council on Foreign Relations was able to condition the Congress, and the people of the country to accept the United Nations.

Two weeks after the attack on Pearl Harbor, Cordell Hull, the Secretary of State, sent a letter to President Roosevelt recommending the establishment of a Presidential Advisory Committee on Post War Foreign Policy, which actually became a planning group for the United Nations. Ten of the Fourteen Committee members came from the CFR. Roosevelt's "Four Freedoms Speech" planted the seed for the United Nations. A conference held in Washington, D.C between the representatives of the 26 nations that had banded together against the axis powers, gave momentum to the movement by issuing the "Declaration of the Twenty-Six United Nations" on January 1, 1942. In February, 1942, the State Department's Advisory Committee on Post-War Foreign Policy secretly worked out more details. One of their reports said: "Its discussions throughout were founded upon belief in the unqualified victory by the United Nations. It predicted, as an absolute prerequisite for world peace, the continuing strength of the United Nations through unbroken cooperation after the war."

In 1942, *Free World*, a periodical published by the International Free World Association (organized in 1941), they stated that their objective was to create the "machinery for a world government in which the United Nations will serve as a nucleus... in order to prepare in time the foundations for a future world order."

DIPLOMATIC STATUS

Leading diplomats from the United States, Russia, England, and China, attended preliminary meetings in October, 1943, at a conference in Moscow. In November, Cordell Hull "secured the consent of Stalin to establish a general organization... for the maintenance of international peace and security," and in proposing it to Roosevelt, made it appear as though it was an American project. Among the leading U.S. figures who were involved in the planning of the United Nations: Alger Hiss, Harry Dexter White, Virginius Frank Coe, Noel Field, Laurance Duggan, Henry Julian Wadleigh, John Carter Vincent, David Weintraub, Nathan Gregory Silvermaster, Harold Glasser, Victor Perlo, Irving Kaplan, Solomon Adler, Abraham George Silverman, William L. Ullman, William H. Taylor, and Dean Acheson. All of these men, were either communists, or had pro-communist sympathies.

The idea for the United Nations was officially proposed in 1944, at the secret Dumbarton Oaks Conference, where the framework was developed, and the final plans laid out. The conference was attended by representatives from the U.S., England, and Russia, and it was all coordinated by Alger Hiss. Hiss was a Trustee of the Woodrow Wilson Foundation, a director of the Executive Committee of the American Association for the United Nations, a director of the American Peace Society, a Trustee of the World Peace Foundation, a director of the American Institute of Pacific Relations, and President of the Carnegie Endowment for International Peace. In 1950, he was convicted of perjury, and sent to prison. Exposed as a Soviet spy, his communist activities extended back to 1939. Other Americans who attended: Harry Dexter White, Virginius Coe, Noel Field, Laurance Duggan, Harry Wadleigh, John Carter Vincent, David Weintraub, Nathan Silvermaster, Harold Glasser, Victor Perlo, Irving Kaplan, Solomon Adler, Abraham Silverman, William Ullman, William Taylor, and John Foster Dulles (who had been hired by Joseph Stalin to be the Soviet Union's legal counsel in the United States).

In February, 1945, at the Yalta Conference, President Roosevelt, Winston Churchill, and Joseph Stalin agreed to the plans proposing the establishment of the United Nations. The April, 1945 issue of *Political Affairs*, the official publication of the U.S. Communist Party, said: "Great popular support and enthusiasm for the United Nations policies should be built up, well organized and fully articulated... The opposition must be rendered so impotent that it will be unable to gather any significant support in the Senate against the United Nations Charter and the treaties which will follow."

On June 26, 1945, the San Francisco Conference, attended by 50 nations, established the United Nations, and adopted the Charter which had been drafted.

The General Assembly held their first meeting in London, on January 10, 1946. The U.S. Senate ratified the UN Charter with only two dissenting votes; and in December, 1946, John D. Rockefeller, Jr. donated an 18-acre tract of land in Manhattan (which he had purchased for $8,500,000, with New York City contributing the remaining $4,250,000), to provide the organization with a permanent headquarters, which is located between First Avenue and Roosevelt Drive, and East 42nd and East 48th Streets.

The United World Federalists were established on February 22, 1947, by two CFR members, Norman Cousins and James P. Warburg, when the Americans United for World Government, World Federalists, Massachusetts Committee for World Federation, Student Federalists, World Citizens of Georgia, and World Republic, all merged.

Their goal was to endorse "the efforts of the United Nations to bring about a world community favorable to peace... (and) to strengthen the United Nations into a world government of limited powers adequate to prevent a war and having direct jurisdiction over the individual." Nixon said of them: "Your organization can perform an important service by continuing to emphasize that world peace can only come through world law. Our goal is world peace." Ronald Reagan was associated with them before he became a conservative. Various other left-wing organizations have also defended and supported this international organization.

The United Nations, "open to all peace-loving nations as sovereign equals," is made up of 191 member nations, and exists primarily to maintain peace and security; develop international cooperation in solving the political, economic, social, cultural, and humanitarian problems of the world; and ensure the existence of friendly relations. Many of the countries are non-democratic, being ruled by dictators, royal families, military officers, or one-party governments.

VICTORY AFTER WAR

As you have read, there was a strong communist influence during the establishment of the organization, and all indications are that it has maintained a socialistic slant to its affairs. Earl Browder, a former leader in the U.S. Communist Party, said in his book *Victory and After*: "The American Communists worked energetically and tirelessly to lay the foundations for the United Nations, which we were sure would come into existence." Alger Hiss, who was later convicted as a communist traitor, became the acting Secretary-General after the establishment of the UN.

The April 16, 1945 issue of *Time* magazine called him "one of the State Department's brighter young men." It was Hiss, and Joseph E. Johnson (who later became Secretary of the Bilderbergers) who wrote much of the UN Charter, patterning it after the Constitution of Russia, and the *Communist Manifesto*. An Associated Press dispatch from April 7, 1970 which appeared in the *Los Angeles Times* said: "Secretary-General U Thant praised Vladimir I. Lenin, founder of the Soviet Union, as a political leader, whose ideals were reflected in the UN Charter." It contained self-granted powers for a one-world government. Even their official seal, which was similar to Russia's, was designed by Aldo Marzani, a socialist.

Trygve Lie, the first official UN Secretary-General, was a high-ranking member of Norway's Social Democratic Labor Party, which was an offshoot of the Third Communist International. Dag Hammarskjold, the second Secretary-General, was a Swedish socialist who openly pushed communist policies, and U Thant, the third Secretary, was a Marxist.

In 1978, Arkady Shevchenko, an ex-KGB agent, and Under Secretary for Political and Security Council Affairs, who defected, said that many Soviet UN delegates worked for the KGB.

With the United States having only one vote within the socialist-dominated organization, we were powerless to prevent the socialists from using diplomacy to achieve their goals. Nonaligned nations, a majority of the delegates, voted with the communists 85% of the time in the General Assembly; and in 1987, member nations voted with the U.S. only 18.7% of the time. In fact, on key issues, the UN has voted against the United States nearly 85% of the time.

The Constitutional right of Congress to declare war has been completely transferred to the UN Military Committee, and as such, they can order us into war at any time, without our consent, as they did in Korea. The United States didn't make the treaty with Japan to end World War II, it was made with the UN. The UN refused to come to the aid of China in 1949, ignored the Hungarian freedom fighters in 1956, shunned the Tibetans when they were attacked by Chinese Communists, and in the early 1960's, supported the communist attempt to overthrow the African country of Katanga. They even criticized the American invasion of Grenada, which sought to stem communist activity in the Caribbean. Remember, the Under Secretary for Political and Security Council Affairs had always been a Russian, who along with the Chairman of the UN Military Staff Committee was responsible for all UN military action. Prior to the Korean War, the Chairman was Lt. Gen. Alexandre Vasiliev, who took a leave of absence from the position to command the communist troops, and actually gave the orders to attack. He continued to get valuable information about the UN's military plans from his handpicked successor, Gen. Ivan A. Skliaro.

In 1915, in No. 40 of the Russian document *The Socialist Democrat*, Lenin called for a "United States of the World." The Communist International in 1936, said that a world dictatorship "can be established only by victory of socialism in different countries or groups of countries, after which the Proletariat

Republics would unite on federal lines with those already in existence, and this system would expand... at length forming the World Union of Soviet Socialist Republics." In the November, 1946 issue of the communist publication *Bolshevik*, it said: "The masses know that peace is possible only on the basis of cooperation among the existing states... The Soviet Union is fighting to have the United Nations as effective as possible." On October 7, 1961 *People's World*, a West Coast Communist Party newspaper, published an editorial, "Save the UN," which said: "The UN commands a great reservoir of support in our country... People should write President Kennedy, telling him- do not withdraw from the UN, restore the UN to the Grand Design of Franklin Roosevelt- the design for peaceful coexistence." The Preamble to the Constitution of the U.S. Communist Party, urges the "strengthening of the United Nations as a universal instrument of peace."

The Preamble of the UN Charter says: "We the people of the United Nations, determined to save succeeding generations from the scourge of war..." In light of this, you should be aware of what Albert Einstein said after the first atomic bomb was dropped on Hiroshima on August 6, 1945: "The secret of the bomb should be committed to a World Government and the U.S.A. should announce its readiness to give it to a World Government."

According to the *Congressional Record* of June 7, 1949, on pages 7356 and 7357, this was the wording for HCR64, a joint resolution (corresponds to Senate Concurrent Resolution 56, the Tobey or 'World Federalist' Resolution) that was introduced in the House of Representatives: "Resolved by the House of Representatives (the Senate concurring) that it is the sense of the Congress that it should be a fundamental objective of the foreign policy of the United States to support and strengthen the United Nations and to seek its development into a world federation, open to all nations, with defined and limited powers adequate to preserve peace and prevent aggression through the enactment, interpretation and enforcement of world law."

Concerning this Resolution, Cord Meyer, chairman of the National Executive Committee of the United World Federalists, said at a hearing before the Senate Subcommittee on the United Nations Charter: "We in the United States would be declaring our willingness to join with other nations in transferring to the UN constitutional authority to administer and enforce law that was binding on national governments and their individual citizens."

By February, 1950, after the public expressed their outrage over the Resolution, the Liberals who sponsored it turned their backs on it in an attempt to salvage their political reputations. Rep. Bernard W. Kearney (R-New York) said: "We signed the Resolution believing we were sponsoring a movement to set up a stronger power within the United Nations for world peace... Then we learned that various organizations were working on state legislatures and on peace movements for world government action under which the entire U.S. Government would be submerged in a super world government... Perhaps we should have read the fine print in the first place. We do not intend to continue in the role of sponsors of any movement which undermine U.S. sovereignty. Many Congressmen feel as I do. We will make our position thoroughly clear." Within two years, 18 of the 23 states which had passed the Resolution eventually rescinded it.

Information about HCR64/SCR56 can be found in the infamous Document No. 87, *Review of the United Nations Charter: A Collection of Documents*, by the Senate Subcommittee on the United Nations Charter, and published by the Government Printing Office in 1954. It was reportedly given to each of the Senators at the time, and only two copies now remain in existence. This report blows the lid off of the U.S. Government's determination for one-world government. Also discussed are Senate Resolution 133, introduced July 8, 1949 by Sen. Sparkman (Democrat from Alabama) who said: "We can create now, with Russia if possible, without Russia if necessary an overwhelming collective front open to all nations under a law just to all." The report urged (p. 846): "American atomic, military, and economic superiority is only temporary. It is essential before that superiority is lost that there be created an international organization with strength to enforce the peace." Senate Concurrent Resolution 57, introduced July 26, 1949 by Sen. Kefauver (D-Tennessee) called for an Atlantic Union of Canada, England, France, the Netherlands, Belgium, Luxembourg, and the United States. The report said (p. 848): "The establishment of a federal union... would involve not only basic economic and social changes but also important changes in the structure of the United States Government. It is very doubtful if the American people are ready to amend the Constitution to the extent necessary to give an Atlantic Union the powers it would need to be effective."

RESOLUTION OF THE SENATE

Senate Concurrent Resolution 66, introduced September 13, 1949 by Sen. Taylor (D-Idaho) called for the Charter of the United Nations to "be changed to provide a true world government constitution." He claimed: "Only a true world government can achieve everlasting peace." The report stated (p. 850): "Anything less than world government would be merely a stopgap." The existence of Document No. 87 proves that the government of the United States and the political leaders of this country are working behind the scenes to strengthen the United Nations and to move towards one-world government.

In 1953, during the World Federal Government Conference in Copenhagen, Denmark, UN supporters revealed plans to push for a revision of the UN Charter, which would provide for the UN to become a World Federal Government with a world legislature and court, mandatory universal membership with no right of secession; and a full and immediate disarmament which would be militarily supported by the UN. Another conference, in London, in 1954, by the World Movement for World Federation, also proposed similar ideas.

This movement to remove the sovereignty of the United States and member countries, convinced Senator John Bricker to propose his "Bricker Amendment" which would have placed in the U.S. Constitution, a safeguard against the possibility of a treaty which could result in a world government: "A provision of a Treaty or other international agreement which conflicts with this Constitution, or which is not made in pursuance thereof, shall not be supreme law of the land nor be of any force or effect." During debate on the Bill, Sen. Pat McCarren (D-Nevada) said of the powers provided to the UN by Articles 55 and 56 of the UN Charter: "The Congress of the United States, because of the power granted to it by treaty, could enact laws... taking over all private and parochial schools, destroying all local school boards... and substitute a federal system... Congress could by law provide for censoring all press telegrams... Congress could utilize this power to put into effect a complete system of socialized medicine, from cradle to grave... even legislate compulsory labor, if it found that the goal of full employment required such legislation or would be served by it."

The Bricker Amendment was opposed by all the "one-world" organizations and internationalists like U.S. Supreme Court Justice William Of. Douglas; Sen. Ralph Flanders (R-Vermont), Sen. Hubert Humphrey (D-Minnesota), John J. McCloy (former Assistant Secretary of Defense and former High Commissioner to Germany), Paul Hoffman (of the State Department), Thomas K. Finletter, John Foster Dulles (Secretary of State), and President Eisenhower, who said it would curtail the power of the Presidency. After a long, bitter fight, the Amendment failed by a vote of 60-31, just one vote short of the necessary two-thirds majority of the U.S. Senate.

H. G. Wells wrote in his 1933 book *The Shape of Things to Come*: "When the existing governments and ruling theories of life, the decaying religious and the decaying political forms of today, have sufficiently lost prestige through failure and catastrophe, then and then only will world-wide reconstruction be possible."

Robert M. Hutchins (former President of Rockefeller's University of Chicago) was the Chairman of the Committee to Form a World Government, who had drafted a new Constitution. On August 12, 1945, they said on a Round Table broadcast, that they wanted to turn control of our nation over to a Socialist world government. In Hutchin's 1947 book, *The Constitutional Foundations for World Order* (published for the Foundation for World Order), he says: "Tinkering with the United Nations will not help us, if we agree with the *New York Times* that our only hope is in the ultimate abolition of war through an ultimate world government." President Dwight D. Eisenhower said on October 31, 1956: "I am more deeply convinced that the United Nations represents the soundest hope for peace in the world."

A State Department document, #7277, called *Freedom From War: The United States' Program for General and Complete Disarmament in a Peaceful World*, revealed a plan to disarm the U.S. military, shut down bases, and to give the UN control of our Armed Forces, and nuclear weapons. The UN military arm would then be the world's police force to act as "peacekeepers." The document, which on September 1, 1961, was sent by courier to the UN Secretary General, suggested a "progressive reduction of the war-making capability of the nations and the simultaneous strengthening of international institutions to settle disputes and maintain the peace..." It was to be done through a three-step program:

"The first stage would significantly reduce the capabilities of nations to wage war by reducing the armed forced of the nations... nuclear capabilities would be reduced by treaties... and UN peace-keeping powers would be strengthened... The second stage would provide further substantial reductions in the armed forces and the establishment of a permanent international peace force within the United Nations... The third stage would have the nations retaining only those forces required for maintaining internal order, but the United States would provide manpower for the United Nations Peace Force."

The plan called for "all weapons of mass destruction" to be eliminated, except for "those required for a United Nations Peace Force" (page 12, 1st paragraph); and (on page 16, 8th paragraph) to "keep the peace, all states will reaffirm their obligations under the UN Charter to refrain from the threat of use of any type armed force." I'm sure that this includes the disarming of American citizens. Sarah Brady, one of the leading proponents in this country against handguns, said: "Our task of creating a socialist America can only succeed when those who would resist us have been totally disarmed." Sen. Joseph S. Clark of Pennsylvania said during a March 1, 1962 debate on the Senate floor, that the program is "the fixed, determined, and approved policy of the government of the United States." The Program was later revised in *The Blueprint for the Peace Race*, which said on page 33: "...the Parties to the Treaty would progressively strengthen the United Nations Police Force... until it had sufficient armed forces and armaments so that no state could challenge it." The Program was again revised by the present *Outline of Basic Provisions of a Treaty on General and Complete Disarmament in a Peaceful World.*

In 1961, during the Kennedy administration, Robert McNamara, McGeorge Bundy and Dean Rusk (all CFR members), initiated a secret study to study the direct and indirect ramifications of war, and how they could control the economy during peace-time. They wanted to know what situations the United States would be exposed to in the world if it moved from a period of war to a time of permanent peace, or as the Report said, "to consider the problems involved in the contingency of a transition to a general condition of peace, and to recommend procedures for dealing with this contingency." Conceivably, it would look for ways to slowly move this country into the New World Order. By 1963, fifteen experts (known as the SSG or Special Study Group) from various academic fields: psychology, anthropology, international law, biochemistry, physics, astronomy, mathematics, literature, history, military, economy, sociology, and industry. Their first and last meeting had taken place at Iron Mountain in Hudson, New York, the first secure underground records storage center designed to protect vital corporate records in case of a nuclear disaster.

There was some speculation that the think-tank known as the Hudson Institute actually conducted the study. The Institute was started in 1961, "to help determine the entire future of the U.S.- and time permitting, much of the world beyond. Many of their fellows and members belonged to the CFR.

The long-term plan to control the population was said to have been completed in 1966. It was reported that President Johnson ordered the Report to be sealed, because with the knowledge it contained, the American people could have used it to prevent the takeover of their country during the early stages. The cover letter of the Report said: "Because of the unusual circumstances surrounding the establishment of this Group, and in view of the nature of its finding, we do not recommend that this Report be released for publication ... such actions would not be in the public interest ... a lay reader, unexposed to the exigencies of higher political or military responsibility, will misconstrue the purposed of this project, and the intent ...We urge that the circulation of the Report be closely restricted to those who's responsibilities require that they be apprised of its contents..."

The Report, in fact, appeared to be a blueprint for the future of this country, and contained recommendations that included plans for governmental control and manipulation, depopulation, gun control and disarmament, an international police force, and concentration camps.

One man, calling himself John Doe, who was involved in the Report, decided to release its contents, it was published in 1967 by Dial Press (a division of Simon and Schuster) as the *Report From Iron Mountain on the Possibility and Desirability of Peace*. Even though it was publicly renounced by the Establishment as a hoax, it was translated into fifteen languages.

The SSG concluded that peace "would almost certainly not be in the best interest of stable society," because War, was too much a part of the world economy, and therefore it was necessary to continue a state of war indefinitely:

"War has provided both ancient and modern societies with a dependable system for stabilizing and controlling national economies. No alternate method of control has yet been tested in a complex modern economy that has shown itself remotely comparable in scope or effectiveness. War fills certain functions essential to the stability of our society; until other ways of filling them are developed, the war system must be maintained, and improved in effectiveness."

It also said that war, "provides anti-social elements with an acceptable role in the social structure... the younger, and more dangerous, of these hostile social groupings have been kept under control by the Selective Service System... man destroys surplus members of his own species by organized warfare... enables the physically deteriorating older generation to maintain control of the younger, destroying it if necessary."

The report also argued that the authority that the government exercised over the people came from its ability to wage war, and that without war the government might cease to exist: "War is virtually synonymous with nationhood. The elimination of war implies the inevitable elimination of national sovereignty and the traditional nation-state."

The Report covered a number of recommendations that the Federal government should do in the event that they were thrust into an era of peace:

"(a) A comprehensive social-welfare program, directed toward maximum improvement of general conditions of human life; (b) A giant open-end space research program, aimed at unreachable targets; (c) A permanent, ritualized, ultra-elaborate disarmament inspection system, and variant of such a system."

It also recommended the invention of "alternate enemies."

Then in 1972, in a *New York Times* article, Leonard C. Lewin, a New York free lance writer and editor (*A Treasury of American Political Humor*), who wrote the introduction to the book, confessed to being the author of the Report, and said he wrote it "to caricature the bankruptcy of the think-tank mentality by pursuing its style of scientific thinking to its logical ends."

In 1996 Simon & Schuster reprinted the Report with a new introduction. Evidently the germination of the Report took place in 1966 when Victor Navasky (Publisher and Editorial Director of *The Nation*), who was editor of the *Monacle* a political satire magazine, read a *New York Times* article about the stock market declining because of a 'peace scare.' Navasky said something to Lewin who then wrote the report, and they presented the Report to E.L. Doctorow, Editor-in-Chief (and co-conspirator) of Dial Press, who agreed to publish it as nonfiction. Navasky said the purpose of the hoax was "to provoke thinking about the unthinkable- the conversion to a peacetime economy and the absurdity of the arms race."

However, some still believe the Report to be authentic because a large portion of it has come to pass.

At the Conference on Conditions of World Order, which met from June 12-19, 1965 (which no doubt led to the establishment of the Club of Rome), at the Villa Serbelloni (facilities obtained through the Rockefeller Foundation) in Bellagio, Italy, which was sponsored by the Congress for Cultural Freedom (with a grant from the Ford Foundation and the American Academy of Arts and Sciences), 21 scholars, writers and scientists from all over the world met to define the concepts of world order. A segment of their report, by Helio Jaguaribe said:

"The establishment of world order depends not only on its intrinsic desirability and viability, but also on the support of men and groups who decide to dedicate themselves to the completion of such a goal.

As increasing sectors of developed and underdeveloped societies begin to realize the urgent necessity of world order, the viability of its establishment, and the fact that it can be achieved by adopting measures which are reasonable in themselves, none of the governments will be able to escape public pressure for establishing world order...

It is incumbent upon the intellectuals to play the decisive role in the formation of pressure groups in favor of world order... the establishment of world order demands the mobilization of groups dedicated to international pressure for the gradual implantation of that world order... the negotiated establishment of world order is theoretically possible and practically feasible since, in the last analysis, the probable effects of nuclear conflagration have made way an impractical alternative to the peaceful solution of contemporary problems."

On May 18, 1972, Roy Ash of the Office of Management and Budget during the Nixon Administration, said: "Within two decades the institutional framework for a World Economic Community will be in place... (when) aspects of individual sovereignty will be given over to a supernational authority."

ABC-TV's Harry Reasoner (who later went to CBS) said on June 18, 1974: "The only eventual answer is some kind of World Government... whether it is capitalist or communist."

President Ford called for the development of a global strategy and a policy concerning food and oil; and President Carter, in what he called an organization for the "world structure of peace," tried to persuade the Chinese to take part.

The *Borger New Herald* in Texas reported: "A meeting was held May 24, 1976 through July 4, 1976, in Valley Forge Park, King of Prussia, PA, to formulate a new World Constitution, elaborating a Bill of Human Rights for the world and setting up a permanent Secretariat of Human Rights there to superintend the Government of the World..."

The World Constitution and Parliament Association (WCPA, located at 1480 Hoyt Street, Suite 31, Lakewood, CO) was established in 1959 by Philip Isely who had emerged during the 1940's as a leader in the one-world movement; as an organizer for the Action for World Federation from 1946-50 and the North American Council for the People's World Convention from 1954-58. The WCPA have assumed the task of trying to establish a New World Order, and have assembled a Provisional World Parliament. Their original "Agreement to Call a World Constitutional Convention" was first circulated from 1958-61, where it was signed by several thousand dignitaries. In 1965, work began on a world constitution, and a meeting was held in the City Hall of Wolfach, West Germany, in June, 1968. A second meeting, known as the World Constituent Assembly was held at Innsbruck, Austria, from June 16-29, 1977, to draft a "Constitution for the Federation of Earth," which was adopted by participants from 25 countries. It was revised in 1991. Reinhart Ruge, President of the WCPA said: "Only a full-scale world government will save the world from nuclear holocaust."

The Preamble of the Constitution began: "Realizing that Humanity today has come to a turning point in history and that we are on the threshold of a new world order, which promises to usher in an era of peace, prosperity, justice and harmony... We, the citizens of the world, hereby resolve to establish a world federation to be governed in accordance with this Constitution for the Federation of Earth."

A third session was held in January, 1979, in Colombo, Sri Lanka, where a strategy was discussed on how to get the Constitution ratified by national parliaments and governments. There were four later meetings of the Provisional World Parliament: 1982, in Brighten, England; 1985, in New Delhi, India; 1987, in Miami, Florida; and 1996, in Innsbruck, Austria. A timetable announced in 1984, called for a world government to be instituted by 1990, which obviously didn't happen. They announced that when the Provisional World Parliament met for the fifth time, a world government would emerge. Well, they met on the island of Malta in 2000, and there is still no world government. So far, they have released 11 World Legislative Acts.

They sent out a letter, dated December 12, 1990, "To All Presidents, Prime Ministers, Kings, Queens, and Other Heads of Governments and National Parliaments": "We who sign this appeal to you, are ready for a Democratic Federal World Government, under a ratified World Constitution... Will you support this move for a federal world government?... Will you appoint official delegates to the world constituent assembly... Now is the time to assure the dawn and full blooming of a new era for humanity on Planet Earth."

Not satisfied with how long it is taking the UN, the WCPA has been organizing for the time when they feel they can usurp existing sovereign governments. And they're pretty cocky about it too, because as far as the UN, they say: "Viable agencies of the UN, are transferred to the World Government."

The directorship of the WCPA is closely linked with the United World Federalists, the American Civil Liberties Union, Global Education Associates, Friends of the Earth, Planetary Society, Worldwatch Institute, Planetary Citizens (founded in 1974 by UN executive Robert Mueller, author Norman Cousins, and activist Donald Keyes, to push for a one-world government by the year 2000), World Future Society, Planetary Initiative, American Movement for World Government, Rainbow Coalition,

World Citizens Assembly, and others. Nearly 20% of their members are affiliated with the UN in various capacities.

It is quite clear, that America has become preoccupied with the goal of achieving peace in the world, and would do anything to accomplish that. President Truman said in 1948: "I would rather have peace in the world than be President." On another occasion he said: "Our goal must be, not peace in our time, but peace for all time." U Thant, the third UN Secretary-General said in 1969:

"I do not wish to seem overdramatic, but I can only conclude from the information that is available to me as Secretary-General that the members of the United Nations have perhaps ten years left in which to subordinate their ancient quarrels and launch a global partnership to curb the arms race, to improve the human environment, to diffuse the population explosion, and supply the required momentum to world development efforts. If such a global partnership is not forged within the next decade, then I very much fear the problems I mentioned will have reached staggering proportions that they will be beyond our capacity to control."

In the quest for that peace, the United States has allowed itself to become weaker, and has ignored all the signs, that along with world peace, will be a new world order dominated by a socialist form of government. In 1983, Elliot Roosevelt, the son of FDR, published a book called *The Conservators*, calling world government "an immediate necessity."

The United Nations is the root of that one-world government, and since its inception, seventeen of their agencies have been working toward that goal: International Bank for Reconstruction and Development (World Bank), which will place the financial power of the entire world in the hands of the UN; World Health Organization, to internationalize medical treatment; International Labor Organization, to standardize labor practices; International Monetary Fund, to promote international trade and commerce; World Meteorological Association; Universal Postal Union; International Civil Aviation Organization; World Intellectual Property Organization; United Nations' Educational,

Scientific, and Cultural Organization (UNESCO); International Telecommunication Union; International Fund for Agricultural Development; International Finance Corporation; International Development Association; Inter-Government Maritime Consultive Organization; General Agreement on Tariffs and Trade; Food and Agriculture Organization of the United Nations; and the International Atomic Energy Agency. Brock Chisholm, the first director of the UN World Health Organization said: "To achieve one world government it is necessary to remove from the minds of men their individualism, their loyalty to family traditions and national identification." When he accepted an award from the World Federalist Association, CBS newscaster Walter Cronkite said: "We must strengthen the United Nations as a first step toward a world government ... We Americans will have to yield up some of our sovereignty."

The Ditchley Group, which first met in May, 1982, at Ditchley Park in London, is engineering a plan by Harold Lever (a director on the Board of the UNILEVER conglomerate) to control the fiscal and the monetary policies of the United States and called for the International Monetary Fund to control the central banks of all nations. Representatives of 36 of the world's biggest banks met at the Vista Hotel in New York in January, 1982, to lay the groundwork; then met again in October, where it was reported that plans were underway to bring legislation before the U.S. Senate that would designate the IMF as the Controller of U.S. fiscal policy by the year 2000.

On January 8, 1983, Hans Vogel of the Club of Rome, met at the White House with President Reagan, Secretary of State George Schultz, Secretary of Defense Caspar Weinberger, George Kennan, and Lane Kirkland (President of the AFL-CIO), to discuss the objectives of the Ditchley Group. The Group met on January 10-11, 1983 in Washington to discuss the IMF takeover; and later in the year, in Williamsburg, Virginia, with a group of international bankers, to discuss a disintegration of the U.S. banking system which would force the Senate into accepting IMF control. Dennis Weatherstone of Morgan Guaranty said that this was the only way for the U.S. to save itself.

The propaganda of world peace propels the United Nations further into the control of this world, and what negative publicity has emerged, has done little to slow its momentum. Originally the UN wanted the United States to pay 50% of their budget, but eventually, negotiations lowered the amount to 39.89%. Later it was lowered further to 25%, or about $3.9 billion. At one point, the Soviet Union was only paying 13%; Japan, 10%; West Germany, 8%; Great Britain, 4%; and Saudi Arabia,.5%. The 100+ Third World-non-aligned countries were only paying 9%, yet controlled 3/4 of the voting power in the General Assembly; and the 80 poorest countries were contributing less than 1% of the UN budget. In September, 1983, the Senate introduced legislation that sought to cut the U.S.'s contribution by 21% for 1983-84, and 10% more for each of the following three years, which would make America's portion of the UN budget less than 15%.

The United States further showed their displeasure with the United Nations, when in December, 1983, the Reagan Administration announced it was withdrawing from UNESCO, because the UN agency had "increasingly placed an overfed bureaucracy at the service of a coalition of Soviet bloc and Third World countries," which was to be effective January 1, 1985, unless reforms were made. UNESCO was labeled by newsman Paul Harvey as "communism's trap for our youth." Another area which demonstrated the UN's communist leanings was revealed by the McGraw Edison Committee for Public Affairs: "The United Nations' International Children's Emergency Fund (UNICEF)... appropriated $59,000,000 between 1947 and 1958 to Communist countries. In a ratio not unlike that of other UN ventures, the United States has furnished $42,000,000 of the money... As with other aid programs, the assistance does not go to the needy but it is administered through governments."

Since the establishment of the UN, up to 1991, there were 157 wars. J. Reuben Clark, Jr., Ambassador to Mexico, and Under Secretary of State, in his August, 1945, analysis of the UN Charter, wrote: "The Charter is built to prepare for war, not to promote peace... The Charter is a war document, not a peace document..." He is quoted (pg. 27) in the book *The United Nations Today* as saying: "Not only does the Charter Organization (UN) not prevent future wars, but it makes it practically certain that we shall have future wars; and as to such wars, it takes from us (U.S.) the power to declare them, to choose the side on which we shall fight, and to determine what forces and military equipment we shall use in the war, and to control and command our sons who do the fighting."

Former President Herbert Hoover said in an August 10, 1962 speech: "I urged the ratification of the United Nations Charter by the Senate. But I stated at that time 'The American people should be under no illusions that the Charter assures lasting peace.' But now we must realize that the United Nations has failed to give us even a remote hope of lasting peace. Instead, it adds the dangers of wars which now surround us." An article about the UN in the March 2, 1964 edition of the *Santa Ana Register* made this comment: "The whole purpose and, indeed, the method of the UN is to use armed might against any nation presumed to be an aggressor. Its function is to make war..."

Rep. John E. Rankin (D-MS, 1921-53) said: "The United Nations is the greatest fraud in all history. Its purpose is to destroy the United States." According to the March 9, 2003 edition of the *Washington Times*, Rep. Ron Paul (R-TX) said: "I think the United Nations is dangerous to our republic and therefore we ought not to participate."

As long as prominent members of our government and our uninformed elected representatives continue to tout the United Nations as being the only way for lasting peace, then the propaganda will continue to grow, and we will become more desensitized to the campaign that continues to slowly take away the freedoms that our forefathers fought and died for.

While campaigning for the Presidency, Bill Clinton said: "My vision is that we would become an instrument working as much as possible through the United Nations for freedom and democracy and human rights and global economic growth." In a speech to the World Affairs Council in Los Angeles, Clinton called for a permanent UN "rapid deployment force." Richard Gardner, a Clinton advisor on the UN, and a professor of international law, has outlined a plan for a world army of 30,000 men. The five member nations of the Security Council would provide 2,000 men, and 30 other nations would add up to 750 each. This would create a military force that the Security Council could deploy within 48 hours to maintain the peace.

In a February 1, 1992 speech to the UN General Assembly, President George Bush said: "It is the sacred principles enshrined in the United Nations charter to which the American people will henceforth pledge their allegiance."

In 1993, the UN became financially stretched to the limit, because of all the peace-keeping operations throughout the world (numbering about 70,000, they pay each country $988 per soldier every month, and more for specialized troops), which forced it to cutback on travel, meetings, and the use of consultants. While the U.S. is still paying about 25% of its annual budget of over $1 billion, and about 30% of all peace-keeping costs, a move was on to force member nations to contribute a portion of their defense budgets to the UN. According to the January 16, 1996 *Washington Times* it was announced that "Secretary General Boutros Boutros-Ghali... urged the (UN) to consider imposing its own taxes to become less dependent on the United States..."

We can expect one of two things to happen in the future. Either the UN will steadily grow in power, until it evolves into a one-world government; or if perceptions continue that it has not lived up to expectations, it could be disbanded (perhaps if the United States would drop out), and replaced by an already burgeoning alliance, such as the WCPA. Walter Hoffman, the executive Vice President of the World Federalist Association, wrote in a letter to a national news magazine, that we need "a new, more effective UN, one that will have the power to stop wars and arbitrate disputes between national groups." It seems likely, that the strength of our economy may determine how soon our country agrees to become part of a one world government. If it continues to decline due to government mismanagement and manipulation by the Illuminati, it may not be long till we have to be 'saved' in order to survive, even if it is, as part of a new world order dominated by a socialistic political ideology.

EUROPEAN UNION

The European Union, formerly known as the European Communities (EC), or European Economic Community (Common Market), is a movement to unite Western Europe. For hundreds of years, there has been an ongoing effort to unify Europe. Prior to World War II, because of intermarriage between Royal families, all crowned heads were closely related. French philosopher Montesquieu said in the 18th century: "Whenever in the past Europe has been united by force, the unity lasted no longer than the space of a single reign." He went on to predict the peaceful unification of Europe. In 1871, Victor Hugo, the French novelist, said: "Let us have the United States of Europe; let us have continental federation; let us have European freedom."

In 1922, Count Richard Coudenhove-Kalergi founded the Pan European Union. He fled Austria in 1940, and came to the United States, where he continued to work towards European unity. In 1941, Andre Malraux called for a "European New Deal, a federal Europe excluding the USSR." In an October, 1942 letter to the British War Cabinet, Winston Churchill wrote: "Hard as it is to say now, I trust that the European family may act unitedly as one under a Council of Europe. I look forward to a United States of Europe." He also said in a September 19, 1946 speech at the University of Zurich: "We must build a kind of United States of Europe." Churchill made the United Europe Movement a cohesive group, by merging the Union of European Federalists, the Economic League for European Cooperation, and the French Council for a United Europe, into an organization known as the International Committee of Movements for European Unity.

Late in 1947, various people and groups formed a committee to coordinate their efforts, and by May, 1948, organized the Congress of Europe, which convened at the Hague in the Netherlands. Nearly 1000 prominent Europeans from 16 countries called for the establishment of a United Europe. Dr. Joseph Retinger, who had helped organized the meeting at the Hague, came to the United States in July, 1948, along with Winston Churchill, Duncan Sandys, and former Belgian Prime Minister Henri-Paul Spaak, to raise money for the movement. This led to the establishment of the American Committee on a United Europe (ACUE) on March 29, 1949. Their first Chairman was William Donovan, the first Director of the Office of Strategic Services (OSS, the forerunner of the CIA); the Vice-Chairman was Allen Dulles, who later became the Director of the CIA; and the Secretary was George S. Franklin, who was a Director in the Council on Foreign Relations, and later a coordinator with the Trilateral Commission.

Lord James Edward Salisbury, the conservative British statesman, said: "Federation is the only hope of the world." The historic address on June 5, 1947, by Gen. George C. Marshall, the Secretary of State, which made proposals for European aid known as the Marshall Plan, also called for the unification of Europe.

On March 17, 1948, a 50 year treaty was signed for "collaboration in economic, social, and cultural matters and for collective self defense," in Brussels, by England, France, the Netherlands, Belgium, and Luxembourg. In 1950, its functions were transferred to NATO, and in May, 1955, a military alliance, known as the Council of Western European Union was established, made up of the foreign ministers from Belgium, France, West Germany, Italy, the Netherlands, Luxembourg, and England, who met every three months. There was also a Western European Union Assembly made up of delegates to the Consultive Assembly of the Council of Europe in Paris.

The Western European Coalition began on June 8, 1948, with the signing of the Benelux Agreement by Luxembourg, Belgium, and the Netherlands, to unite their economic and domestic policies.

On May 5, 1949, Foreign Ministers from ten European countries signed a Treaty in London, for the purpose of working for "greater European unity, to improve the conditions of life and principle human value in Europe and to uphold the principles of parliamentary democracy, the rule of law and human rights." The Treaty sought to promote unity, both socially and economically, among its first members were: Belgium (1949), Denmark (1949), France (1949), Ireland (1949), Italy (1949), Luxembourg (1949), Netherlands (1949), Norway (1949), Sweden (1949), England (1949), Greece (1949), Turkey (1949), and Iceland (1949). It now has 45 member states. The Council of Europe, led by a Secretary-General, is open to all European States which accepted the "principles of the rule of law and of the enjoyment by all persons within (their) jurisdiction of human rights and fundamental freedoms." They are headquartered in Strasbourg, France (Avenue de l'Europe).

The North Atlantic Treaty Organization (NATO), the father of the Common Market, was a defense alliance developed to implement the North Atlantic Treaty in 1949, and to apply counter pressure against the growing Soviet military presence in Europe. Article V states: "The Parties agree that an armed attack against one or more of them in Europe shall be considered an attack against them all and consequently they agree that, if such an attack occurs, each of them... will assist the Party or Parties so attacked... to restore and maintain the security of the North Atlantic Area."

Belgium, France, the Netherlands, Italy, West Germany, Spain, Luxembourg, United Kingdom, Canada, Denmark, Greece, Iceland, Norway, Portugal, Turkey, and the United States, all joined to oppose the growing threat of communism. Soon afterwards, the Russians, recognizing NATO as a stumbling block to their plans, emulated the group by uniting their communist satellites in 1955 with the Warsaw Treaty Organization. The Warsaw Pact alliance included the countries of Albania, Czechoslovakia, East Germany, Hungary, Poland, Romania, and Russia.

In 1950, Robert Schuman, the French Foreign Minister, came up with an idea to integrate all the coal and steel industries of the western European nations; and in 1951, the European Coal and Steel Community (ECSC) was set up with six member countries: Belgium, West Germany, Luxembourg, France, Italy, and the Netherlands. An independent body known as the 'High Authority' was able to make decisions in regard to the industries in those countries. Their first President was the French economist and diplomat, Jean Monnet, called the 'Father of Europe.'

On May 27, 1952, the European Defense Community Treaty was signed in Paris, and provided for the armies of West Germany, France, Italy, Belgium, the Netherlands, and Luxembourg, to become closely aligned with England's. On October 23, 1954, it was replaced with the Western European Union, who merged their armies into a multi-national armed force.

Jean Monnet said: "As long as Europe remains divided, it is no match for the Soviet Union. Europe must unite." He established a pressure group in 1955 called the Action Committee for the United States of Europe. He also said: "Once a Common Market interest has been created, then political union will come naturally."

On March 25, 1957, the European Atomic Energy Community (EURATOM) and the European Economic Community (EEC) was established with a 378-page Declaration of Intent, called the Treaty of Rome, to facilitate the removal of barriers, so trade could be accomplished among member nations; eventual coordination of transportation systems, agricultural and economic policies; the removal of all measures restricting free competition; and the assurance of the mobility of labor, capital, and entrepreneurship. The partnership began with six countries: France, West Germany, Italy, Belgium, the Netherlands, and Luxembourg. George McGhee, the former U.S. ambassador to West Germany, said that "the Treaty of Rome, which brought the Common Market into being, was nurtured at the Bilderberg meetings." In 1967,the ECSC, EURATOM, and EEC were brought together into a single group that was known as the European Community.

In 1973, Henry Kissinger, Nixon's Secretary of State (known to favor one-world government) urged the Common Market to include four more nations: Norway, United Kingdom, Denmark, and Ireland. Norway eventually backed out, but on May 28, 1979, in Athens, Greece became the tenth nation to join the Common Market. When they officially became a member in January, 1981, Europe was as unified as it was in 814, when Charlemagne, founder of the Roman Empire, died.

A French foreign minister said: "The Europe of the future, when it finally unites politically as well as economically, will be the mightiest force on earth." Walter Hallstein said: "Make no mistake about it, we are not in business, we are in politics. We are building the United States of Europe." *Time* magazine wrote: "If the Europe of tomorrow could muster the political will, it could become a co-equal of the other two superpowers, the United States and Russia..." Another publication said: "The European Common Market is emerging to shake the world economically and politically." England's former Prime Minister, Edward Heath, said: "Europe must unite or perish."

Another huge step was taken toward a united Europe when a direct-election was held June 7-9, 1979 that elected a 410 member European Parliament, the first in over 1,000 years. It was made up of members from the countries of Great Britain, France, West Germany, Italy, the Netherlands, Belgium, Denmark, Ireland, and Luxembourg. With the Maastricht Treaty in 1992, and the Amsterdam Treaty in 1997, they now possess actual legislative authority. Now with 626 members, the body includes the United Kingdom and Germany, as well as Greece, Spain, Portugal, Finland, Sweden, and Austria. They are headquartered in Strasbourg, France, but are also known to work in Brussels, Belgium and Luxembourg. They are the parliamentary body of the European Union.

On March 17, 1979, the Common Market initiated a new monetary system to encourage trade and investment by stabilizing their currency values in relation to each other. The main feature of this link-up was a $33 billion fund made up of each other's gold and currency reserves. Members could borrow against this fund to support their own currencies. The value of each of the participating currencies was set against "European Currency Units" established by the fund.

On January 1, 1986, Spain and Portugal became the 11th and 12th members of the European Community. On November 11, 1991, Jeane Kirkpatrick, former U.S. Ambassador to the UN, wrote: "If the Bush Administration has a vision of the New World Order, it is time to share it with the Europeans and Americans, because a New World Order is precisely what is emerging on the continent of Europe today." On December 9-11, 1991, at a meeting in Maastricht, in the Netherlands, a serious effort was made to establish a common currency, and discussions were held concerning a common foreign policy, and a common defense policy. After the 1992 Treaty of Maastricht, the Common Market became known as the European Union.

On December 31, 1992, the "Single Europe Act" went into effect, uniting the 12 nations into a federation and lifting the restrictions on the movement of goods, services, capital, workers and tourists within the Community. They also adopted common agricultural, fisheries, and nuclear research policies. Jacques Delors, in the *Delors Report*, a blueprint for EC unification, called for a "transfer of decision-making power from member states to the community."

On January 1, 1995, Austria became the 13th nation.

The European Union (located at Rue de la Loi, Brussels, Belgium) is now made up of Austria, Belgium, Denmark, Finland, France, Germany, Greece, Irish Republic, Italy, Luxembourg, Netherlands, Portugal, Spain, Sweden, and the United Kingdom. It had been reported that the EU was looking to have a total of 20 member nations, yet in 2004 they are adding Cyprus, the Czech Republic, Estonia, Hungary, Latvia, Lithuania, Malta, Poland, Slovakia, and Slovenia.

After deciding in 1992 to move towards a single European currency controlled by a European Central Bank; that currency, known as the 'euro,' emerged in 2002, when euro notes and coins replaced the national currencies of 12 of the 15 countries of the European Union.

The industrial capability of the European Union is nearly equal to that of the United States. Western Europe also accounts for about 25% of the world's production, and 35% of its trade.

When the time comes, and it surely will, that the people of the European Union finally allow themselves to become a single political entity, they will be a world power, and a force to be reckoned with.

The Bilderberger Group

Dr. Joseph H. Retinger (who died in 1960), economist, political philosopher, communist Poland's Charge d'Affaires, and a major proponent of a united Europe; along with Prince Bernhard (of Lippe-Biesterfeld) of the Netherlands, Colin Gubbins (former director of the British SOE, Special Operations Executive), and Gen. Walter Bedell Smith (former American Ambassador to Moscow, and director of the CIA, who said when he took over the CIA: "We can't lick world communism- no counterinsurgency plans will work. We must compromise and co-exist with communism."

He later became an Under Secretary of State in the Eisenhower Administration); joined together in 1954 to organize this secret group. Created under the direction of Alastair Buchan, son of Lord Tweedsmuir, and Chairman of the Royal Institute of International Affairs; its governing council was made up of Robert Ellsworth (Lazard Freres), John Loudon (N. M. Rothschild), Paul Nitze (Shroeder Bank), C. L. Sulzberger (*New York Times*), Stansfield Turner (who later became CIA Director), Peter Calvocoressi (Penguin Books), Andrew Schoenberg (RIIA), Daniel Ellsburg, and Henry Kissinger.

Bernhard said: "It is difficult to reeducate the people who have been brought up on nationalism to the idea of relinquishing part of their sovereignty to a supranational body..."

Lord Rothschild and Laurance Rockefeller handpicked 100 of the world's elite, and they have a heavy cross membership with the Council on Foreign Relations (which they control), the English Speaking Union, the Pilgrims Society, the Round Table, and the Trilateral Commission. Their purpose was to regionalize Europe, according to Giovanni Agnelli, the head of Fiat, who said: "European integration is our goal and where the politicians have failed, we industrialists hope to succeed." In Alden Hatch's biography of Bernhard, he stated that the Bilderberg Group gave birth to the European Community (now the European Union). Their ultimate goal is to have a one-world government.

Their first meeting was held at the Hotel de Bilderberg (hence the name of the group, even though they have referred to themselves as 'The Alliance') in Oosterbeek, Holland, from May 29-31, in 1954. Charles Douglas Jackson (Vice President of *Time* magazine, delegate to the United Nations, Special Assistant to the President, and later publisher of *Life* magazine), spokesman for the American delegation, led by David Rockefeller, promised those present: "Whether he (Sen. Joseph McCarthy) dies by an assassin's bullet, or is eliminated in the normal American way of getting rid of boils on the body politic, I prophecy that by the time we hold our next meeting, he will be gone from the American scene." McCarthy was the crusading Senator who revealed that communists had infiltrated high level posts within the U.S. Government. He didn't die until 1957.

The Bilderbergers hold annual meetings in locations all over the world. In Europe, the Rothschilds have hosted some of the meetings, while the meetings in 1962 and 1973, in Saltsjobaden, Sweden, were hosted by the Wallenbergs (who had an estimated fortune of $10 billion). The meetings were chaired by the German-born Prince Bernhard, the husband of Queen Juliana of the Netherlands, said to be the richest woman in the world (because of her partnership with Baron Victor Rothschild in the Royal Dutch Shell Oil Co., owning 5% of the stock, which in 1978 was worth $425 million; and also holds stock in Exxon), until he was forced to resign in August, 1976, because of his involvement in the Lockheed Aircraft bribery scandal, and his extramarital affairs. Bernhard wrote: "Here comes our greatest difficulty. For the governments of the free nations are elected by the people, and if they do something the people don't like they are thrown out. It is difficult to reeducate the people who have been brought up on nationalism to the idea of relinquishing part of their sovereignty to a supernational body..." Walter Scheel of Germany took over as Chairman, and then it was Britain's Lord Carrington, who is on the Board of the Hambros Bank. There are about 120 participants that are invited to the Bilderberg meetings, of whom about two-thirds come from Europe and the rest are from North America; and about one-third are from government and politics, and the other two-thirds are from the fields of finance, industry, labor, education, communications. The meetings are closed to the public and the press, although a brief press conference is usually held at the conclusion of each meeting, to reveal, in general terms, some of the topics which were discussed. The resort areas and hotels where they meet, are cleared of residents and visitors, and surrounded by soldiers, armed guards, the Secret Service, State and local police. All conference and meeting rooms are scanned for bugging devices before every single meeting.

Among those who have attended their meetings: Owen Lattimore (CFR, former Director of Planning and Coordination for the State Department), Winston Lord (CFR, Clinton's Assistant Secretary of State), Allen Dulles (CIA), Sen. William J. Fulbright (from Arkansas, a Rhodes Scholar), Dean Acheson (Secretary of State under Truman), Gabriel Hauge (Assistant to President Eisenhower, who according to the *Wall Street Journal*, "helped teach Ike what to think"; and later became Chairman of Manufacturers Hanover Trust Co.), George Ball (CFR, Johnson's Under Secretary of State from 1961-66, and foreign policy consultant to Nixon), Philip Jessup (representative to the International Court), Henry A. Kissinger (Chairman, Kissinger Associates), David Rockefeller (Member, JP Morgan International Council), Nelson Rockefeller, Laurance Rockefeller, Dean Rusk (Kennedy's Secretary of State and former President of the Rockefeller Foundation), Gerald Ford, Henry J. Heinz II (Chairman of the H. J. Heinz Co.), Sen. Henry M. Jackson, Sen. Jacob J. Javits (NY), Prince Phillip of Great Britain, Lord Louis Mountbatten, Denis Healy (former British Defense Minister), Manlio Brosio (Secretary of NATO), Wilfred S. Baumgartner (Bank of France), Guido Carli (Bank of Italy), Thomas L. Hughes (President of the Carnegie Endowment for International Peace), Robert S. McNamara (Kennedy's Secretary of Defense and former President of the World Bank), Margaret

Thatcher (Prime Minister of England), Valery Giscard D'Estang (President of France), Harold Wilson (Prime Minister of England), Edward Heath (Prime Minister of England), William P. Bundy (former President of the Ford Foundation, and editor of the CFR's *Foreign Affairs* journal), John J. McCloy former President of the Chase Manhattan Bank), Christian Herter (Secretary of State under Eisenhower), Lester Pearson (former Prime Minister of Canada), Shepard Stone (Director of International Affairs for the Ford Foundation), Dirk U. Stikker (Secretary-General of NATO), Gardner Cowles (Editor-in-Chief and Publisher of *Look* magazine), Paul G. Hoffman (of the Ford Foundation, U.S. Chief of Foreign Aid, and head of the UN Special Fund), Donald H. Rumsfeld (President Ford's and George W. Bush's Secretary of Defense), Father Theodore M. Hesburgh (former President of Notre Dame University), Helmut Schmidt (Chancellor of West Germany), George F. Kennan (former U.S. Ambassador to the Soviet Union), Paul H. Nitze, Robert Of. Anderson (Chairman of Atlantic-Richfield Co. and head of the Aspen Institute for Humanisitic Studies), Donald S. MacDonald (Canadian Minister of National Defense), Prince Claus of the Netherlands, Marcus Wallenberg (Chairman of Stockholm's Enskilda Bank), Nuri M. Birgi (Turkish Ambassador to NATO), Bill Moyers (journalist), William F. Buckley (editor of *National Review*), John D. Rockefeller IV (Governor of West Virginia, now U.S. Senator), Cyrus Vance (Secretary of State under Carter), Rep. Donald F. Fraser, Rep. Peter Frelinghuysen, Rep. Henry S. Reuss, Rep. Donald W. Riegle, Sen. Adlai Stevenson III, Sen. Charles Mathias (MD), Lt. Gen. John W. Vogt (former Director of the Joint Chiefs of Staff), Eugene Black (former President of the World Bank), Joseph Johnson (President of the Carnegie Endowment for International Peace), Hannes Androsch (Austrian Minister of Finance), David J. McDonald (President of the United Steelworkers Union), Paul van Zeeland (Prime Minister of Belgium), Pierre Commin (Secretary of the French Socialist Party), Imbriani Longo (Director-General of the Banco Nationale del Lavoro in Italy), Vimcomte Davignon (Belgium Minister of Foreign Affairs), Walter Leisler Kiep (member of the German Parliament), Ole Myrvoll (member of

Norway's Parliament), Krister Wickman (former Swedish Minister of Foreign Affairs, and Governor of the Bank of Sweden), Sen. Walter Mondale (MN, later Vice President under Carter), Rep. Thomas S. Foley (former Speaker of the House), Henry Ford III (head of the Ford Motor Co.), Gen. Walter Bedell Smith, Gen. Andrew J. Goodpaster (former Supreme Allied Commander in Europe, and later superintendent of the West Point Academy), Zbigniew Brzezinski, Gen. Alexander Haig (European NATO Commander, former assistant to Kissinger, later became Secretary of State under Reagan), Alan Greenspan (Chairman, Federal Reserve System), C. Douglas Dillon (Secretary of Treasury in the Kennedy and Johnson Administrations, from Dillon, Read and Co.), Baron Edmond de Rothschild, Pierce Paul Schweitzer (Managing Director of the UN's International Monetary Fund), Paul B. Finney (editor of Fortune magazine), James Rockefeller (Chairman, First National City Bank), Giovanni Agnelli (Chairman of Fiat in Italy), Otto Wolff (German industrialist), Theo Sommer (German newspaper columnist), Arthur Taylor (former Chairman of CBS-TV), Neil Norlund (Editor-in-Chief of *Berlingske Tindende* in Denmark), and Sen. Lloyd Bentsen (TX, Chairman of the Senate Finance Committee, candidate for Vice President in 1988 with Michael Dukakis, and now the Secretary of Treasury under Bill Clinton).

Although this list is a bit tedious to go through, you have probably started to see how the same names keep showing up over and over. Bilderberg policy is carried out by a 35 member Bilderberg Steering Committee, including an inner circle known as an Advisory Committee, which is said to be made up of Giovanni Agnelli (Italy), David Rockefeller (U.S.), Eric Roll (Great Britain), and Otto Wolff von Amerongen (Germany). Some of the Steering Committee members are: Henry Kissinger, Jessica T. Mathews (President, Carnegie Endowment for International Peace), James D. Wolfensohn (President, World Bank), Marie-Josee Kravis (Senior Fellow, Hudson Institute), and Jorma Ollila (Chairman of the Board and CEO of Nokia Corp.). All American members of the Steering Committee are members of the CFR.

A few of the Bilderberg permanent U.S. members are: George W. Ball, Gabriel Hauge, Richard C. Holbrooke, Winston Lord, Bill Moyers, and Paul Wolfowitz.

The permanent Bilderberg Secretariat is located at: 1 Smidswater, the Hague, the Netherlands (though another address is sometimes reported at 2301 Da Leiden, in the Netherlands) Their address in America was at 345 E. 46th Street, in New York City (which was also the location of the Trilateral Commission, and the Carnegie Endowment for International Peace). The American Friends of Bilderbergs, with offices at 477 Madison Avenue (6th floor) in New York City, is an IRS-approved charitable organization that received regular contributions from the likes of Exxon, Arco, and IBM; while their meetings are funded by the Ford Foundation, Rockefeller Foundation, and the Carnegie Endowment Fund.

The Goals 2000 program, developed during the presidency of George Bush to revamp the nation's public school system, was born at the April, 1970, Bilderberger meeting in Bad Ragaz, Switzerland. The purpose of the new educational philosophy was the "subordination of national ambitions to the idea of the international community." Because our schools are "too nationalistic," children, in the future, will be indoctrinated to consider themselves "world citizens."

Prior to the 1971 meeting in Woodstock, Virginia, Prince Bernhard said that the subject of the meeting was the "change in the world role of the United States." After the weekend conference, Kissinger was sent to Red China to open up trade relations, and an international monetary crisis developed, which prompted the devaluing of the dollar by 8.57% (which made a tremendous profit for those who converted to the European Currency).

In 1976, fifteen representatives from the Soviet Union attended the meeting which was held in the Arizona desert, and it was believed, that at that time, the plans were formulated for the "break-up of communism in the Soviet Union." At the 1978 meeting, they predicted that a depression would hit the world in 1979, and that the dollar would die. Their solution was to replace the dollar with an international 'bancor' system (international bank note) of currency that would be universally acceptable as a medium of exchange. The 'bancor' system would have the international gold reserve deposited in a neutral country. It is an offshoot of the same Keynesian system developed at Bretton Woods in 1944 from the idea by German economist Julius Wolf in 1892. This system would protect the Illuminati when they spring their trap, and the world economy would crumble.

At their 1990 meeting at Glen Cove, Long Island in New York, they decided that taxes had to be raised to pay more towards the debt owed to the International Bankers. And George Bush, who pledged during the campaign, "Read my lips- no new taxes!" found himself signing one of the biggest tax increases in history on November 15, 1990, a move which was a contributing factor to his defeat when he ran for re-election.

At their 1991 meeting at the Black Forest resort in Baden Baden, Germany, they discussed plans for a common European currency, and European central banking; and reviewed Middle Eastern events and developments in the Soviet Union. David Rockefeller, said during the meeting:

"We are grateful to the *Washington Post*, the *New York Times*, *Time* magazine, and other great publications whose directors have attended our meetings and respected their promises of discretion for almost forty years... It would have been impossible for us to develop our plan for the world if we had been subject to the bright lights of publicity during these years. But, the world is now more sophisticated and prepared to march towards a world government. The supernational sovereignty of an intellectual elite and world bankers is surely preferable to the national auto-determination practiced in past centuries."

Then Governor of Arkansas, Bill Clinton (a Rhodes Scholar, who attended Oxford University in England), was invited to speak, and a decision was made to endorse his candidacy (according to Jim Tucker, a *Spotlight* reporter, who had a source within the group, code-named 'Pipeline'). No wonder

Clinton was able to survive all the media attacks regarding his personal life and lack of experience. One of his top money men was investor and international banker Jackson Stephens, who also donated $100,000 to the Bush campaign. His wife was the Co-Chairwoman of the national "Bush for President" organization in 1988. Also in attendance, were Michael Boskin, Chairman of Bush's Council of Economic Advisors, who was a speaker; Nicholas Brady, U.S. Treasury Secretary; and Vice President Dan Quayle, who impressed the group enough, that there was talk of supporting him for the Republican nomination in 1996. In fact, after the meeting, Bilderberger member Katherine Graham, head of the *Washington Post*, published a series of positive articles on Quayle.

At their 1992 meeting, the group discussed the possibility of "conditioning the public to accept the idea of a UN army that could, by force, impose its will on the internal affairs of any nation." Henry Kissinger, who attended the meeting, said: "Today, Americans would be outraged if UN forces entered Los Angeles to restore order. Tomorrow, they will be grateful."

The official press release for their 2002 Conference said: "Bilderberg's only activity is its annual Conference. At the meetings, no resolutions are proposed, no votes taken, and no policy statements issued." They are just "a small flexible, informal and off-the-record international forum in which different viewpoints can be expressed and mutual understanding enhanced." However, Phyllis Schlafly wrote in *A Choice Not An Echo*, that the Bilderbergers are a "little clique of powerful men who meet secretly and plan events that appear to 'just happen'."

Atlas Shrugged

In 1957, a 1,168 page book by Ayn Rand, called *Atlas Shrugged*, was published. According to one source, Rand was alleged to be a mistress to Philippe Rothschild, who instructed her to write the book in order to show that through the raising of oil prices, then destroying the oil fields and shutting down the coal mines, the Illuminati would take over the world. It also related how they would blow up grain mills, derail trains, bankrupt and destroy their own companies, till they had destroyed the economy of the entire world; and yet, they would be so wealthy, that it would not substantially affect their vast holdings. The novel is about a man who stops the motor of the world, of what happens when "the men of the mind, the intellectuals of the world, the originators and innovators in every line of industry go on strike; when the men of creative ability in every profession, in protest against regulation, quit and disappear."

If we are to believe that the book represents the Illuminati's plans for the future, then the following excerpts may provide some insight to the mentality of the elitists who are preparing us for one-world government.

One of the characters, Francisco d'Anconia, a copper industrialist and heir to a great fortune, the first to join the strike, says:

"I am destroying d'Anconia Copper, consciously, deliberately, by plan and by my own hand. I have to plan it carefully and work as hard as if I were producing a fortune- in order not to let them notice it and stop me, in order not to let them seize the mines until it is too late... I shall destroy every last bit of it and every last penny of my fortune and every ounce of copper that could feed the looters. I shall not leave it as I found it- I shall leave it as Sebastian d'Anconia found it- then let them try to exist without him or me!"

A bit later, d'Anconia says: "We produced the wealth of the world- but we let our enemies write its moral code." Still later, he says: "We'll survive without it. They won't."

Dagney Taggart, the main character of the book, is the head of the Taggart Transcontinental Railroad. Her goal was to find out who John Galt was. She discovered that he was a young inventor with the Twentieth Century Motor Company, who said he would put an end to the regulations which bound a man to his job indefinitely. Before disappearing, he said: "I will stop the motor of the world."

He told her: "Dagney, we who've been called 'materialists'... we're the only ones who know how little value or meaning there is in material objects... we're the ones who create their value and meaning. We can afford to give them up... We are the soul, of which railroads, copper mines, steel mines, and oil wells are the body- and they are living entities that beat day and night, like our hearts, in the sacred function of supporting human life, but only so long as they remain our body, only so long as they remain the expression, the reward and the property of achievement. Without us, they are corpses and their sole product is poison, not wealth or food, the poison of disintegration that turns men into hordes of scavengers... You do not have to depend on any material possessions, they depend on you, you create them, you own the one and only tool of production... leave them the carcass of that railroad, leave them all the rusted nails and rotted ties and gutted engines- but don't leave them your mind."

Later in the book, Galt says: "And the same will be happening in every other industry, wherever machines are used- the machines which they thought could replace our minds. Plane crashes, oil tank explosions, blast furnace breakouts, high tension wire electrocutions, subway cave-ins, and trestle collapses- they'll see them all. The very machines that made their life so safe- will now make it a continuous peril... You know that the cities will be hit worst of all. The cities were made by the railroads and will go with them... When the rails are cut, the city of New York will starve in two days. That's all the supply of food its got. It's fed by a continent three thousand miles long. How will they carry food to New York? By directive and ox-cart? But first, before it happens, they'll go through the whole of the agony- through the shrinking, the shortages, the hunger riots, the stampeding violence in the midst of the growing stillness... They'll lose the airplanes first, then their automobiles, then their trucks, then their horsecarts... Their factories will stop, then their furnaces and their radios. Then their electric light system will go."

Francisco d'Anconia, who blew up all the copper mines in the world, said of Galt: "He had quit the Twentieth Century. He was living in a garret in a slum neighborhood. He stepped to the window and pointed at the skyscrapers of the city. He said that we had to extinguish the lights of the world, and when we would see the lights of New York go out, we would know that our job was done."

Galt led the men of the mind, on strike, and they retired to a self-supporting valley, where a character, Midas Mulligan, says that "the world is falling apart so fast that it will soon be starving. But we will be able to support ourselves in this valley." Galt said: "There is only one kind of men who have never been on strike in human history... the men who have carried the world on their shoulders, have kept it alive, have endured torture as sole payment... Well, their turn has come. Let the world discover who they are, what they do and what happens when they refuse to function. This is the strike of the men of the mind."

The book describes what resulted from the strike: "But years later, when we saw the lights going out, one after another, in the great factories that had stood like mountains for generations, when we saw the gates closing and the conveyer belts turning still, when we saw the roads growing empty and the streams of cars draining off, when it began to look as if some silent power were stopping the generators of the world and the world was crumbling quietly..." And the culmination of their efforts: "The plane was above the peaks of the skyscrapers when suddenly, with the abruptness of a shudder, as if the ground had parted to engulf it, the city had disappeared from the face of the earth. It took them a moment to realize that the panic had reached the power stations- and the lights of New York had gone out." The men of the mind had taken over the world.

Ayn Rand, author of *Atlas Shrugged*, which was a bestseller; had previously written *We the Living* (1936); *The Fountainhead* (1943), which became a 1949 movie starring Gary Cooper as an architect willing to blow up his own work, rather than see it perverted by public housing bureaucrats; and *Anthem* (1946). She later wrote *For the New Intellectual* (1961), *Capitalism: The Unknown Ideal* (1966), and *The New Left: The Anti-Industrial Revolution* (1970). She also published a monthly journal (with Nathaniel Branden, a psychological theorist) called *The Objectivist.*

Rand based her novel on her philosophy which she calls Objectivism. As she puts it: "We are the radicals for capitalism... because it is the only system geared to the life of a rational being... The method of capitalism's destruction rests on never letting the world discover what it is that is being destroyed." She also said about the book: "I trust that no one will tell me that men such as I write about don't exist. That this book has been written- and published- is proof that they do."

In the book *Capitalism: The Unknown Ideal,* in a chapter titled "Is Atlas Shrugging" she wrote that "the purpose of this book is to prevent itself from being prophetic." She also quoted several news stories which seemed to indicate that the world was indeed being depleted of its brains and intellectuals.

Is *Atlas Shrugged* a coded blueprint for the Illuminati's plans of bringing this world to a point where they can institute a one world government? It certainly is thought provoking, and it is included only for the sake of conjecture. Being that the Illuminati is destroying our economy, and they do control the corporate structure of the United States, if not the world, there just may be something to this book, and maybe we should consider it a warning.

The Seven Sisters

One oil cartel is the Organization of Petroleum Exporting Countries, known as OPEC, which is made up of Iran, Iraq, Venezuela, Kuwait, Saudi Arabia, Algeria, Indonesia, Libya, Nigeria, Qatar, and the United Arab Emirates. The group was created on September 14, 1960, for the purpose of setting oil prices by controlling oil production. They were originally thought to be primarily Arabian, in ownership, however, it is actually an international group, which includes Americans. The cartel was established from an agreement signed on September 17, 1920, by Royal Dutch Shell, Anglo-Iranian, and Standard Oil, for the purpose of fixing oil prices. By 1949, the cartel was made up of Anglo-Iranian, Socony-Vacuum, Royal Dutch Shell, Gulf,

Esso, Texaco, and Calso. In the early 1950's, revelations surfaced that the oil companies would pump the oil from the Middle East, then split the profits with the government of the country where the oil was produced. OPEC was formed to make people believe that the Arabian oil reserves were not owned by non-Arabian oil companies.

Those non-Arabian oil companies are another cartel, which had been informally called "The Seven Sisters," and control what is shipped to the United States, and how much is refined into gas and heating oil. Originally, it was made up of the Rockefeller-controlled Exxon (previously known as Standard Oil of New Jersey, or Esso), Mobil (Socony or Standard Oil of New York, which merged with Vacuum Oil), and Chevron (Socal or Standard Oil of California); the Mellon's Gulf Oil; Shell (Royal Dutch Petroleum), Texaco, and British Petroleum (Anglo-Iranian). They controlled 90% of crude exports to world markets by controlling every important pipeline in the world, such as the 753-mile Trans Arabian Pipeline, from Qaisuma in Saudi Arabia to the Mediterranean Sea, which was owned by Exxon, Chevron, Texaco, and Mobil. Exxon owned the 100-mile Interprovincial Pipeline in Canada; and also the 143-mile pipeline in Venezuela. The 799-mile Alaskan Pipeline was owned by British Petroleum and Exxon. By controlling these, and other vital arteries, they can restrict the flow of oil, limiting supplies to refineries.

You could also see their link, through the joint ownership of the major crude oil production companies:

Abu Dhabi Marine Areas (British Petroleum)-	66-2/3%
Compagnie Francaise de Petroles-	33-1/3%
Kuwait Oil Co. (British Petroleum)-	50%
Gulf-	50%
Iran Consortium (Gulf)-	7%
Shell-	14%
Exxon-	7%
Chevron-	7%
Compagnie Francaise des Petroles-	6%

Texaco-	7%
British Petroleum-	40%
Mobil-	7%
other-	5%
Abu Dhabi Petroleum Co. (Shell)-	23.75%
Exxon-	11.875%
Compagnie Francaise des Petroles-	23.75%
British Petroleum-	23.75%
Mobil-	11.875%
other-	5%
Iraq Petroleum	
(Compagnie Francaise des Petroles)-	23.75%
British Petroleum-	23.75%
Mobil-	11.875%
Shell-	23.75%
Exxon-	11.875%
other-	5%
Aramco Saudi Arabia (Exxon)-	30%
Chevron-	30%
Mobil-	10%
Texaco-	30%
Bahrain Petroleum Co. (Chevron)-	50%
Texaco-	50%

The Sisters were also interlocked with eight of the largest banks in the country, and with each other: Exxon had ties to Mobil, Chevron, and Texaco; and Mobil had ties to Exxon, Shell, and Texaco. When six of the nation's major commercial banks held their Executive Board meetings, the directors of the top eight oil companies, with the exception of Gulf and Chevron, met with them. When the Bank of America had a Board meeting, the directors of Chevron and Getty Oil met with them. Chevron also had ties with Western Bancorp. Shell and Mobil directors were present at the Board meetings of First National City Bank. Mobil also had ties with Bankers Trust, and Chemical

Bank. Exxon was tied in with the Chase Manhattan Bank (a holding company for hundreds of smaller oil companies, including Humble Oil and Creole Petroleum), Morgan Guaranty, and Chemical Bank. Amoco (Standard Oil of Indiana) was tied in with Chase Manhattan, Continental Illinois, and National Bank and Trust.

Some of the oil executives who were members of the Council on Foreign Relations: Lawrence G. Rawl (Chairman of Exxon), Lee R. Raymond (President of Exxon, and Trilateral Commission member), Jack G. Clark, Sr. (Vice President of Exxon); Alfred C. Decrane, Jr. (Chairman of Texaco), John Brademas (a Director of Texaco, and Trilateral Commission member), William J. Crowe, Jr. (a Director of Texaco, and Trilateral Commission member); Allan E. Murray (Chairman & President of Mobil, and Trilateral Commission member), Lewis M. Branscomb (a Director of Mobil), and Helene L. Kaplan (a Director of Mobil).

The Seven Sisters also controlled 70% of the U.S. coal supply, which during World War II, the Germans used to make pollution-free synthetic fuel. Their philosophy was "to mine it now, it's coal; to mine it later, it will be like gold."

These seven companies announced their alliance with the statement: "We have formed a very exclusive club... And we are now united. We are making history." Remember, in 1914, Congress referred to Standard Oil as "the invisible government." The oil companies are powerful, and their power was never more apparent, then it was during the manufactured crisis of 1973.

On October 6, 1973, as synagogues in Israel observed Yom Kippur, the Jewish Day of Atonement, Syrian MiG-21's attacked a group of Israeli jets. Egypt, Syria, Jordan, and eight other Arab nations had mobilized against Israel. Egypt attacked the Sinai Peninsula with 4,000 tanks, knocking out many Israeli tanks; while Syria attacked the Golan Heights with 1,200. New Soviet-made SAM-6 missiles plucked Israeli planes out of the sky with ease. However, within a few days, the tide was turned. Israel regained control of the Heights, and took a large part of Syria. On October 12, they were only 18 miles from Damascus.

With 12,000 soldiers, and 200 tanks, they swept across the Suez Canal in two directions to surround the Egyptian Third Army, which had been caught on the east side, and came within 12 miles of Cairo.

Since the first day of the war, Russia had been airlifting supplies to the Arabs, so to counter that move, the United States said they intended to supply Israel "with whatever it needs." Once Israel began smashing their way to victory, Russia sent a Naval force of 71 ships, including 16 submarines, to the Mediterranean, and put their seven airborne divisions on full alert.

On October 12th, the Chairmen of Exxon, Texaco, Mobil, and Chevron (who made up the production company of Aramco in Saudi Arabia), sent Chief of Staff Gen. Alexander Haig (who later became Reagan's Secretary of State) a memo warning against any increased aid to Israel, by saying it would "have a critical and adverse effect on our relations with the moderate Arab producing countries." On October 17th, Omar Saqqaf, the Foreign Minister of Saudi Arabia, gave President Nixon a letter from King Faisal, which said that if the U.S. did not discontinue their shipment of military supplies to Israel within two days, there would be an embargo. Nixon stated that he was committed to supporting Israel. The U.S. Sixth Fleet of 49 ships, including 2 aircraft carriers, was sent to the Mediterranean, where they maintained a state of combat readiness.

OPEC met and decided to raise the price of oil to $5.12 a barrel, which was 70% higher than they had agreed to before the Arab-Israeli War. The next day, the Arab countries met, and decided to cut oil production by 5%, however, the Saudis later decided to cut back production by more than 20%, and by October 20th, had embargoed all oil shipments to the U.S., and countries that were partial to Israel.

As the Israeli counterattack continued, Egypt and Syria were in serious trouble, and Russia urged the UN to call a ceasefire. Jim Akins, the ambassador to Saudi Arabia sent a message to Aramco that the oil embargo would not be lifted "unless the political struggle is settled in a manner satisfactory to the Arabs." Two days later, the Saudis requested from the Aramco directors, information concerning the amount of oil used by the U.S. military, which they supplied. The Saudis then instructed them to stop all supplies to the military. In December, OPEC announced a price of $11.65 a barrel, and the result was economic chaos in the United States and Western Europe.

Though Aramco claimed that they had no choice in what they did, and that they weren't acting as agents of a foreign government against the United States, the cry went out that the oil industry was putting "profits before patriotism." Before the embargo, America was importing 1.2 million barrels oil a day; and by February, only 18,000 barrels, which was a drop of 98%. The rush was on to reallocate other sources of oil (Venezuela and Iran had not joined the boycott), and to distribute it throughout the world. The global emphasis of the American oil companies were revealed, when they refused to favor the U.S. at the expense of the other countries, causing us to lose a higher percentage of the available oil supply.

In Egypt, Sadat's terms for a ceasefire, was that Israel had to withdraw from all territories that it had won during the 1967 war; thus pressure from the United States and the Soviets, forced Israel to turn their victory into a negotiated compromise.

To add insult to injury, when the winter was at its worst during the shortage, the announcement that oil companies were experiencing record profits, left a very sour taste in the mouths of Americans. Exxon announced that their third quarter profits were up 80% over the previous year, while Gulf was up 91%. Exxon ended up the year with a profit that was an all-time record for any company, in any industry.

By March, 1974, the embargo was lifted from the U.S., and the oil companies scrambled to salvage their shattered reputations. However, the incident would never be forgotten, because it shocked the American people back to the reality of just how much control a foreign government, and multinational corporations could exert over our nation. The price of oil never went down to their pre-embargo levels, and the threat of another shortage would always remain as the Arabs realized that they could achieve political leverage by using oil to blackmail the world.

There have been many changes in the oil industry since the inception of the Seven Sisters. In 1984, Chevron (Standard Oil of California) bought, and merged with Gulf Oil; and then in 2001, merged with Texaco (who in 1984 had bought Getty Oil), to become Chevron Texaco, the 2nd largest oil company in the country, and 5th largest in the world. In 2002, Shell Oil acquired a couple of Texaco's interests. In 1998, Exxon (Esso, Standard Oil of New Jersey) merged with Mobil (Socony, Standard Oil of New York) to become Exxon Mobil, the biggest oil company in the country, and third largest company in the U.S. In 1987 British Petroleum purchased the remaining 45% of Sohio (Standard Oil of Ohio) that they didn't already own, then in 1998, merged with Amoco (Standard Oil of Indiana), and in 2000 merged with Arco (Atlantic Richfield).

The Seven Sisters are now the Four Sisters, so what you have now is an expanded amount of power and influence that is concentrated in less hands, as oil companies have sought to consolidate their interests because of economic concerns. It's uncanny in that it has happened in less than 20 years. It's almost as if the old Standard Oil Company was coming back together. In 2001, Conoco (Continental Oil) and Phillips Petroleum (Phillips 66) merged, to make Conoco Phillips, the 3rd largest oil company, the 12th largest company, and the 6th largest oil company in the world. If this trend continues, it will make it all the more easier for oil companies to manipulate and control a crucial commodity like gasoline and oil.

Club of Rome

This think-tank of Anglo-American financiers, scientists, economists, politicians, heads of state, and industrialists from ten different countries, met in April, 1968 at Rockefeller's private estate in Bellagio, Italy, at the request of Aurelio Peccei, the Italian industrialist who had close ties to Fiat and the Olivetti Corporation. He claimed to have solutions for world peace and prosperity, which could be accomplished through world government. The Club of Rome (COR) was established with a membership of 75 prominent scientists, industrialists, and economists from 25 countries, which along with the Bilderbergers, have become one of the most important foreign policy arms of the Roundtable group. Many of the COR executives were drawn from NATO, and they have been able to formulate a lot of what NATO claims are its policies. Through Lord Carrington, they were able to split NATO into two factions, a left-wing political group (whose doctrine was formed on the basis of Peccei's book *Human Quality*), and its former military alliance.

The first Club of Rome conference in the U.S. was in 1969, where the American branch was organized as the "American Association of the Club of Rome." Among its members were: Norman Cousins (honorary Chairman of Planetary Citizens), John Naisbitt (author of *Megatrends*), Amory Lovins (a speaker at Windstar, John Denver's New Age center in Snowmass, Colorado), Betty Friedan (founding President of NOW, the National Organization of Women), Jean Houston and Hazel Henderson (New Age authors and speakers), Robert Of. Anderson and Harlan B. Cleveland (CFR members and part of the Aspen Institute for Humanistic Studies), Sen. Claiborne Pell (D-RI), and Rep. Frank M. Potter (staff director of the House Subcommittee on Energy).

Their first book, called *The Limits to Growth*, was published in 1972, and described their vision for the world: "We believe in fact that the need will quickly become evident for social innovation to match technical change, for radical reform of the institutions and political processes at all levels, including the highest, that of world polity. And since intellectual enlightenment is without effect if it is not also political, The Club of Rome also will encourage the creation of a world forum where statesmen, policy-makers, and scientists can discuss the dangers and hopes for the future global system without the constraints of formal intergovernmental negotiation."

For the most part, the Club (main office at 193 Rissener Landstr. In Hamburg, Germany) functions as a research institute on economic, political, and social problems, and claim that "there is no other viable alternative to the future survival of civilization than a new global community under a common leadership." Their website claims: "The Club of Rome's mission is to act as a global catalyst of change that is free of any political, ideological or business interest. The Club of Rome contributes to the solution of what it calls the world problematique, the complex set of the most crucial problems-political, social, economic, technological, environmental, psychological and cultural- facing humanity. It does so taking a global, long term and interdisciplinary prospective aware of the increasing interdependence of nations and the globalization of problems that pose predicaments beyond the capacity of individual countries."

It almost sounds like the Club of Rome is the A-Team of internationalist groups. Just like how the proposals suggested by the Bilderbergers seem to gain acceptance, we have to worry that the same thing will happen with the COR.

On September 17, 1973, they released a Report called the "Regionalized and Adaptive Model of the Global World System," which was prepared by Directors Mihajlo Mesarovic and Eduard Pestel (part of the "Strategy for Survival Project"), which revealed the Club's goal of dividing the world into ten political/economic regions (which have been equated to the 10 "Kingdoms" of Bible prophecy), which would unite the entire world under a single form of government. These regions are: North America, Western Europe, Eastern Europe, Japan, Rest of Developed World, Latin America, Middle East, Rest of Africa, South and Southeast Asia, and China. The same plan was published in a Club of Rome book called *Mankind at the Turning Point*, which said: "The solution of these crises can be developed only in a global context with full and explicit recognition of the emerging world system and on a long-term basis. This would necessitate, among other changes, a new world economic order and a global resources allocation system..."

In 1976, they published *RIO: Reshaping the International Order* which called for a new international order, including an economic redistribution of wealth.

Howard T. Odum, a marine biologist at the University of Florida, who is a member of the Club of Rome, was quoted in the August, 1980 edition of *Fusion* magazine, as saying: "It is necessary that the United States cut its population by two-thirds within the next 50 years." He didn't say how this would be accomplished. Their 1972 book, *The Limits to Growth* (which sold 12 million copies in 27 languages), dealt with the problem of worldwide overpopulation, and stated that "if the world's consumption patterns and population growth continued at the same high rates of the time, the earth would strike its limits within a century."

During the Carter Administration, a task force was appointed to expand upon this report, and on July 24, 1980, a two-volume document called "Global 2000 Report," which had been written by former Secretary of State Cyrus R. Vance, was presented to President Carter, and then Secretary of State Edward S. Muskie. It attempted to project global economic trends for the next twenty years, and indicated that the resources of the planet were not sufficient enough to support the expect dramatic increase in the world population. The report called for the population of the U.S. to be reduced by 100 million people by the year 2050.

AIDS CAMPAIGN

About six months later, the Council on Environmental Quality made recommendations based on the Report, called "Global Future: A Time to Act." They suggested an aggressive program of population control which included sterilization, contraception and abortion. In August, 1982, the *Executive Intelligence Review* published a report called "Global 2000: Blueprint for Genocide" which said that the two aforementioned Presidential reports "are correctly understood as political statements of intent- the intent on the part of such policy centers as the Council on Foreign Relations, the Trilateral Commission, and the International Monetary Fund, to pursue policies that will result not only in the death of the 120 million cited in the reports, but in the death of upwards of two billion people by the year 2000."

Peccei wrote (based on a report by COR member Harland Cleveland, U.S. Ambassador to NATO, who believed that Third World countries should decide for themselves who should be eliminated): "Damaged by conflicting policies of three major countries and blocs, roughly patched up here and there, the existing international economic order is visibly coming apart at the seams... The prospect of the necessity of the recourse to triage deciding who must be saved is a very grim one indeed. But, if lamentably, events should come to such a pass, the right to make such decisions cannot be left to just a few nations because it would lend themselves to ominous power over life of the world's hungry."

Throughout the world, the Club of Rome has indicated that genocide should be used to eliminate people who they refer to as "useless eaters."

This would be accomplished by using limited wars in advanced countries, and even a limited nuclear strike at a strategic location; as well as starvation through created famines and diseases in Third World countries.

In the 1976 novel *Ceremony of the Innocent* by Taylor Caldwell, she effectively explains the rationale behind their actions: "...there will be no peace in the tormented world, only a programmed and systematic series of wars and calamities-until the plotters have gained their objective: an exhausted world willing to submit to a planned Marxist economy and total and meek enslavement- in the name of peace."

Have their plans for genocide already started? AIDS (Acquired Immunodeficiency Syndrome) has become a plague in our society, spreading to 91 nations. In the early 1990's the *U.S. News and World Report* stated: "If there is not a cure for AIDS within the next thirteen years, tens of millions will die." Even though there has been a lot of talk about AIDS awareness and prevention, the full danger of it has been covered-up by the Center for Disease Control, and the media, which has increasingly shown its pro-homosexual bias.

In 1969, at a House Appropriations hearing, the Defense Department's Biological Warfare unit requested funds to develop, through gene-splicing, a new disease that would be resistant to treatment, and break down a victim's immune system. They received $10 million (H.B. 15090), to produce "a synthetic biological agent, an agent that does not naturally exist and for which no natural immunity could have been acquired."

In the 1972 Bulletin of the UN's World Health Organization (WHO), volume 47, page 251, it says: "An attempt should be made to see if viruses can in fact exert selective effects on immune function. The possibility should be looked into that the immune response to the virus itself may be impaired if the inflicting virus damages, more or less selectively, the cell responding to the virus." This sounds like the AIDS virus, so why is it being discussed by a health organization?

Derivatives from sheep and cattle have been commonly used to manufacture vaccines, however, certain viruses common to these animals can interact indefinitely, forming a new strain of deadly viruses called retro-viruses. In 1974, the National Academy of Sciences recommended that "Scientists throughout the world join with members of this committee in voluntarily deferring experiments (linking) animal viruses."

Dr. Robert Strecker, a practicing gastroenterologist, with a Ph.D. in pharmacology, who was hired as a consultant to work on a health-care proposal for Security Pacific Bank, said: "I don't think there is any doubt that AIDS is a man-made problem. The question is whether it was created either accidentally or intentionally. I believe the AIDS virus was requested, predicted, produced, and deployed."

The most common theory about the origin of AIDS was that it came from green monkeys in Africa. Yet several virologists have said that the AIDS virus does not occur naturally in any animal. Besides, it would have been statistically impossible to reach the point we are at now, just from a single episode. If the AIDS virus had originated with the monkeys, then the disease would have surfaced with the Pygmies, who are closer to them, and use them as a food source, yet, it appeared first in the cities. Further damaging evidence comes from the fact that AIDS practically occurred simultaneously in the United States, Haiti, Brazil, and Central Africa.

Strecker's research indicated that the AIDS virus (code-named 'MKNAOMI') was developed by the Frederick Cancer Research Facility of the National Cancer Institute, in cooperation with the WHO, in their laboratories at Fort Detrick, Maryland (which until 1969 was part of the U.S. Army's germ warfare unit, known as the Army Infectious Disease Unit, or Special Operations Division); by combining bovine (cow) leukemia virus and visna (sheep) virus, and injecting them into human tissue cultures.

The bovine leukemia virus is lethal to cows, but not to humans; and the visna virus is deadly to sheep, but not to man. However, when combined, they produce a retro-virus that can change the genetic composition of the cells that they enter. He said:

"If one analyzes the genes of the human AIDS virus and the genes of the bovine leukemia virus of cattle and the visna virus of sheep, and compares them, the genes appear related. How is it possible that the bovine visna virus- which looks like AIDS and produces an AIDS-like disease, and which produced pneumocystis carinii pneumonia in chimpanzees in 1972- has not been analyzed and compared with AIDS... until 1987 when 'Characterization and Molecular Cloning of Bovine Lente (Latin for 'slow') Virus Related to Human Immunodeficiency Virus' was published in *Nature* magazine. Matthew Gonda, the author, described a virus that looks like AIDS, named bovine visna virus, and suggested that it was most closely related to AIDS and may well be its precursor."

On August 11, 1988, Ted Strecker, Dr. Strecker's brother was found shot to death in his home in Springfield, Missouri. His death was ruled a suicide. On September 22, 1988, Illinois State Representative Douglas Huff of Chicago was found dead in his home. The autopsy revealed that he died of a stroke as a result of an overdose of cocaine and heroin. Rep. Huff just happened to be a very vocal supporter of Dr. Strecker's work to publicize the AIDS cover-up. Coincidence or conspiracy?

There was a vaccination program for Smallpox in Africa by the WHO. Some researchers believe that the Smallpox vaccination program in 1972 was used to introduce the virus into the population. On May 11, 1987, the *London Times* ran an article called "Smallpox Vaccine 'Triggered AIDS Virus'," written by Science Editor Pearce Wright, who linked the mass vaccination program of the World Health Organization in the 1970's to the outbreak of AIDS, because Central Africa was the focus of the program, and they have become the most affected area in the world.

Though in Africa, AIDS is generally regarded as a heterosexual disease, in the United States, it has the stigma of being a 'gay' disease. Prior to 1978, there was no sign of the AIDS virus here, yet in 1978, the killer disease struck with a vengeance within the homosexual community. The evidence points to the introduction of an experimental Hepatitis B vaccine. In 1969, Dr. W. Schmugner, a Polish physician, who was educated in Russia, came to the United States, where he became head of the New York City Blood Bank. He set up guidelines for a Hepatitis vaccine study, and only promiscuous males between the ages of 20 and 40 were included in the study, which has led some to believe that this was how the virus was introduced into the gay population.

In 1978, more than 1,000 non-monogamous gay adult males received an experimental vaccination against Hepatitis B, which was sponsored by the National Institute of Health and the Center for Disease Control. With the Hepatitis vaccine, which is not produced from a human tissue culture, it is impossible to have an accidental contamination, which seems to indicate that the AIDS virus was intentionally put in the vaccine. In 1981, the Center for Disease Control reported that 6% of those receiving the Hepatitis vaccine were infected with AIDS, but in 1984, they admitted that it was actually 64%. These Hepatitis vaccine studies are now in the possession of the Justice Department in Washington, DC.

To allow the disease to become entrenched within the population, various facts were covered-up and glossed-over. A great deal of emphasis had been put on the prime cause of

AIDS infection, being the exchange of body fluid, through sexual activity and intravenous drug use, which has brought a campaign for the importance of using clean, unused needles, and condoms. The use of a condom does not guarantee protection against the transmission of the AIDS virus. All it takes is one AIDS virion (a complete virus particle with its outer coat intact), and the smallest sperm is 500 times larger that one such virion. In addition, the quality of condoms have become highly suspect, since failure rates of 30-50% have been reported.

The risk of casual contact has been played down when in fact AIDS is a highly contagious disease which demands that a quarantine be placed on those who suffer from the disease. Rather than treat the disease as the epidemic it is, the government has concerned itself with giving AIDS carriers more rights and more exposure to the general population. There is concrete medical evidence that indicates that the virus can survive up to 7 days on a dry petri dish, and up to 15 days, in an aqueous (wet) environment.

This raises the question, what would happen if an AIDS carrier would sneeze into a punch bowl or a salad bowl. It can incubate 10-15 years before causing any noticeable signs of illness, which means that sexual relations exposes you to every sexual contact your partner has had in that period of time.

A February, 1985 report in the British medical journal *Lancet*, said: "There is little evidence for homosexual activity among African AIDS patients (and it) appears to be transmitted through heterosexual contact or exposure to blood through insect bites..." On September 9, 1985, a research team of researchers from the National Cancer Institute, the Laboratory of Tumor Cell Biology and the Institute of Tropical Medicine, said that "human retroviruses could be transmitted by mosquitoes or within the parasite itself." In a report published in the October, 1981, issue of *Science*, Boston hematologist Dr. Jerome Groopman, and researchers with the National Institute of Health said that recovery of the AIDS virus "from saliva suggests that direct contact with this body fluid should be avoided..."

On January 11, 1985, the Center for Disease Control reported: "There is a risk of infecting others by... exposure of others through oral-genital contact or intimate kissing ('french' kissing)." Dr. Richard Restak, a Washington neurologist, made this statement:

> *"At this point live AIDS virus has been isolated from blood, semen, serum, saliva, urine and now tears. If the virus exists in these fluids, the better part of wisdom dictates that we assume the possibility that it can also be transmitted by these routes. It seems reasonable, therefore, that AIDS victims should not donate blood or blood products, should not contribute to semen banks, should not donate tissues or organs to organ banks, should not work as dental or medical technicians, and should probably not be employed as food handlers."*

Professor William Haseltine of the Harvard Medical School, in a presentation to a University audience, said that anyone "who tells you categorically that AIDS is not contracted by saliva is not telling you the truth. AIDS may in fact be transmissible by tears, saliva, bodily fluids, and mosquito bites."

AIDS is an epidemic that will not be stopped. The scientists that created this deadly virus, have created a virus that multiplies 100 times faster than influenza. There are more than 180 different AIDS viruses, and 300 strains, which makes blood testing meaningless. The virus is constantly mutating, which makes it impossible to develop a general vaccine that would be effective with everyone. Quite simply, AIDS is a world-wide, modern-day plague, and every year, the number of those affected increases drastically. In the March, 1987 issue of *Vanity Fair*, Dr. William Grace, chief of Oncology at St. Vincent's Hospital in New York, is quoted as saying: "I think AIDS is going to devastate the American medical system." Besides not being able to combat it medically, the disease will progress to being an economic drain, especially if national health care is instituted."

If its purpose was to glean out the population, it certainly will be successful. It must be assumed that the progenitors of this disease must have a measure of protection to prevent themselves from being exposed. The elite have already segregated themselves from the general population by virtue of their position, so from that aspect, there is little risk from being contaminated. In the event of medical treatment, they have access to the best medical treatment that money can buy, and most likely possess a private, untainted blood supply. Somehow, I just can't help thinking, that when their goal of limits to the population have been reached, how will they end the scourge which they have placed upon the earth. Just as the saying goes, that a lawyer in court doesn't ask the witness a question that he doesn't already have the answer for; the same reasoning would seem to apply here, that the Illuminati would not unleash a disease that they didn't already have a cure for.

Bro. R. G. Stair, a well-known radio evangelist, had received an anonymous letter which seemed to confirm this theory. The writer claimed to be a molecular biologist who worked in the same laboratory with Dr. Robert C. Gallo (the molecular biologist noted for his involvement in the co-discovery of the AIDS virus). The writer claimed that there is an AIDS vaccine that is now available, and that 500,000,000 doses have been produced and is now available. Now the bombshell. The writer accidentally discovered that Gallo had actually created the AIDS virus, and found a couple letters in his office, from high government officials which mentioned the New World Order.

In 1961, in a Litton Bionetics laboratory (who was working with the Navy's Biomedical Research Laboratory, in association with the Univeristy of California), retroviral experiments with African Green Monkeys and Human T-Cell Leukemia were being conducted under the auspices of the National Institute of Health (contract # SVCP PR#8 NIH #71-2025). It consisted of taking monkey viruses that were harmless to humans, recombined them with DNA, RNA and enzymes from other animal viruses that were known to cause leukemias, lymphomas, and sarcomas; then got them to jump species, and cultured the new mutant viruses into human white blood cells in some studies, and in other studies- human fetal tissues, which produced an "immune-system destroying, cancer-causing viruses" for which "no natural immunity could have been acquired, and no cure exists." The scientist who was directing the tests was Dr. Robert Gallo.

In 1975, Gallo and eight other scientists (working at the Bethesda Cancer Research Center in Maryland) had been working to modify the genetic structure of the virus so that it can be more easily transmitted. That same year, after Fort Detrick had become demilitarized, the newly established Frederick Cancer Research Facility was placed under the direction of the Bethesda Cancer Research Center, where Gallo was the Director. One investigation revealed that in March, 1976, a special federal government virus development program began producing the AIDS virus, and it was headed by Dr. Gallo and Dr. Novakhatskiy of the Ivanosku Institute in Russia. Gallo would later be investigated and found guilty of scientific misconduct, but President Clinton pardoned him.

In response to the charges that AIDS was developed as a military biological warfare weapon, in February, 1987, Army Col. David Huxsoll said: "Studies at army laboratories have shown that the AIDS virus would be an extremely poor biological warfare agent." He later denied saying it.

Whether AIDS is the vehicle of elimination, that the Club of Rome has referred to, or a precursor, just like Gulf War Syndrome, Ebola, and SARS, is undoubtedly open to speculation, even in light of all the questions raised. However, you can't deny how neatly this little piece of the puzzle fits into the entire picture of preparing the world for a one-world government.

INDEPENDENT COMMISSION ON INTERNATIONAL DEVELOPMENT ISSUES

The Toronto Globe and Mail, on April 7, 1980, reported the story of a conference to be hosted by Canadian Prime Minister Trudeau, that fall, which would "reshape global structures." The Summit, known as the "North-South Dialogue," which would "make recommendations on ways of breaking through existing international political impasse in North-South negotiations for global development," was sponsored by the

Independent Commission on International Development Issues, and was to include President Jimmy Carter, *Newsweek* and *Washington* Post publisher Kathryn Graham, Robert McNamara, former British Prime Minister Edward Heath, and West German Chancelor Helmut Schmidt.

On January 14, 1977, Robert McNamara, President of the World Bank, proposed the establishment of an international commission of politicians and economists who would meet, not as government representatives, but independently to discuss "basic proposals on which global agreement is both essential and possible." Willy Brandt, the former West German Chancellor was asked to chair the commission.

On September 28, 1977, Brandt announced his intention to launch the Independent Commission on International Development Issues, and said that it "would not interfere with ongoing international negotiations, and would make recommendations to help improve the climate of North-South relations." Brandt wanted the Commission, consisting of 18 members, to represent many views, and to be politically and regionally balanced, with a majority coming from developed countries. Their initial meeting was in December, 1977.

There was two phases to what is more commonly referred to as Brandt's Commission. The funding for the first ($750,000) in 1980, producing *North-South: A Program for Survival*, was provided by the Dutch Government, as well as Denmark, Finland, India, Japan, Republic of Korea, Norway, Saudi Arabia, Sweden, United Kingdom, the Commission of the European Communities, OPEC Special Fund, German Marshall Fund of the United States, the Ford Foundation, Friedrich-Ebert and Friedrich-Naumann Foundations of the Federal Republic of Germany, and the International Development Research Center of Canada.

Subsequent funding was provided by the governments of Denmark, the Netherlands, Norway, Sweden, United Kingdom, and the OPEC Special Fund.

The funding for the second phase ($350,000), which produced the 1983 report *Common Crisis: North-South Cooperation for*

World Recovery, came from the governments of Canada, the Federal Republic of Germany, the Netherlands, Kuwait, the Commission of the European Communities, and the German Marshall Fund of the United States.

In short, the Brandt Reports "called for a full-scale restructuring of the global economy," and the purpose of the Commission was "to influence public opinion to help change government attitudes, as well as to make proposals for revitalizing North-South negotiations."

In the 380-page report called *North-South*, which called for the "instant" redistribution of wealth from the richer, to poorer nations, and a stepping up of world disarmament. They wanted "greater power for the International Monetary Fund and the World Bank." Their rationale was that the "transfer of wealth must be tackled, not out of charity, but to ward off economic collapse... Hence, the global super summit now. Worldwide security is not achieved by granting more aid, but by reshaping global structures, by greater regionalized planning and development." In *Common Crisis* they recommended that a supernational authority be established to regulate world commerce and industry, international currency, and an international police force, under the direction of the UN Security Council.

Bibliography

Alan, B.: *Management of Electronic Media*, Belmont, Wadsworth/Thompson Learning, 2002.

Anthony, R. and John Williams Tebbel: *American Media History*, Belmont, Thomson/Wadsworth, 2005.

Arant, David: *Perspectives: Ethics, Issues and Controversies in Mass Media,* St. Paul, Coursewise Publishing, 1999.

Bagdikian, Ben: *The Media Monopoly,* Boston, Beacon Press, 1997.

Berkman, I. : *Digital Dilemmas: Ethical Issues for Online Media Professionals*, Ames, Iowa State Press, 2003.

Berry, David: *Ethics and Media Culture*, Woburn, Focal Press, 2000.

Bertrand, Jean: *An Arsenal for Democracy: Media Accountability Systems,* Cresskill, Hampton Press, 2003.

Cannadine, David: *History and the Media*, New York, Palgrave Macmillian, 2004.

Charles, Ramirez: *Latin Looks: Images of Latinos and Latinas in U.S. Media,* Boulder, CO: Westview, 1996.

Chermak, Steven M.: *Victims in the News: Crime and the American News Media,* Boulder, Westview Press, 1995.

Christians, G.: *Media Ethics: Cases and Moral Reasoning,* Boston, Allyn & Bacon, 2004.

Craig, Richard: *Online Journalism: Reporting, Writing and Editing for New Media*, Belmont, CA: Thomson/Wadsworth, 2005.

Dahlgren, Peter and Colin Sparks: *Communication and Citizenship: Journalism and the Public Sphere in the New Media Age,* New York: Routledge, 1991.

Daniel, Webster: *The Media in America,* Santa Barbara, ABC-CLIO, 1995.

Darrell, M.: *The Rise and Fall of the Media Establishment,* Boston MA: Bedford/St. Martin's, 2001.

Day, A: *Ethics in Media Communications*, Belmont, Wadsworth, 2003.

Downing, John: *Ethnic Minority Media: An International Perspective,* Thousand Oaks, CA: Sage, 1992.

Earl, R.: *Writing for Mass Communication,* White Plains, NY: Longman, 1996.

Emery, Michael: *The Press and America: An Interpretive History of the Mass Media*, Boston, Allyn and Bacon, 1999.

Ericson, Richard: *Crime and the Media,* Brookfield, Dartmouth Publishing, 1995.

Fallows, James: *Breaking the News: How the Media Undermine American Democracy,* New York, Pantheon, 1995.

Finberg, Howard, and Bruce D. Itule: *Visual Editing: A Graphic Guide for Journalists,* Belmont, CA: Wadsworth, 1990.

Fiske, John: *Media Matters: Everyday Culture and Political Change*, Minneapolis MN: U. Minnesota Pr., 1996.

Gillmor, Dan: *We the Media: Grassroots Journalism by the People, for the People*, Sebastopol, CA: O'Reilly Media, 2004.

Goldstein, Tom: *Killing the Messenger: 100 Years of Media Criticism,* New York, Columbia University Press, 1989.

Good, Howard : *Media Ethics Goes to the Movies,* Westport, Praeger, 2002.

Gordon, A. David: *Controversies in Media Ethics,* White Plains, Longman Publishers, 1999.

Hiley, H.: *Mainsteams of American Media History,* Needham Heights, MA: Allyn & Bacon, 1997.

Hudson, Robert V.: *Mass Media,* New York, Garland Publishing, 1987.

Hutchison, Earl R.: *Writing for Mass Communication,* White Plains, NY: Longman, 1996.

Jewkes, Yvonne: *Media and Crime,* Thousand Oaks, Sage, 2004.

John Williams Tebbel: *American Media History,* Belmont, Thomson/Wadsworth, 2005.

Kelly, A.: *Police and the Media,* Springfield, Thomas Books, 1987.

Land, Mitchell : *Contemporary Media Ethics,* Spokand, Marquette Books, 2006.

Langman, Larry: *The Media in the Movies,* Jefferson, NC: McFarland & Company, 1997.

Merrill, C.: *Journalism Ethics: Philosophical Foundations for News Media,* New York, St. Martin's Press, 1997.

Mouritsen, H.: *Case Studies in Media Management,* Boston, McGraw-Hill, 2001.

Nacos, Brigitte L.: *Terrorism & the Media,* NY, Columbia University Press, 1994.

Norris, Pippa: *Women, Media and Politics,* Oxford, Oxford University Press, 1997.

Patterson, Philip : *Media Ethics: Issues and Cases,* Boston, McGraw Hill, 2002.

Ripley, Jr. Casey: *The Media and the Public,* New York, H.W. Wilson, 1994.

Robert, V.: *Mass Media,* New York, Garland Publishing, 1987.

Scott, K.: *Human Resource Management in the Electronic Media,* Westport, Quorum Books, 1998.

Seiter, Ellen: *Gender, Race and Class in Media,* Thousand Oaks, CA: Sage, 1995.

Sohn, Ardyth: *Media Management: A Casebook Approach,* Mahwah, Lawrence Erlbaum Associates, 2003.

Surette, Ray: *Justice and the Media,* Springfield, Thomas Books, 1984.

Teeter, Jr.: *Voices of a Nation: A History of Mass Media in the United States,* Needham Heights, Allyn & Bacon, 1997.

Warner, Charles: *Media Management Review,* Mahwah, Lawrence Erlbaum Associates, 1997.

West, Darrell M.: *The Rise and Fall of the Media Establishment,* Boston MA: Bedford/St. Martin's, 2001.

INDEX